TESTING
IN GUIDANCE
AND COUNSELING

GUIDANCE, COUNSELING, AND STUDENT PERSONNEL
IN EDUCATION SERIES

WALTER F. JOHNSON, *Consulting Editor*

Bennett   Guidance and Counseling in Groups
Berdie, Layton, Swanson, and Hagenah   Testing in
Guidance and Counseling
Hoppock   Occupational Information
Johnson, Stefflre, and Edelfelt   Pupil Personnel and Guidance Services
Jones   Principles of Guidance

TESTING IN GUIDANCE AND COUNSELING

RALPH F. BERDIE

WILBUR L. LAYTON

EDWARD O. SWANSON

THEDA HAGENAH

McGRAW-HILL BOOK COMPANY, INC.

New York   San Francisco   Toronto   London

TESTING IN GUIDANCE AND COUNSELING

PREFACE

The first purpose of counseling is of immediate concern to the individual because it involves his satisfactions, anxieties, pleasures, and emotions. The second purpose of counseling is immediately relevant for the community and centers around the individual's achievement, productivity, influence on others, and contribution to society. These two purposes are not independent of one another, but the first purpose sometimes is referred to by counselors as their mental health purpose, the second purpose as their manpower purpose.

The achievement of these mutually dependent purposes depends on how well the individual understands himself, and counselors often are concerned with this instrumental purpose of self-understanding. Underlying much of counseling is the assumption that satisfaction, mental health, achievement, and productivity depend on self-understanding. This assumption is verified by much everyday experience, although little research evidence supports it. It is an assumption basic to what appears in this book.

Self-understanding is a process best defined in terms of behavior. We infer that a person understands himself when he accurately describes his own experiences and has logical explanations for his behaviors, when he describes reasonable relationships between various experiences, when he accurately predicts his own behavior and exerts control over this behavior, when his behavior leads toward his goals, and when he functions efficiently and effectively.

Observations of behavior which lead to the inference that psychological conflict is present suggest lack of self-understanding.

When two incompatible reaction tendencies are simultaneously aroused, there is a conflict. The reaction tendencies themselves cannot be observed. The stimuli and the responses are observed and the reaction tendencies are inferred to exist in the organism. The inference of conflict in behavior is not a mysterious process. When the observer notices an organism-environment pattern similar to previous patterns which have preceded certain responses a greater number of times than chance could allow, he declares on the basis of this experience that the organism is in a state preparatory to reaction or shows a reaction tendency for those responses. When two patterns exist simultaneously and the observer predicts on the basis of past experience that both anticipated reactions cannot occur or cannot be brought to fulfillment, he declares a conflict is present. Knowledge of a person's attitudes, beliefs, habits, innate reaction patterns, and present environment enables the observer to make this inference. (Berdie, 1943)

Self-understanding consists of a verbal component and a feeling component. Some persons are able to describe their own experiences with great accuracy, but do not have any genuine self-understanding. Other persons behave as if they had self-understanding, but cannot verbally describe themselves. Information about oneself and incorporation of this information into the total behavior pattern are the two essential ingredients of self-acceptance. Development of this self-acceptance is one of the primary goals of a counselor.

A second assumption underlying this book is that if the counselor is to help the counselee obtain better self-understanding, the counselor also must understand the pupil. The counselor wishes the pupil to learn more about himself and to behave according to this understanding. In order to do this, the counselor must make new information available to the pupil, including information about the pupil, help the pupil as he attempts to interpret this information, and aid the pupil to incorporate the information into his existing perceptions and into his total behavior. To provide information to pupils is not enough; to attempt to increase self-understanding without increasing the pupil's knowledge of himself is futile.

The purpose of this text is to help counselors learn how to learn about pupils. We shall emphasize but not dwell exclusively on the use of tests for this purpose. The process of learning about pupils consists of determining what information is needed and what methods are available for obtaining this information; selecting and using the most appropriate methods; evaluating the adequacy of the obtained information; interpreting the information in light of other available information; presenting the information to the pupil; aiding the pupil to interpret, evaluate, and understand the information; and working with the pupil as he explores the implications of the new information for his own behavior.

In order to use tests in counseling, a counselor must know many things other than testing. He must know much about the physical and psychological development of the pupil; about the pupil's family and social development; about educational and school influences on the pupil; about the pupil's learning processes; about the pupil's personality dynamics; about the organization of the work world, the labor force, and occupations. To know any one of these things well is in itself a lifetime career. No counselor can be an expert in all, or perhaps even in many, of the things he will have to know. Nevertheless, he must know enough about each of these things to effectively use the knowledge when necessary.

Few counselors have the time or the inclination to become experts in testing. To know even a small part of what is known about testing requires many years of careful study. Merely to read the research currently published on psychological testing is a full-time job and leaves little time for other professional reading. No one person can study in great detail more than a few of the many hundreds of educational and psychological tests in use today. Many persons make a full-time career of studying one interest inventory, one type of reliability, a single scale on a personality inventory, or a method of interpreting results from an individual intelligence test. Most counselors cannot be test experts.

But as long as counselors use tests, and they must use tests, they must be well informed about tests and have a basic familiarity with them. Even though they do not have a profound acquaintance with technical test problems, particularly as they relate to test construction, evaluation, and standardization, they should have an easy acquaintanceship with the general purposes of tests, the role of tests in the counseling process, and the uses that can be made of tests as they work with individual students. The purpose of this text is not to make test experts of prospective or present counselors, but rather to provide to these persons information about tests that counselors have found useful in the past.

If one is to discuss meaningfully tests in counseling, one also must discuss many aspects of counseling. That is why we have included here discussions of other methods of personality evaluation; occupational, vocational, and educational information; interviewing relationships and responsibilities of the counselor; and research in counseling. Testing is not something apart from counseling; it is an integral part of counseling and as such must be considered along with other aspects of the counseling process.

This is not an orthodox text on testing; neither is it a traditional text on counseling. It is designed for the use of counselors who will be using tests in their counseling, and its purpose is to help these counselors see testing as an important part of counseling, not as the entire counseling process and not as merely an interesting adjunct to counseling.

This text will be most meaningful to counselors who are already acquainted with books such as Leona Tyler's *The Work of the Counselor* (1961) and basic texts in testing such as those of Anastasi (1961), Cronbach (1960), or Thorndike and Hagen (1961). And no counselor can use tests for long without having to refer frequently to the *Mental Measurements Yearbook* (Buros, 1959).

The present text, although the first edition, nevertheless is the fourth in a series of publications all having the same purpose. Since 1949, the authors have been attempting to help Minnesota counselors incorporate into their counseling the information provided by the tests included in the Minnesota Statewide Testing Programs. A short manual first was prepared for school counselors in 1949 and was entitled *The Counseling and Guidance Use of Test Scores*. A few years later, this manual was revised and expanded and published under the title of *Using Tests in Counseling*. In 1959, a greatly expanded manual, *Counseling and the Use of Tests*, was published and distributed to school counselors. Each of these publications aroused from school counselors, teachers, and principals many comments and suggestions that provided bases for improvements in the manuscript. Visits to schools, comments at state conferences, and discussions in graduate classes all provided the authors with insights into the questions counselors have about testing; and this is how the present book came into being.

The authors are indebted to the many persons who have provided both information and inspiration in preparing the text. None of these persons, of course, can be held responsible for what the authors have produced, but a debt of gratitude must be expressed. The late Professor Donald G. Paterson, one of the pioneers in psychological testing and one of the founders of the Minnesota Statewide Testing Program, is foremost among this group. Dean E. G. Williamson, who for long years has had ultimate responsibility for testing in Minnesota, has made this project possible. Professor Timothy O'Keefe of St. Thomas College, and more recently Dean Martin Quanbeck of Augsburg College, served as chairman of the Minnesota High School–College Relations Committee and in many ways aided the authors. Dean Martin Snoke, for many years secretary of this committee, has been a staunch supporter. The members of the Association of Minnesota Colleges and of the Minnesota Association of Secondary School Principals, through their support of the Minnesota Statewide Testing Program, have earned the authors' gratitude. Most important have been the contributions of the many counseling psychologists who over the years have served on the staff of the Student Counseling Bureau at the University of Minnesota. These counselors, through making their counseling experiences with more than 50,000 high school and college students available to the authors, have added to this text the "counselor's flavor."

Ralph F. Berdie
Wilbur L. Layton
Edward O. Swanson
Theda Hagenah

REFERENCES

Anastasi, Anne. *Psychological testing.* (2nd ed.) New York: Macmillan, 1961.

Berdie, R. F. Psychological processes in the interview. *J. soc. Psychol.,* 1943, **18**, 3-31.

Buros, O. K. (Ed.) *The fifth mental measurements yearbook.* Highland Park, N.J.: Gryphon Press, 1959.

Cronbach, L. J. *Essentials of psychological testing.* (2nd ed.) New York: Harper & Row, 1960.

Thorndike, R. L., & Hagen, E. *Measurement and evaluation in psychology and education.* (2nd ed.) New York: Wiley, 1961.

Tyler, Leona. *The work of the counselor.* (2nd. ed.) New York: Appleton-Century-Crofts, 1961.

CONTENTS

CHAPTER 1

Counseling and Education

If you subscribe to the statements made below, the discussion in this and the succeeding chapters will be meaningful to you; otherwise, what follows in this text will be hollow and senseless.

Individual students differ from one another in their abilities, rates of learning, needs, and personalities; these individual differences are crucially significant in education.

The school must help the individual student adapt to the demands of society and at the same time must adapt itself to the unique characteristics of the student.

The purposes of education predicate the many current and future roles of the student as a citizen, as a spouse and parent, as a worker, and as a supporter of the culture and wisdom of his community.

The school and the educator must be concerned with both the happiness and satisfaction of the individual and the welfare of the community to which he belongs.

The purpose of the school is to encourage diversity and uniqueness and at the same time to develop conformity to and respect for the requirements of society.

Behavior of the student always reflects both his reasoning processes and his emotions, both conscious and unconscious, and no behavior is exclusively cerebral or visceral.

All that can be discussed or described meaningfully about persons is behavior; and the referent for concepts, constructs, or abstract ideas in such discussion or description always must be behavior.

Persons with specialized competencies are needed to manage today's schools. The tasks to be done by educators require varying types of abilities, interests, and training. Educational specialists such as administrators, classroom teachers, counselors, nurses, school psychologists, social workers, and main-

tenance staff are required. The effectiveness of the educational
enterprise depends on the relationships among these persons
and the goodwill and integrity of all.

The above statements do not provide a comprehensive summary of
an educational philosophy for school counselors, but in capsule form
they are the major assumptions counselors must make when they explain
and justify their existence.

Counseling is not new in education or in the community. It always
has been one of the more important types of social interrelationships,
and persons in many professions, in law and medicine, as well as in education, have provided counseling to those with whom they work. Only
recently, however, has a group emerged to which counseling has been
assigned as a primary responsibility. Professional counselors with specialized graduate training devoting most of their time to counseling are
a new phenomenon, and they must be viewed in light of the society and
the school from which they emerged.

Counselors in schools should be differentiated from the many other
persons who use the occupational title *counselor*. The counseling psychologist is a counselor whose training is primarily as a psychologist,
and although he also may be a school counselor, his primary responsibility is that of a psychologist. Insurance counselors, investment counselors, and vacation counselors are salesmen who attempt to tailor their
products or services to fit the needs of the individual. School counselors
are educators trained in psychology who use their counseling skills to
maximize the constructive effects of the school on the pupil.

The counselor gives "primary attention to the differential needs of
each individual student, which stem from the wide individual differences in abilities, interests, and personality characteristics which exist
and which can be measured. It is the development of the individual student as a unique entity which is the center of emphasis of the counseling
function" (AAAS, 1958).

Three aspects of our society must be considered if this emerging profession of counseling is to be understood. They are (1) the values that
predominate in our social life, (2) the resources available to transform
these values to overt behavior, and (3) the social organization that
facilitates and makes possible this actualization of values.

DOMINANT VALUES

Historically, the individual has been the center of our society. For the
most part, group action, governmental legislation, and institutional activity have been evaluated in terms of their effects on individuals. Any

action that harms individuals is disapproved; any action that benefits individuals is approved. Insofar as every group action benefits some persons and harms others, much social conflict can be explained by this ambiguity. The viewpoint of social action, however, is that of the individual.

Many phrases in current use reflect this value: "the worth of the individual," "the rights of man," "the dignity of the person," "the integrity of personality." These and other similar phrases are used to explain or justify group action and in their many interpretations are accepted by most persons.

These statements and related attitudes can be traced back at least as far as Thomas Paine, who wrote in *Rights of Man* (1817):

> Government is nothing more than a National association; and the object of this association is the good of all, as well individually as collectively. Every Man wishes to pursue his occupation, and to enjoy the fruits of his labors, and the produce of his property in peace and safety, and with the least possible expence. When these things are accomplished, all the objects for which Government ought to be established are answered.

The school's concern with individuals reflects this value, and the counselor's task results from the responsibility assumed by the community and school for aiding each pupil to achieve a satisfying individuality.

Another set of values centers around materials and ideas, possessions and experiences, progress and emotion, the Philistine and the children of the light. Americans are prone to regard themselves as materialists, and critics of America frequently have contended that the value placed on material possessions is a mark of our nation. On the other hand, Americans are religious and have many religious institutions. They publish many books and make ideas available to all economic groups. All parts of the community are concerned with music, both classical and popular. The country supports thousands of artists; art galleries are visited by hundreds of thousands; and many other characteristics belie the oversimplified description of a materialistic society. American society places great value on physical well-being, but no other society has shown greater concern for problems of ethics, justice, and mercy.

The counselor's assignment is influenced by this value. Counselors are not classification officers concerned only with productivity and efficiency. Neither are they concerned only with the spiritual or intellectual development of their pupils. Their work encompasses both the matter and the mind.

Our society is characterized by the attitudes of persons toward their past, their present, and their future. This time orientation is reflected in our feelings about history, in our concern about a man's precedents, in our ideas of progress, in our tendencies to project ourselves into the future, and in our anxiety about our fate after death.

Our ambivalence toward the past is revealed when we say that any American child can become President and at the same time grant prestige to members of old families and to foreign nobility and royalty. We say a man's ancestry is unimportant and at the same time evaluate his importance on the basis of his ancestry. We stress the desirability of social mobility and at the same time derive satisfaction from the election to high office of a descendent of an old and famous family.

We consider the present better than the past and know without doubt that in spite of temporary delays, the future must be better than the present. Man's destiny is on the ascent, and this defines our goal. Counseling is directed toward the future and would not exist in a past-oriented society.

A fourth value underlying our society is expressed through the individual's need for acceptance. The opinions of others, what others think about a person, how a person is perceived by others, these all determine the behavior of the individual. Children are reared to behave so they obtain approval from others; the threat of rejection molds their behavior.

Our entire social hierarchy of status and prestige reflects this basic value. Persons strive to move upward in order to obtain increased recognition and to be seen by others in a more favorable light. Motivation rarely consists solely of the need for status, but many vocational and educational decisions are so influenced.

The counselor's task often consists of aiding pupils to understand these hierarchies and of helping pupils find their places in them. The profession of counseling is a product of a mobile society and is one solution to problems resulting from this mobility.

A final value consists of the attitudes in our society toward authority. Most apparent is the ambivalence of these feelings. Submission to authority is accepted as necessary and inevitable, but at the same time is resented. Careful controls are established to limit authority, and "authoritarian" has become a nasty word. These ambivalences, having their origin in the home as a result of increasing confusion about the authority role of parents, have generalized to others in the community, particularly to the school, teachers, and counselors.

As society becomes more complex, the need for specialists and finely trained experts becomes more obvious, but their work is made difficult by the resistance they arouse as figures of authority. Students react to counselors in some instances as they do to parents, and this is an expression of more than the individual's unique behavior.

These social values that characterize our contemporary communities are derived from many sources. Some precede the Judaic-Christian philosophy. Some have their roots in the oppressions and liberations of the Middle Ages. Some more recently reflect the Industrial Revolution, the concept of evolution, and the influences of psychoanalysis.[1]

SOCIAL RESOURCES

The formative values of our society exist in their present form only because we have had resources to give these values meaning and relevance. The extent to which value is placed on the individual depends in part on the ability of society to provide opportunity for the individual. The extent to which individuals can devote time to philosophy, religion, and art depends on the availability of time that need not be used to search for food or clothing or to fight to protect oneself from the elements. Time must be available and so must materials. The writer must have his paper, the painter his paint, and both must have time in which to contemplate and perform. We must recognize the extent to which hundreds of square miles of fertile land, mountains of iron and copper, and abundant timber have allowed us to define our values and direct our behavior. The counselor particularly must see how counseling students preparing for a life of abundance differs from counseling those in a society of severe deprivation.

SOCIAL ORGANIZATION

Finally, the manner in which society organizes itself is directly related to the tasks and the methods of the counselor. In a fluid social organization, counselors have more opportunity and greater need to encourage self-exploration than they do in a more rigidly structured society. The greater the responsibility given to individuals for their own decisions and behaviors, the greater the concern of the counselor with stimulating self-understanding and self-exploration. In a society where the state assigns persons to training programs and occupations most appropriate for their abilities, aptitudes, and interests, the task of the counselor is quite different from that in a state which allows persons a free choice (Berdie, 1960). The greater the social mobility in a community, the more the counselor can help students to identify and actualize their potentials. The clearer the definition of occupational and social groups, the more the counselor can emphasize rational learning. This clarity of occupational definition, however, may characterize a rigid or old society and may result in fewer rational work decisions.

The values of a society, its resources, and its organization provide the

---

[1] An interesting discussion of the history of American attitudes and values is presented in *The Americans: The Colonial Experience* by Daniel J. Boorstin (1958).

social context from which counseling emerges. The counselor who understands his work must be aware of the anthropology of the groups in which he lives, the sociology of his community, and the social psychology of his counselees.

THE SCHOOLS AND COUNSELING

The purpose of the schools is to influence the nature of society, but at the same time society determines the objectives and the structure of the schools. Schools must reflect the values of society, and changes in the schools must be correlated in time with corresponding though not necessarily identical changes in society. Perhaps we should not say that schools reflect society, but rather that both the schools and other social institutions have been affected by a broad range of common influences, and to understand one, the other must be understood. The school can be a powerful force for social change, and the nature of the desired change is one of society's most controversial issues.

The school counselor exists today as a result of certain needs and developments in the educational enterprise. In order to understand further his profession, the school counselor must be aware of the schools which gave rise to this profession. Any summary of the history of education must overgeneralize and oversimplify, so no such summary will be made here (Brubacher, 1947).

The objectives of American schools are not neatly defined, and any objectives that obtain wide agreement must be so general that they will have little utility. Phrases such as "education for life," although aptly describing at one level the objectives of education, are of little help in deciding what should be taught or how to teach it. Needless to say, however, the accepted objectives of American education are broad. The schools attempt to achieve many ends; these objectives encompass, in addition to liberal education, preparing for an occupation, training for citizenship, attaining mental and emotional maturity, and reaching personal values which share maximum congruence with one another.

Conant (1959) summarized the three functions of the high school:

Provide a good general education for *all* the pupils as future citizens of a democracy, provide elective programs for the majority to develop useful skills, and educate adequately those with a talent for handling advanced academic subjects.

The intellectual functions of the teacher, and by implication the functions of the school, were summarized by J. B. Johnston (1930):

1. To make the materials for study available. To organize the content of a proposed course of study and present it in lectures, by reading references, or otherwise.

2. To stimulate interest or to connect up the subject-matter at hand with such interests as the student has.

3. To awaken new interests, to arouse intellectual curiosity.

4. To guide and direct the student; to show the way to intellectual attainment.

5. To give the student training in the technique of acquiring knowledge. This must include the critical attitude and self-criticism.

6. To elucidate difficulties, to initiate the student from time to time into new and higher forms of investigation or creative effort by applying for him and with him new techniques, new avenues of approach or new combinations or modes of attack.

7. To infuse and maintain intellectual integrity.

8. To evaluate the results of the student's efforts.

President Coffman of the University of Minnesota once spoke about liberal education in this way (1939):

A liberal education is not a matter of studying certain subjects; it may flow from any subject. It implies something more than a knowledge of the social sciences, of art, of literature, and of mathematics. Indeed, one may graduate from a liberal arts college without having been liberalized at all. The most important by-product of every subject of study should be a liberal mind. And what do we mean by a liberal mind? We mean a mind that has broad interests, wide knowledge, cultivated tastes, appreciation, and sound perspective. We mean a mind that is open and tolerant, ready and willing to face new situations and to interpret them in terms of knowledge as it relates to social welfare. We mean a mind that includes a standard of ethics and a keen sense of responsibility. The education I am describing—and the type of mind that is its choicest by-product—cannot thrive where there is regimentation or where students in the name of self-expression determine the programs and processes of instruction. The essence of democracy is an enlightened give and take. This, likewise, is the essence of a liberal education. Totalitarianism and untutored self-expression are accordingly incompatible with both sound democracy and sound education.

In another publication (Coffman, 1934), he defines the objective of education by describing the educated person:

What does the truly educated American believe in? He believes that his institutions are social in origin and in nature, not the product of any individual nor of any group of individuals, that they represent the soul hungers and the spiritual expressions of the common people. He believes that the only natural rights anyone has are those that he uses for collective welfare. He believes in equal rights before the law. He believes in equality of opportunity. He believes that potentially the achievement of the individual is measureless. He believes that a generous education for himself and a better one for his children are the only safeguard of democracy. These are the priceless possessions of his creed, the articles of his faith which he desires to have transmitted and made available to mankind everywhere.

Liberal education, in this sense, is not a prerogative of certain intellectual groups nor only of groups who have attained the collegiate levels in our education hierarchy. As Coffman has stated in the same volume:

Where trained intelligence exists, there we seem to have the best citizenship. And is not citizenship a function which all classes of people are expected to exercise? Shall we deny those who are to traverse the humbler walks of life the outlook of the trained mind?

Long ago they [the state universities and public schools] learned that genius and talent do not belong to any class because of wealth or social position. The only differences they recognize are differences due to ability and to a desire to achieve. They recognize that all cannot achieve alike nor move forward at equal rates of speed. They know that some must fall by the way and that some attempt work which they are not qualified to pursue. But they are not willing to condemn those of less talent merely because they have less talent. They propose for them just what they propose for the more talented—that each shall be permitted to progress as rapidly as his abilities will permit to the approximate limits of his attainment. The student of few talents shall not be denied his opportunity while the student of many talents is given his.

Our schools have a broad range of objectives and are concerned with a broad variety of students. No one type of student per se is more important than any other type, and the responsibility of the school is to provide to each the kind of education most suitable for his abilities, interests, and needs.

The fact that our public schools function as community institutions also determines the role of the counselor. The schools are managed by members of the community. The boards that control our schools consist of businessmen, lawyers, carpenters, and farmers who constantly are concerned with the relationship between the school and the remainder of the community. Students satisfy not only their intellectual needs in the school but also many of their social and recreational needs. Schools have assumed many broad community responsibilities, and many of these are shared with the church, the family, and community agencies.

"The framework in which the counselor operates depends upon school policy" (Conant, 1959). The counselor, to work effectively with others in the school, both members of the staff and students, must have a thorough appreciation of the educational philosophies characterizing different schools and must be well aware of the conditions that have influenced American schools to become the schools they are today. Only with this understanding can the counselor understand his role and perform it effectively.

THE NATURE OF COUNSELING

Within this social and educational context, a new counseling has emerged. The teacher, the parent, the pastor, the family physician, and many others continue to provide counseling and advice as they always have, but the service provided by the person trained as a counselor is a new aspect of our schools.

The counselor, more than persons in other professions, is aware of and sensitive to questions and knowledge resulting from modern psychology. The psychological concepts particularly important for the task of the counselor include individual differences, motivation, learning, emotions, the unconscious, social psychology and group dynamics, and psychological development. All of these concepts directly touch the adjustment of the student, and all must be the concern of the counselor who works with him. Not equally as much is known about each of these concepts, and the counselor's activities, although influenced by all, are influenced to a greater extent by certain ones.

The topic in psychology about which most is known is that of *differences among individuals*. The nature, the measurement and observation, the consistency and predictability, and the implications of individual differences all have received intensive and prolonged study, and volumes of research are available to counselors to help them learn how and why one person differs from another and what these differences mean (Anastasi & Foley, 1949; Tyler, 1956).

The school counselor must know about the psychology of learning, how students acquire skills, how their educational backgrounds develop, and how their learning responds to teaching methods (Deese, 1958). Counselors also must know about the psychodynamics of the individual, and the relationships between his emotional reactions and his earlier emotional history as it involves his parents, his siblings, and his peers (Shaffer & Shoben, 1956). Counselors must be sophisticated about the development of the individual as he passes through one stage to another, as his motor skills develop, as his intellectual competencies grow (Goodenough & Tyler, 1959). All this knowledge is important if the counselor is to perform his job satisfactorily, but if a priority can be assigned, the topic to receive first place will be *individual differences*.

Counseling can be defined as listening and talking with an individual about the needs, characteristics, traits, and behaviors which make him similar to or different from other persons, with particular emphasis in the discussion on the rational meaning and the emotional implication of these characteristics as they relate to his educational and vocational behavior. The marriage counselor will be concerned with differences related to the marital behavior of the person; the rehabilitation counselor will be concerned with differences as they relate to the rehabilitation process; but the school counselor primarily will be concerned with differences that have educational and vocational implications, with full recognition that differences in emotional attitudes, family relationships, and physical maturity all have vocational and educational bearing.

The principal function of the school counselor is to communicate with the student, his family, and his teachers about these individual differences so that this knowledge is meaningfully integrated into the total behavior pattern of the student. It is not enough for the counselor to observe systematically and report about these differences; he must realize that for this knowledge to become functional, learning must occur, emotional blocks and resistances overcome, and motivation and interests stimulated. In a sense the counselor works as does the athletic coach. He provides to the student information about methods and skills, and then he observes the student as he attempts to use them. He asks questions to emphasize certain points, indicates dangers and hazards, makes suggestions concerning errors as they are made, recognizes and acknowledges progress as it occurs, and provides new and advanced information as the student's readiness develops. This analogy is a rather idealized picture of what the counselor should do, but it is presented to provide an objective for counselors as they work with their students.

Historically, the task of the professional counselor was to help students find appropriate occupations and training leading to these jobs (Kitson, 1925). However, when counseling was beginning to develop, another psychological specialty, clinical psychology, was evolving, and this specialty focused attention on psychologically disturbed or poorly functioning individuals. Counselors were influenced by this new psychology. In response to school administrators and teachers faced with problems they were unable to solve satisfactorily, counselors developed disproportionate concern with students who were in difficulty. In a sense, the function of the counselor was seen as a remedial or therapeutic one.

The possibilities of counseling as a preventive were quickly seen, and one of the main jobs of the counselor was to prevent small problems from becoming large ones. The counselor, working with others in the school, was expected to detect students who were showing incipient problems and help solve these problems.

More recently, and particularly because of increasing awareness of the need to aid gifted children, counselors again have been given a responsibility that is neither therapeutic nor preventive, but rather developmental and educational (Berdie, 1949; Williamson, 1947). The assumptions introducing this chapter were not meant to apply only to students who had problems or to pupils who might have problems, but rather to all pupils. Each pupil, regardless of his abilities, his current adjustment, or his plans and ambitions, deserves an opportunity to have the fullest possible knowledge concerning his own potential. Each pupil must have a complete appreciation of the differences that make him an individual unique from other persons. Each person must be able to take advantage of the unique and appropriate opportunities provided by his school and by his community. Each pupil must have a chance to learn how his own emotions and his own intellectual processes influence his behavior. Each pupil must have an opportunity to select his own goals and objectives from the many within his view and to review periodically his progress toward these goals and their continuing appropriateness.

In this sense the counselor serves as an educator. Classroom teachers are concerned with the individual student and with the content of instruction, but the subject matter in most classes is not the student but rather the course content. The counselor serves a similar educational role, but his course content is the student himself. This educational role is the most important one assigned to the counselor.

UNDERSTANDING INDIVIDUAL STUDENTS

Counseling, as it has been defined here, requires that the counselor possess a great deal of information about students. Every counselor, just as every effective teacher, must know the students with whom he works, and we will make the following important assumption: *The more information we have about students, the better we can work with them.* Some types of information about students are not relevant to the purposes of most teachers, and some types of information may not be needed for counseling purposes. In many instances, however, whether information is helpful or not can be determined only after it is examined. Thus, a senior high school counselor who has incomplete records concerning the progress of a student in junior high school may wonder whether to request information from the junior high school counselor. Actually, there is no way for this counselor to determine whether the information from the junior high school will be helpful or not until he obtains and examines it. After this examination, he may decide that the report is of little relevance as far as his work is concerned, or on the other hand he may discover that the data are most helpful. Counselors and teachers seldom have too much information about those with whom they work; more often they have too little.

In this text we shall be concerned mainly with the kinds of information needed for counseling individual students, regardless of whether the counseling is done by teachers, principals, or professional counselors. We shall not be concerned as much with the kinds of information needed for effective classroom teaching or for effective administration, but we must recognize that these types of information cannot be easily separated and many data about students are helpful to both counselors and others in the school. Different types of information are used by counselors in different ways. A counselor combines information about high school records and scores on engineering aptitude and mathematics achievement tests to predict how well a student will do in engineering school. Another student may be perplexed by his poor grades, and the counselor, on the basis of a review of his school record and a reading test profile, may refer him to a remedial reading specialist.

To discuss some questions, a counselor must have a comprehensive understanding of the individual with whom he is concerned. He may have to obtain an adequate understanding of the personality characteristics of the student, his needs, his motivations, his attitude toward himself, toward his elders, and toward his school, and the psychological mechanisms that have been developed or that are developing as means of solving his conflicts. The counselor will use many kinds of information while attempting to understand the pupil's personality. Test scores, particularly scores on personality inventories, may provide clues or hints about other sources of information that should be explored to understand the pupil. Scores may suggest that a counselor meet with parents or teachers, or that he consult with the visiting teacher or school nurse.

Some information is used not to make direct predictions, but rather because it suggests ways for the counselor to integrate other kinds of information so that a systematic and consistent picture of the student can be obtained. A counselor may have information about a pupil's school achievement, his relationships with his friends, his family background, his abilities, and his measured interests. Information and understanding are not synonymous. A case may arise in which the counselor will be bewildered by an array of facts which do not seem to provide a real understanding of the pupil, but an additional bit of information may suggest a theme to the counselor, an idea that integrates the available information. The counselor may have a rather complete picture of a student, but may not really understand him until he learns that the pupil has only recently found out that he was adopted at a relatively early age. The additional information might give meaning to the other information concerning the pupil's emotions and attitudes. Another pupil might be overly dependent on teachers and have difficulty establishing relationships with other pupils, and this pupil also might show much educational and vocational indecision. A score on the Minnesota Counseling Inventory might suggest a family conflict, and following this lead, the counselor may be able to increase his understanding of this person and help him resolve his conflict.

In this text, much attention will be given to methods for collecting and interpreting information. We should never forget, however, the importance of making each bit of information about a student fit into the total picture. Seldom will we be able to form a picture that encompasses all of our information, one that completely satisfies us as adequately describing the pupil. At best, we can obtain a concept of each person that allows us to make some inferences regarding his goals and objectives and to help that person, his family, and his teachers explore means of reaching those goals or of finding new ones.

QUESTIONS FOR STUDY

1. The professionally trained school counselor is a product of the mid-twentieth century. What conditions explain his appearance during that epoch?
2. What would a counselor's role have been in a medieval society? What would it be in a communistic state?
3. Why should a counselor be concerned with the liberal education of his counselees?
4. Discuss reasons why counselors should have information about their counselees. In what ways could such information hinder counseling?

REFERENCES

American Association for the Advancement of Science. *Identification and guidance of able students*. Conference on Testing and Counseling, University of Michigan, May 28–31, 1958.

Anastasi, Anne, & Foley, J. P., Jr. *Differential psychology*. New York: Macmillan, 1949.

Berdie, R. F. Counseling—an educational technique. *Educ. psychol. Measmt*, 1949, 9, 89–94.

Berdie, R. F. The counselor and his manpower responsibilities. *Personnel Guid. J.*, 1960, 38, 458–463.

Boorstin, D. J. *The Americans: the colonial experience*. New York: Random House, 1958.

Brubacher, J. S. *A history of the problems of education*. New York: McGraw-Hill, 1947.

Coffman, L. D. *The state university: its work and problems*. Minneapolis: University of Minnesota Press, 1934.

Coffman, L. D. *Freedom through education*. Minneapolis: University of Minnesota Press, 1939.

Conant, J. B. *The American high school today*. New York: McGraw-Hill, 1959.

Deese, J. E. *The psychology of learning*. (2nd ed.) New York: McGraw-Hill, 1958.

Goodenough, F. L., & Tyler, Leona E. *Developmental psychology*. New York: Appleton-Century-Crofts, 1959.

Johnston, J. B. *The liberal college in changing society*. New York: Century, 1930.

Kitson, H. D. *The psychology of vocational adjustment*. Philadelphia: Lippincott, 1925.

Paine, T. *Rights of man*. London: W. T. Sherwin, 1817.

Shaffer, L. F., & Shoben, E. J., Jr. *The psychology of adjustment: a dynamic and experimental approach to personality and mental hygiene*. Boston: Houghton Mifflin, 1956.

Tyler, Leona E. *The psychology of human differences*. New York: Appleton-Century-Crofts, 1956.

Williamson, E. G. Counseling and the Minnesota point of view. *Educ. psychol. Measmt*, 1947, 7, 141–156.

CHAPTER 2

Learning about the Physical Development of Pupils

Individual differences in physique are greater among persons in the early teens than at any other stage in the life span. For example, variability in height and weight increases gradually from birth to the beginning of adolescence, shows a sharp increase during the adolescent growth spurt, and returns almost to the preadolescent level at maturity (Tuddenham & Snyder, 1954).

Obviously, classification into grades by chronological age results in physically heterogeneous groups of adolescents. This heterogeneity in physical development leads to many problems in education. Some will not be discussed in this book, since they more properly belong in the broader domain of psychology of secondary and higher education. We are concerned, however, with the implications for counseling of individual differences in physical characteristics.

Pupils are aware of and sensitive to the wide range in physical development among their contemporaries. Adolescence is a time of great concern with social acceptance and desire to belong to a group. The adolescent knows that physical characteristics are important determiners of status in his peer group. As the pupil's physical characteristics change during puberty and adolescence, he often is painfully concerned with how his physical appearance may affect his relations with others. Normal, delayed, or accelerated biological development of the individual can have varying effects on the individual and his relationships with his peers, parents, and school staff.

In addition to physical growth and development, the health of pupils is of concern to counselors. At pubescence, health problems and physical defects including those of sensory acuity increase. Health problems may include poor nutrition, skin diseases such as acne, low energy level, generally poor health, the loss of limbs or other orthopedic disability, and

14

the loss of sight or hearing. Other major or minor physical impairments may result from accident or disease. A related problem is that of imagined physical handicaps, such as a pupil's feelings of being too short, of having unattractive ears or teeth, or of being too fat or too thin.

The counselor can make a significant contribution to the school health program by being sensitive to the health and physical condition of his counselees and referring pupils he suspects of needing treatment to the school nurse. Health is also of direct and immediate relevance for counseling. A knowledge of normal and abnormal physical development aids us to understand the individual and his needs, and thus it is directly significant for educational and occupational counseling. The counselor must consider all of the pupil's characteristics, his needs, interests, abilities, and desires. All of these characteristics interact to produce the total individual. The health and physical status of a pupil have a direct bearing on his educational and vocational plans.

SOCIAL IMPLICATIONS OF PHYSICAL APPEARANCE

Physique has social stimulus value, and people react to physical appearance. To most persons, the physical appearance of another individual is his most obvious characteristic. People tend to react more quickly to physical manifestations of the individual personality than they do to psychological or social characteristics. They tend to analyze and evaluate these latter characteristics before reacting. Chapter 4 discusses in detail the concern adolescents have about relationships with others. Having friends, being sought after by one's peers, and belonging to a group are highly valued by adolescents. Consequently, they are concerned with anything which might affect their social relationships. Recognizing the importance of physical appearance, the adolescent is keenly aware of the changes taking place in his physical structure and appearance. During his earlier years of growing up, he had developed certain notions about himself and his physique and its impact on others. As his body rapidly changes in adolescence, he must evaluate the effect of these changes on his relationships with others.

The social stimulus value of physical appearance is culturally determined. Consider the changing standards for female attractiveness over the past seventy-five years in this country. Reflect on the beauty and charms of Lillian Russell, those of the flapper in the twenties, of Marilyn Monroe, Brigitte Bardot, and the pinup girls featured in illustrated magazines. Anthropologists have documented how values placed on various aspects of physique differ from culture to culture and determine standards of beauty and desirability (Benedict, 1934; Hanks & Hanks, 1948; Klineberg, 1954).

ARBITRARY CULTURAL STANDARDS

The standards used in assessing the values of physique and physical appearance often are quite arbitrary. The armed services, for example, have set minimum height and weight standards for induction. Physical health standards also must be met by the inductee. Police departments in large cities have similar physical standards. Girls must meet certain criteria of height, weight, and attractiveness in order to become airline hostesses. Thus, physical makeup can be related to vocation as well as to social stimulus value.

PHYSICAL HANDICAP

Very obvious is the difference in the social stimulus value of a person who suffers from a physical handicap and of one who does not. However, what constitutes a handicap also is determined culturally, and one part of the body and its impact on other persons can temper their reaction to other bodily characteristics. How many women were repelled by Clark Gable's big ears, for example? Jimmy Durante has capitalized on his abnormal nose. Thus, there is interaction and compensation of the various aspects of physical appearance with the culture determining the total effect of a person on others. Meyerson (1955) has made the following generalization about physique and disability:

A disability exists only when a person lacks an adequate physical tool for behavior and this lack is perceived by the culture in which the person lives as making the person less able than his fellows. If a particular tool is not differentiated or required by a culture, its lack or impairment in a person cannot be a disability. If the tool is differentiated with a "higher" physical, social, and psychological ability, the lack or impairment will not be perceived as a disability.

ATTITUDES TOWARD ONE'S PHYSIQUE

The developing individual is aware of societal standards of physical appearance and interprets them as they apply to himself. He realizes that physique is one criterion for assigning a person to a social role, and thus it causes one's peers to expect certain behavior from a person in that role. For example, studies have indicated that children larger in height and weight tend to show leadership, popularity, social success, and good adjustment more frequently than smaller children (Barker et al., 1953; Jones, 1946; Jones & Bayley, 1950). These expectations influence a person's perception of himself directly, and as he compares himself with others, he develops certain beliefs about himself. Sometimes the expectations or attitudes of an individual about himself are misinterpretations or overinterpretations of his impact on others. Consequently, the attitudes of the individual toward himself are important, and these attitudes often are things with which the counselor must deal.

Helen, a high school freshman, was large for her age and not particularly attractive or popular. Her hair was straight and her facial features were plain. She used to sit for hours on a soda fountain stool in the local teen-age hangout. As she ate sundaes or sodas, she was fascinated by her image in the mirror behind the fountain. She told everyone who would listen that she had the most beautiful mouth in the world, especially when she was chewing. Helen illustrates the teen-agers' need for social approval and acceptance, their concern with their physical appearance, and their perceptions of their own and others' expectations of themselves as a function of physique.

Variations in physical development and physique may not result in ability or behavioral limitations or be responsible for social handicaps, but the person involved may use these variations as a defense against facing other problems. Physical differences can provide a rationalization for rather than a cause of negative attitudes and maladjustment. A girl may use a large and spectacular pimple as an excuse for not attending a social function of which she is afraid, whereas on another occasion she will treat and hide as best she can an equally disfiguring blemish to attend a function she has anticipated with pleasure.

Normal variations in physique are a cause for concern by some children and not for others, and the degree of concern depends in part on adequacy of adjustment. Sometimes parents and siblings ridicule a slight physical variation in a child as a means of teasing or expressing hostility. This attacking causes the child to become sensitive about that part of his body. Each of four children in one family had some body part about which he was particularly sensitive and concerned. One boy felt he had abnormally large and protruding teeth; the other felt his head was "funny shaped"; one girl thought she had a large ugly nose; and the other was so sensitive about her ears that she refused to wear her hair in a style which revealed them. None of the children differed to an abnormal degree in physical appearance, but their parents first and they later referred to these physical attributes as abnormal. The family was poor and the parents had unsatisfactory social lives. Possibly they were looking for reasons to explain the unhappy social lives they feared for their children.

In order to understand better the social reactions of persons to changes in their physical appearance, consider the variations in attitude among children when they are required to wear glasses for the first time. Their own reactions to the glasses include their reactions to the

fancied and real attitudes of their playmates and families. Consider also
the varied reactions of adults who must adjust to the physical and psychological aspects of beginning to wear bifocal glasses.

PHYSICAL DEVELOPMENT

Since this book is written primarily for high school counselors, we will
discuss physical development just before, during, and slightly after adolescence. As emphasized above, the counselor must know much about
normal physical development. This knowledge will enable him to gauge
whether or not a student who has certain physical characteristics is in
need of further attention. This knowledge also assumes an understanding
of biological characteristics and of the development of the large individual differences among teen-agers.

The transition from childhood to adolescence is known as pubescence.
The period from puberty to complete maturation is known as adolescence. Maturity, we commonly say, is reached when a person is grown-
up, but because different aspects of the individual mature at different
rates, we more appropriately should speak of specific maturities occurring at different ages.

Puberty is preceded by a period of rapid growth during which ossi-
fication of bones is accelerated. Anatomical and endocrine changes may
occur a year or more earlier in some persons, but sharp physiological
differences are not found between different age groups.

The menarche, or appearance of first menstruation in girls, is an outstanding time mark in puberty and is used as a reference point. The age
of girls at the first menstruation varies widely. About one-half of American girls first menstruate between the twelfth and the fourteenth birthday, the average being about the thirteenth year. Yet, among healthy
girls, the range of age at menarche appears to be at least from the ninth
year to the twentieth year. Some girls are in late adolescence at the age
of ten, and a few are in early adolescence at the age of twenty.

Boys have no such well-defined point as the menarche. A traditionally
used indication of puberty in boys is the appearance of the first pigmented pubic hair, but authorities do not agree on this being analogous
to the menarche in girls. Boys have the same age range as girls in reaching puberty, but some research indicates that boys reach puberty from
one to two years later than girls. The appearance of pigmented pubic
hair in boys appears on the average at approximately thirteen years of
age. The acceleration in growth of boys is delayed from one to two years
as compared with that of girls. Among boys and girls, there is a wide
range in chronological age at which puberty is passed and adolescence
begins.

In any one school class primarily based on chronological age, pupils will vary widely in their physical development. Even at the senior high school level, boys and girls who are prepubertal and postpubertal, with all of the accompanying differences in psychological and emotional development, will be in the same class.

Most obvious, however, are differences in physical appearance. As an individual moves from prepuberty into postpuberty, a number of physical changes occur. He grows heavier, taller, and stronger. The difference in strength is more marked in boys than in girls as one compares the postpubertal with the prepubertal period. The long bones of the arms and legs extend and grow so rapidly that height gains of 6 inches in a year have been recorded. Clothes are outgrown soon after they are purchased. As they are altered, the individual has outgrown them almost before the alteration is complete. Boys and girls in the pubertal stage are pictured as gangly, long-legged, and consisting primarily of knees and elbows.

Facial proportions change. The individual loses the childish contour of his face, and boys' faces particularly become more angular. Girls' faces appear softer and more rounded. In both sexes the faces take on a grown-up appearance. The amount of fat underneath the skin decreases in boys and increases in girls. In most cases the boys' shoulders become wider than their hips, whereas in the girls the reverse is true. In boys the larynx, or Adam's apple, becomes noticeably enlarged with an accompanying change in voice. Some teen-age boys develop hoarse, harsh, discordant voices. They may lose control of their voices and suddenly change from a squeak to a bass.

Research reveals no loss in skill or coordination for people going through puberty, but casual observation indicates that they are clumsy and appear to be uncoordinated. This clumsiness may be more apparent than real and may be due to two conditions. As size increases, parents may expect more coordination than the children actually have and hence judge them to be clumsy. In addition, the children are self-conscious about their appearance. They are striving to attain adult roles. Experiences resulting from this striving can be embarrassing and increase self-consciousness, so that awkwardness comes from self-consciousness rather than from lack of coordination.

Other noticeable characteristics are the appearance of secondary sex characteristics. Girls' breasts develop; axillary and pubic hair appear for both boys and girls, and facial hair appears for boys.

The changes in physical size and the appearance of secondary sex characteristics have a great impact on the individuals and on others and may chiefly account for the changes in social behavior accompanying puberty. The increase in sexual sensitivity and interest may influence behavior. Although delinquency as a whole does not seem to be related to adolescence, there may be a shift in the kind of delinquencies, and sexual delinquency may increase.

Research suggests no causal relationship between physical maturity and mental growth within any one individual, although certainly there is a concomitant development of physical maturity and mental growth. That is, the group as a whole tends to develop physical maturity at the same time it develops mental maturity. Physical development and the age of onset of menstruation and puberty appear to be due to hereditary, nutritional, and health factors.

BEHAVIORAL CHANGES

Rapid growth and body changes are likely to be accompanied by fatigue and listlessness. The inadequate diet of many teen-agers accentuates these symptoms. Concomitant with the physical changes are attitudinal and behavioral changes, probably due in part to the physical changes taking place. Psychologically, pubescents demonstrate restlessness, boredom, social antagonism, a desire for isolation from family and friends, resistance to authority, a reluctance to work, heightened emotionality, lack of self-confidence, daydreaming, excessive modesty, preoccupation with sex, and sexual antagonism (Davidson & Gottlieb, 1955; Frank, 1951; Frank & Frank, 1956; Gesell, Ilg, & Ames, 1956; Hurlock, 1959; Liccione, 1955; Stouffer & Owens, 1955).

INTENT OF THE SCHOOL HEALTH PROGRAM

The philosophy underlying most school health programs is that the school has a responsibility for the pupils' health only to the extent that maximum health is important to school achievement. A pupil usually cannot perform his best work if he is not in good physical condition. Parents have the primary responsibility for the health of their children. The family physician and dentist have obviously important roles for maintaining the family's health. Most school systems require pupils to have periodical physical and dental examinations from their family physicians or pediatricians and dentists. These examinations detect many children in need of extensive diagnosis and treatment for conditions which handicap their participation in the regular school program. Most schools also conduct regular gross screening physical examinations, particularly of vision and hearing. Teachers and counselors who are sensitive to the importance of good health to pupil academic achievement serve as "suspecticians," i.e., are alert to signs of poor health. When they suspect a child has poor health, the teachers and counselors refer the pupil to the school nurse. However, the school is not a diagnostic center, and where defects are suspected, referral is made through the parent to the family physician and dentist.

Screening for physical health disabilities is usually most intensively done at the preschool and elementary school levels. However, there is an upsurge of health and physical defects at pubescence. Hence, the counselor of adolescents in his role as detector of poor health will find many pupils in need of physical care. The diet of adolescents, especially girls, is notoriously inadequate (Anon., 1955a, 1955b; Gschneider & Roderuck, 1960; Stearns, 1952). Everson (1960) has succinctly summarized inadequacies of teen-agers' diets:

> Some of the shortcomings in the diets of the adolescent are as follows: too little calcium due to a low consumption of milk; insufficient intake of green and yellow vegetables and fruits, resulting in sub-optimal supplies of vitamin A; too little ascorbic acid; and questionable provision for an amino acid mixture which will support optimal health. In the case of the amino acid intake this may not be as much a matter of protein intake per 24 hr. as it is irregular eating habits, omitting breakfast and poor distribution of protein throughout the day. The teenager is known to enjoy meat, but he doesn't always do a good job of providing a regular mixture of amino acids for most advantageous body use.

Poor nutrition may contribute to poor health, including digestive disturbances and consequent poor educational, social, and vocational adjustment.

HEALTH AND COUNSELING

Even though the school administrator, the school nurse, and the teacher have greatest responsibility for the school program of health instruction and detection and remediation of defects, the counselor can make a unique contribution to the health program. The counselor is aware that poor health and physical condition interfere with the learning process and that the pupil's health and physical status are related to the demands of future jobs and careers. The restrictions placed on children with severe physical disabilities are obvious. These disabilities handicap their participation in many school activities and may limit their vocational choices. Not always obvious is the desirability of encouraging every child to maintain the best health possible in order to promote scholastic and vocational achievement.

The physical demands of certain vocations and the physical risks involved in some must be considered in relationship to the student's physique and emotions. Certain physical characteristics lessen the chances of an individual's vocational success, and the counselor who knows a pupil's physical limitations can help him make choices based on a consideration of them. The physical standards for a career in the Air Force or as an airline stewardess can be correlated with the pupil's attitudes, interests, and health status. Bacteriology or interior decorating would be poor vocational choices for a color-blind person. Flat feet are not compatible with careers in nursing or law enforcement. The tone-deaf person *might* be handicapped in music.

The counselor sees many adolescents when they are highly motivated to do educational and vocational planning. If he is aware of the importance of good health and physical status, he can integrate the pupil's motivation to plan with his concern over his physical appearance. As already discussed, adolescents are interested in their physical appearance and how it might affect their relationships with others. The pupil previously may not have responded to teaching about dental health, but in adolescence the correction of dental defects may be important to him. The effect of food on his weight and complexion may also become important.

A research study conducted in the Denver Public Schools in 1954 revealed the health interests of adolescents (Denver Public Schools, 1954). The counselor can help the pupil relate his interest in a pleasing physical appearance to his health and physical status as they are important to his educational and vocational goals.

CONSULTATION WITH MEDICAL SPECIALISTS

When appropriate, the school nurse or physician or the family physician refer children and their parents to medical specialists such as opthalmologists, otologists, audiologists, otolaryngologists, orthopedists, and physiatrists. The counselor may be doing educational and vocational counseling with pupils who are being treated by these specialists for defects which should modify the pupil's planning for the future. Consequently, the counselor should become familiar with the work of these specialists and consult them about the pupil's capabilities and expectations. Of course, the confidential nature of the medical information may restrict many physicians' participation. Arranging a joint consultation with the parents of the pupil and the physician may solve this problem. Many of the severely disabled pupils will be counseled by the state vocational rehabilitation counselor who has contact with these specialists, and the school counselor need only cooperate with him. However, consultation is also appropriate in the cases of pupils who are not severely disabled.

Physicians recently have become increasingly interested in the health problems of adolescents, and several "teen-age clinics" have been established throughout the country. The counselor working in a school near such a clinic will want to consult the physicians there.

Good school health records resulting from periodic physical and dental examinations are an invaluable resource for the counselor. The counselor must have ready access to these records and be able to consult school medical personnel and other medical specialists.

CONSULTATION WITH OTHERS

Through consultation with school administrators and instructional staff members, the counselor can help them better understand the pupil, his limitations, and his assets. The counselor can interpret to teachers and administrators a pupil's behavior as it is influenced or caused by health or physical limitations. Increased understanding may lead to more sympathetic and productive treatment of the pupil.

SENSORY ACUITY

In addition to routine medical examinations and diagnostic practices in the case of illness, other physical capacities of individuals need to be investigated. The importance of sensory acuity has long been recognized as important in educational endeavors. Obviously, learning can only take place through the avenue of the senses. Of these senses, sight and hearing are of most importance, although in some learning the senses of touch, kinesthesis, taste, and smell are also important.

To learn in the classroom, students must have visual acuity which enables them to see adequately at both near and far points. They should be able to read books or material presented at a distance, such as writing on a blackboard or information projected on a screen. Visual acuity is the ability of a person to perceive fine differences in the visual environment. Most visual screening examinations measure acuity through use of the Snellen charts designed to compare the subject's visual acuity with a standard designated as normal. Anyone who has had his eyes examined by an oculist or optometrist has read from the chart which has letters in rows of decreasing horizontal and vertical size. The largest letter can just be read at 200 feet by normal persons. The next largest letters can just be read at 100 feet, and so on. At 20 feet from the chart, the person who can read the letters which can be read by the normal person is considered to have 20/20 vision. However, if he can read only those letters normally seen at 100 feet he has 20/100 vision. In many states persons with 20/200 vision are considered legally blind. A person with 20/10 vision, of course, has excellent vision since he sees at 20 feet what normal persons see at 10 feet. The Snellen charts generally provide reliable indications as to a person's ability to discriminate visually at a distance of 20 feet.

Some people, however, are able to see adequately at 20 feet, but have difficulty making fine visual discriminations at distances about 14 inches from the eye.

Farsightedness, or hyperopia, the inability to see near objects clearly, and nearsightedness, or myopia, the inability to see far objects clearly, are common defects of vision. Astigmatism, which is due to irregularities in the cornea of the eye, is also quite common and causes the affected person to see, as being in focus, lines oriented in certain directions in a plane, and as out of focus, lines oriented in other directions. A chart with lines radiating in all directions from the center is often used to detect astigmatic persons. Where feasible, visual examinations in the school should make use of refined techniques such as the Orthorater designed for this purpose. However, the teacher who is alert to visual problems is the most effective screening device in most schools. When problems of inadequate vision in pupils are suspected, the pupils should be referred through their parents to a physician for complete diagnosis and treatment.

Visual discrimination of color also is important. Approximately 4 per cent of males and 0.5 per cent of females have observable limitations of color discrimination, the limitation being much less frequent in girls than boys. Why pupils react in different ways to instructions involving colors—"red means stop and green means go"—and why they make use of certain, sometimes weird, color combinations frequently can be understood only by knowing the effectiveness of their color vision. Many easily administered tests of color blindness are available, and the color vision of every pupil should be observed at least once during his elementary school career and again during his high school years.

The Ishihara Test of Color Blindness[1] utilizes pseudoisochromatic plates. These plates use differently colored dots which appear different to persons with normal color vision, but alike to persons with certain types of color blindness. For example, one plate consists of a background of yellowish-green dots upon which is superimposed a number 8 made up of pink and red dots. The number is seen as an 8 by persons with normal color vision, as a 3 by those red-green blind, and is not seen by those totally color-blind.

Effectiveness of hearing, like effectiveness of vision, can be observed directly by noting how the pupil reacts to auditory stimuli. If a person consistently shows signs of not understanding what is said to him, a hearing loss should be suspected. All schools should have pure tone audiometers available to measure the adequacy with which an individual can hear different sound frequencies. Frequently, hearing losses are specific to a given pitch, and the kind of remediation required depends upon the type of hearing loss. Special tests are now available to determine not only the effectiveness with which a person can hear tones, as on an audiometer, but also the effectiveness with which he can hear and understand speech. However, these tests are not available in most

[1] Available from the C. H. Stoelting Company.

schools. Both the visual and the hearing acuity of every pupil should be observed systematically, and adequate provision should be made for remediation of losses in both senses.

The other senses perhaps are not so important for educational purposes. Almost as much difference exists among persons in their ability to sense odors or to respond to tastes as exists in their abilities to see or hear. Counselors and teachers should know that these differences exist and should not assume, as one home economics teacher did, that a girl is uncooperative if she reports she cannot taste paprika, a flavor the teacher thinks very obvious.

SPEECH

The speaking ability of the pupil should also be of concern to the counselor and teacher. Abnormality of speech is a noticeable characteristic that has a profound impact on a pupil and his peers. Speech pathologists have techniques with which to diagnose speech defects resulting from both physical causes and previous learning. The counselor, therefore, should be alert to speech deviations and refer pupils with them to a speech pathologist or speech correctionist.

HEIGHT AND WEIGHT

Much can be learned about the physical status of a person through direct observation. More refined observations can be made with specialized instruments and diagnostic techniques. For example, one can look at a pupil and observe he is overweight, or with a scale one can determine the amount by which he is overweight. By then referring to normative tables, one can determine the status of the individual in respect to others of his age.

The Wetzel Grid for Evaluating Physical Fitness is widely used in schools to compare the developmental status of pupils to the norm. The grid consists of a set of calibrated standards by which each of the following may be assessed by referring to height, weight, and age: growth, development, physique (body build), nutritional grade, physical status, age advancement, maturation, basal metabolism, caloric needs, and net progress. Use of the grid increases in value as observations are accumulated over a period of years during which the child becomes his own standard of comparison. Of course, single observations are valuable since the child's physical status can be compared to general standards.

The Oseretsky Tests of Motor Proficiency were published in Russia in 1923. Edgar Doll (1946) translated them from the Portuguese. They are useful in testing children to detect motor-coordination disorders. Age levels from 4 to 16 are determined in a procedure similar to that of the

Stanford-Binet, and motor ages analogous to mental ages are derived. The tests measure, among other things, postural reactions, gross bodily movements, finger coordination, and control of facial muscles. Readily obtainable materials, such as matchsticks, thread, and paper, are used in the test items.

Pupils worried about their height sometimes can be reassured by predictions of their adult height based on their present height. At age twelve, for example, boys on the average have attained 80 per cent of their mature height. Bayley and Pinneau (1952) present a table giving the percentage of mature height attained by boys and girls at various ages from one month to eighteen years. More accurate predictions can be obtained from a joint consideration of present height and skeletal age as determined by X rays of the hand. Bayley and Pinneau also present tables to be used for these predictions. Of course, the school counselor will not usually be able to obtain hand X rays.

The Meredith Physical Growth Record (Meredith, 1949) is now widely used in schools to record height and weight and refer them to age norms for boys and girls. The age norms range from four to eighteen years. Five normative classifications for height and weight are plotted on the record. These are, for height, tall, moderately tall, average, moderately short, and short. For weight they are heavy, moderately heavy, average, moderately light, and light. After plotting height and weight for a given child, one might describe him, for example, as tall and light. The children on which the norms were based were white children of Northwest European ancestry in Iowa living under better-than-average conditions. The composition of the norm group should be kept in mind when the records are used. Children from other ethnic groups should probably be compared to their own group norms whenever they are available.

The Meredith Physical Growth Record forms are available from the American Medical Association, 535 North Dearborn Street, Chicago 10, Illinois, or the National Education Association, 1201 Sixteenth Street, Northwest, Washington, D.C.

Except for extreme cases, speed of reaction and speed of movements, like physical strength, have little relevance for ordinary learning activities, just as they have little relevance for success in most occupations. In social interaction and in some occupations, however, success is directly dependent on these characteristics, and counselors and teachers must be aware of the implication of extremely slow or fast reaction time.

THE PHYSICALLY HANDICAPPED

A physical *disability* may be considered as an impairment medically or objectively defined, whereas a *handicap* is an impairment which has associated with it restrictions in psychological or social behavior. Within a group of individuals with the same physical structure or the same medically determined disability, one will find a wide range of handicapping. At one extreme will be individuals who are completely incapacitated psychologically and socially by their disability, and at the other extreme will be persons who are not in the least handicapped.

The person with a disability to which he made an adequate adjustment during childhood may again during adolescence become painfully aware of his disability. Most often this awakened awareness is a result of the aforementioned adolescent upsurge of interest in the social impact of one's physique.

The following summary of behavior of crippled children is presented because it has suggestions for the behavior to be expected of persons who are concerned with real or imagined physical disabilities:

Crippled children have a strong need for social acceptance. They are fearful and may avoid social participation in fear of rejection. Physically disabled persons tend to withdraw, are hypersensitive, overinhibited, unstable emotionally, easily discouraged and fatigued. There is a greater frequency of personal maladjustment in the physically disabled group than in the general population, but there is not a personality syndrome associated with physical disability (Barker et al., 1953; Garrett, 1952).

PSYCHOLOGICAL TESTING OF THE PHYSICALLY HANDICAPPED

Although the school psychologist usually is responsible for the testing of handicapped pupils, the school counselor becomes involved in the testing and often will receive test results about handicapped pupils. The purpose of this section is to give the counselor some knowledge about the psychological testing of the physically handicapped and the problems encountered. Chief among these problems is the nonsuitability of testing the handicapped with most standardized tests, since they are constructed using nonhandicapped persons as subjects. It is impossible to communicate adequately the usual test instructions to the blind and the deaf, and many disabled persons cannot respond appropriately even if they do understand what is wanted. If these difficulties of communication and response are overcome, norms based on handicapped persons in various disability groups, such as the deaf, the blind, and the orthopedically handicapped, are necessary. Ideally, with a test one should be able to compare a handicapped child with others of his disability type and with nonhandicapped children of the same age and grade.

A few tests have been constructed and standardized on persons with specific disabilities, e.g., the blind and the deaf. A number of other tests have been adopted for use with other special disability groups. Most attention has been given to the testing of the deaf, the blind, and the orthopedically handicapped, such as the cerebral palsied.

Deaf children and the cerebral palsied who have learned to read can, of course, read test directions and test items; and the deaf at least can respond to performance tests. Blind children can be read the test directions and verbal test items and can respond orally. Obviously, neither blind persons nor the cerebral palsied can respond adequately to the usual performance tests.

Performance tests with instructions given in pantomime are used with deaf persons who have not learned to read. The Pintner-Paterson Performance Scale (Pintner & Paterson, 1917) was the first test of this nature. Revised Form II of the Arthur Point Scale of Performance Tests (Arthur, 1947) reduced the verbal instructions of Form I to make the scale suitable for use with deaf children. The Cornell-Coxe Performance Ability Scale (Cornell & Coxe, 1934) also has been widely used in testing deaf children. The Nebraska Test of Learning Aptitude for Young Deaf Children was developed by Hiskey (1941) for use with deaf and hard-of-hearing children from ages four to ten. The test was standardized on such children. All items included were selected after reference to limitations of deaf children. Age differentiation was the other criterion for selection of items. The following eleven subtests are included in the Nebraska test:

1. Memory for colored objects
2. Bead stringing
3. Pictorial association
4. Block building
5. Memory for digits
6. Completion of drawings
7. Pictorial identification
8. Paper folding
9. Visual attention span
10. Puzzle blocks
11. Pictorial analogies

Norms were based on 466 children, four to ten years old, attending state schools for the deaf in six states.

Learning age, the concept proposed by Hiskey, is similar to mental age but refers to performance norms of deaf children. He reports a split-half reliability of .96. Correlations of subtests with total score range from .63 to .84. The manual discusses general practices of testing deaf children.

Performance tests are not usually applicable to the testing of blind persons. As indicated above, oral adaptations of tests can be used for testing of the blind. Bauman and Hayes (1951) have summarized the intelligence, special aptitude, achievement, and personality tests most commonly used for testing the blind and have presented a good introduction to procedures for such testing. Rawls (1954) is another good source of information.

The Stanford-Binet Intelligence Test, the Wechsler-Bellevue, and the later Wechsler Intelligence Scales are the principal intelligence tests which have been modified for testing blind subjects. Hayes (1942; 1943) modified the 1916 and 1937 forms of the Stanford-Binet. These modifications are labeled the Hayes-Binet and the Interim Hayes-Binet Intelligence Tests respectively. The adaptations of the Binet and Wechsler scales consist chiefly of retaining the verbal subtests and discarding the performance subtests. Several group tests of intelligence also have been adapted for use with the blind. Administration is oral, as are the subject's responses. The Kuhlmann-Anderson Intelligence Tests, the Ohio State University Psychological Test, the Otis Quick-Scoring Mental Ability Tests, and the College Entrance Examination Board Scholastic Aptitude Test, all of which are discussed in Chapter 15, have been used in this way, as have been the Pintner General Ability Tests, Verbal Series.

Several tests have been developed or modified for use in testing the orthopedically handicapped, including the cerebral palsied. Among these tests are the Columbia Mental Maturity Scale (Burgemeister, Blum, & Lorge, 1953); the Full-Range Picture Vocabulary Test (Ammons & Ammons, 1948); the Leiter International Performance Scale (Arnold, 1951; Arthur, 1952; Leiter, 1936, 1952); Porteus Maze Test (Arnold, 1951); and the Raven Progressive Matrices Tests (Raven, 1947, 1956, 1958; Tracht, 1948).

STATE AID TO EXCEPTIONAL CHILDREN

Many states have recognized the need to identify pupils with physical or mental handicaps and the importance of specialized help for these pupils by providing state funds to assist local school systems. Some states provide state aid to allow local school systems to hire school psychologists, speech pathologists and correctionists, remedial reading teachers, and teachers of classes for the mentally retarded. These services are usually available to pupils through high school. Counselors should be aware of such programs in their states and make use of the resources they provide.

A state agency usually is concerned with vocational rehabilitation of people who are in need of habilitation or rehabilitation as a result of accident, disease, or mental impairment. These agencies provide funds for physical restoration, wheelchairs, crutches, and prosthetic devices, and in addition can make funds available to further the training of handicapped people. Rehabilitation counselors or rehabilitation workers in these state agencies work with handicapped people in outlining for them the type of rehabilitation program which best meets their needs. This casework involves the provision of prosthetic devices, the administration of tests, and the provision of counseling services. It may provide for training, such as four years in a college or several years in a trade school. The high school counselor should be aware of these state resources and communicate early with the state division of vocational rehabilitation so that the transition of the counselee from the high school counselor to the rehabilitation counselor in the state agency can be as smooth as possible. In many states the state agency is not allowed to work directly with the handicapped individual until he reaches a specified age. However, the agency is usually very interested in identifying the handicapped as early as possible so its work can begin as soon as the person reaches the legal age.

The efforts of the school counselor and the rehabilitation counselor should be coordinated as early as possible so the pupil's plans can be enacted without delay when he graduates from high school. Many state divisions of vocational rehabilitation have provisions for providing sheltered workshop experiences to aid persons in the transition from illness or disability to training, and from there to the world of work. In some states these agencies are organized under the State Department of Public Welfare, and in others under the State Department of Education.

The counselor will come in contact with pupils with normal and abnormal variations in physical development and physique. Some pupils will have physical disabilities resulting from accident or disease. Other pupils will have nonnormal attitudes toward their physical and health status. The counselor can help his counselees understand and accept their physical abilities and disabilities. He can help disabled pupils understand the nature of their disabilities and help them learn to live (function adequately) within the limitations imposed by the disability. The counselor can also work with parents to help them understand the disability and its implications for psychological and social development. By careful work with the pupil and his parents, the counselor can minimize the handicapping effects of a physical limitation.

SUMMARY

The information most readily obtained from direct observations concerns the physical status of the pupil. We can tell whether he is short or tall, slim or stout, dark or light, merely by looking at him. The color of his hair, the tint of his eyes, the pitch of his voice, the vigor of his walk can all be obtained through direct observation. Sometimes we can use this kind of information without further refinement. A high school basketball coach, for instance, can see that a muscular, well-coordinated boy well over 6 feet in height might be encouraged to try out for the team. A school nurse can tell quickly that an obese girl should be given particular attention regarding her problem of overweight.

Frequently before we can systematically use information about physical status, we must refine it. For instance, we are concerned not only with how large a student is, but also with his rate of growth. Thus, we must measure and then record our measurements. This kind of refinement provides us with information that can be used for comparative purposes and also can be communicated with ease. If we have not measured or weighed a person, we have difficulty in telling others how tall or how heavy he is. Measurements allow us to say, "Fourteen-year-old Dorothy is 4 feet 8 inches tall and weighs 140 pounds." This is more efficient than saying, "Fourteen-year-old Dorothy is quite a bit shorter than the average girl of her age and a great deal heavier."

Adolescence is a time of rapid and large bodily changes. These changes have a great impact on the attitudes and expectations of the pupil, his parents, and his peers since physical appearance is one cue we use to establish a person's social role. Associated with body changes in adolescence is an increase in health defects. Physical examinations and acuity tests help identify those pupils with poor health and physical condition. Alert school staff members can help detect poor health of pupils and refer them for medical diagnosis and treatment. The counselor has an additional important task to perform as he integrates knowledge of the pupil's health and physical condition with the physical demands of his educational and vocational aspirations. The need of the physically handicapped pupil for such counseling is quite obvious. Not so obvious is the need of every pupil to correlate his physical condition with his long-range plans.

Most counselors would not consider counseling a pupil without knowledge about his abilities, interests, and other psychological attributes. Similarly, no counselor should attempt to aid a pupil in attaining educational, vocational, and social maturity without information about the pupil's health and his physical apparatus and its readiness for such development.

QUESTIONS FOR STUDY

1. Consult your family physician about his views on counseling the physically handicapped. Has he followed up such patients to determine their vocational success or failure, and with what results? Is he reluctant to discuss his young patients with their school counselor? With their school nurse?
2. Consider an occupation which you know, such as filling station attendant, and the implications of health and physique for it.
3. List some obvious and subtle physical characteristics which might have some bearing on the success or failure of a person in that job.

4. Can a blind person be an effective counselor?
5. Compile a list of occupations which you think could not be held by the blind or the deaf.
6. Take the list from number 5 and attempt to adapt each occupation in a way which would enable a handicapped person to do the job.

REFERENCES

Ammons, R. B., & Ammons, Helen S. *The full-range picture vocabulary test.* Missoula: Southern Universities Press, 1948.

Anonymous. Adolescent nutrition—I. Physiological requirements. *Dairy Council Digests,* 1955, **26,** No. 4. (a)

Anonymous. Adolescent nutrition—II. Nutritional status studies. *Dairy Council Digests,* 1955, **26,** No. 4. (a)

Arnold, Gwen F. A technique for measuring the mental ability of the cerebral palsied. *Psychol. Serv. Center J.,* 1951, 3, 171–180.

Arthur, Grace A. *Point scale of performance tests. Revised Form II. Manual for administering and scoring the tests.* New York: Psychological Corporation, 1947.

Arthur, Grace A. *The Arthur adaptation of the Leiter International Performance Scale.* Washington, D.C.: Psychological Service Center Press, 1952.

Baller, W. R., & Charles, D. C. *Psychology of human growth and development.* New York: Holt, 1961.

Barker, R. G., et al. *Adjustment to physical handicap and illness. A survey of the social psychology of physique and disability.* New York: Social Science Research Council, 1953.

Bauman, Mary K., & Hayes, S. P. *A manual for the psychological examination of the adult blind.* New York: Psychological Corporation, 1951.

Bayley, Nancy. Growth curves of height and weight by age for boys and girls, scaled according to physical maturity. *J. Pediatrics,* 1956, **48,** 187–194.

Bayley, Nancy, & Pinneau, S. Tables for predicting adult height from skeletal age: revised for use with the Greulich-Pyle hand standards. *J. Pediatrics,* 1952, **40,** 423–441.

Benedict, Ruth. *Patterns of culture.* Boston: Houghton Mifflin, 1934.

Burgomeister, Bessie, Blum, Lucille H., & Lorge, I. *Columbia mental maturity scale. Manual of directions.* New York: Harcourt, Brace & World, 1953.

Cornell, Ethel L., & Coxe, W. W. *A performance ability scale: examination manual.* Tarryton-on-Hudson, N.Y.: World, 1934.

Cruickshank, W. M. (Ed.) *Psychology of exceptional children and youth.* Englewood Cliffs, N.J.: Prentice-Hall, 1955.

Cruickshank, W. M., & Johnson, G. O. (Eds.) *Education of exceptional children and youth.* Englewood Cliffs, N.J.: Prentice-Hall, 1958.

Davidson, H. L., & Gottlieb, L. S. The emotional maturity of pre- and post-menarcheal girls. *J. genet. Psychol.,* 1955, **86,** 261–266.

Denver Public Schools. *Health interests of children: report of a research study of health interests and needs of children as a basis for health instruction, kindergarten through grade 12.* Denver, 1954.

Doll, E. A. (Ed.) *Oseretsky tests of motor proficiency.* Minneapolis: Educational Test Bureau, 1946.

Espenschade, A., Doble, R. R., & Schoendube, R. Dynamic balance in adolescent boys. *Res. Quart. Amer. Phys. Educ. Ass.,* 1953, **24,** 270–275.

Everson, Gladys J. Bases for concern about teenagers' diets. *J. Amer. Dietetic Ass.*, 1960, **36**, 17–21.

Frank, L. K. Personality development in adolescent girls. *Monogr. Soc. Res. Child Develpm.*, 1951, **16**, No. 53.

Frank, L. K., & Frank, M. *Your adolescent at home and in school.* New York: Viking, 1956.

Garrett, J. F. (Ed.) *Psychological aspects of physical disability.* U.S. Federal Security Agency, Office of Vocational Rehabilitation Service Series 210. Washington, D.C.: U.S. Government Printing Office, 1952.

Gesell, A., Ilg, F. L., & Ames, L. B. *Youth: the years from ten to sixteen.* New York: Harper & Row, 1956.

Gschneider, Melba P., & Roderuck, Charlotte E. Nutriture of school girls of different physiques. *J. Amer. Dietetic Ass.*, 1960, **36**, 22–26.

Hanks, J. R., & Hanks, L. M., Jr. The physically handicapped in certain non-occidental societies. *J. soc. Issues*, 1948, **4**, 11–20.

Hayes, S. P. Alternative scales for the mental measurement of the visually handicapped. *Outlook for the Blind*, 1942, **36**, 225–230.

Hayes, S. P. A second test scale for the mental measurement of the visually handicapped. *Outlook for the Blind*, 1943, **37**, 37–41.

Hiskey, M. S. *Nebraska test of learning aptitude for young deaf children: manual.* Lincoln: University of Nebraska Department of Educational and Psychological Measurement, 1941. Rev. manual 1955. Now published by author, 5640 Baldwin, Lincoln, Nebr.

Hurlock, Elizabeth B. *Developmental psychology.* (2nd ed.) New York: McGraw-Hill, 1959.

Jackson, R. L., & Kelly, H. G. Growth charts for use in pediatric practice. *J. Pediatrics*, 1945, **27**, 215–229.

Jones, H. E. Physical ability as a factor in social adjustment in adolescence. *J. educ. Res.*, 1946, **40**, 286–301.

Jones, Mary C., & Bayley, Nancy. Physical maturing among boys as related to behavior. *J. educ. Psychol.*, 1950, **41**, 129–148.

Klineberg, O. *Social psychology.* (Rev. ed.) New York: Holt, 1954.

Kralj-Čereček, Lea. The influence of food, body build, and social origin on the age of menarche. *Human Biol.*, 1956, **28**, 393–406.

Leiter, R. G. The Leiter International Performance Scale. *Univer. Hawaii Bull.*, 1936, **15**, No. 7.

Leiter, R. G. *Part II of the manual for the 1948 revision of the Leiter International Performance Scale.* Washington, D.C.: Psychological Service Center Press, 1952.

Liccione, J. V. The changing family relationships of adolescent girls. *J. abnorm. soc. Psychol.*, 1955, **51**, 421–426.

Lofquist, L. *Vocational counseling with the physically handicapped.* New York: Appleton-Century-Crofts, 1957.

Meredith, H. V. A "physical growth record" for use in elementary and high schools. *Amer. J. Publ. Hlth.*, 1949, **39**, 878–885.

Meyerson, L. Somatopsychology of physical disability. In W. M. Cruickshank (Ed.), *Psychology of exceptional children and youth.* Englewood Cliffs, N.J.: Prentice-Hall, 1955. Pp. 1–60.

Paterson, D. G. *Physique and intellect.* New York: Appleton-Century, 1930.

Pintner, R., Eisenson, J., & Stanton, Mildred. *The psychology of the physically handicapped.* New York: Appleton-Century-Crofts, 1941.

Pintner, R., & Paterson, D. G. *A scale of performance tests.* New York: Appleton-Century-Crofts, 1917.

Pressey, S. L., & Kuhlen, R. G. *Psychological development through the life span.* New York: Harper & Row, 1957.

Raven, J. C. *Progressive matrices (1947), Sets I and II.* Dumfries: Chrichton Royal, no date.

Raven, J. C. *Guide to using progressive matrices (1938).* London: Lewis, 1956. (U.S. distributor: Psychological Corporation, New York.)

Raven, J. C. *Guide to using the coloured progressive matrices (1947), Sets A, Ab, B.* London: Lewis, 1958. (U.S. distributor: Psychological Corporation, New York.)

Rawls, R. F. Objective tests and testing of blind children. *New Outlook for the Blind,* 1954, 48, 39–45.

Stearns, G. Nutritional health of infants, children, and adolescents. In *Proc. Natl. Food & Nutrition Inst., USDA Agric. Hand.,* 1952, No. 56.

Stolz, H. R., & Stolz, L. R. Adolescent problems related to somatic variations. In *NSSE 43rd Yearb.* Chicago: University of Chicago Press, 1944, Part 1.

Stouffer, G. A. W., & Owens, J. Behavior problems identified by today's teachers and compared with those reported by E. K. Wickman. *J. educ. Res.,* 1955, 48, 321–331.

Tracht, V. S. Preliminary findings on testing the cerebral palsied with Raven's "Progressive Matrices." *J. except. Child.,* 1948, 15, 77–79.

Tuddenham, R. D., & Snyder, M. M. *Physical growth of California boys and girls from birth to eighteen years.* Berkeley: University of California Press, 1954, Vol. 1, No. 22.

Wetzel, N. C. Physical fitness in terms of physique, development, and basal metabolism. *J. Amer. med. Ass.,* 1941, 116, 1187.

Wetzel, N. C. *The grid for evalutaing physical fitness.* Cleveland: NEA Service, 1941.

CHAPTER 3

Learning about the Psychological Development of Pupils

Do I have enough ability to take college preparatory mathematics and a foreign language?

Can I pass the shorthand course?

Am I intelligent enough to go to college?

Can I do well in the shop courses?

Do I have enough talent to be a professional musician?

I would like to be a draftsman or an engineer. For which am I best suited? Which will I like better?

These questions, often explicitly asked by pupils, are similar to the ones faced by all children as they make educational and vocational decisions. These decisions depend on many things, including opportunity, interest, and a variety of fortuitous circumstances; but among the most important determinants of a student's plans should be his own evaluations of his abilities, aptitudes, and capacities. The pupil and the counselor both are interested in how well the pupil will do, but underlying this prediction must be a judgment as to what the pupil is capable of doing.

ABILITIES AND THEIR MEANING

The judgment of capacity requires information about a potential, about a characteristic that cannot be seen, but oddly enough, can be measured.

Ability and aptitude refer to what a person *can do*, not to what he will do. Bingham makes several enlightening comments about abilities and aptitudes in his book *Aptitudes and Aptitude Testing* (1937):

Aptitude, then, is a condition symptomatic of a person's relative fitness, of which one essential aspect is his readiness to acquire proficiency—his potential ability—and another is his readiness to develop an interest in exercising that ability. Anyone who has come to a clear realization of his capacities, his informed interests, and the na-

35

ture of the occupations he is considering, has achieved some basis for appraising the relative strength of his aptitudes.

Ability means power to perform responsive acts. . . . We shall use the term "ability" in its broadest sense as meaning power to perform designated responsive acts, without implication as to whether this power is potential or actual, native or acquired. . . . Proficiency refers to the degree of ability already acquired, in contrast to *capacity*, which is potential ability . . . *capability*, like . . . capacity, is . . . maximum ability with further training.

Special abilities peculiar to certain types of performance are distinguished from *general ability*, construed by some writers as the sum of one's specific abilities, and by others as a common factor operative in all or many types of performance. . . .

Talent is a relatively high order of aptitude. More specifically, a talented person is one who is susceptible to an unusually high degree of training.

We should think of behavior, or performance, and it is this behavior that defines the ability which we are considering. An ability is a concept, not a thing. We infer its existence through observing other kinds of behavior, but we never directly observe the ability. We cannot observe a person's musical ability, but we can observe his progress in acquiring musical skills, observe his level of competency, and on the basis of these observations, infer the amount of musical ability he possesses. We infer that a person has a given amount of scholastic aptitude by observing his schoolwork. We make judgments or inferences on the basis of behaviors that we realize are related to the abilities which concern us.

If we define abilities on the basis of different observed behaviors, then the number of abilities could be as great as the possible number of such behaviors. In other words, the number of possible behaviors is limitless, and consequently the number of abilities we must consider may also be infinite. During the past fifty years, however, psychological research (Guilford, 1959) has suggested that abilities and aptitudes are not independent of one another, but rather that they form a somewhat meaningful pattern and that by observing a limited number of behaviors, and thereby inferring the existence of a few related abilities, generalizations can be made to a far greater number of behaviors. Observing how a pupil responds to a test—a vocabulary test for example—allows us to make useful inferences concerning the pupil's academic ability, or his ability to do well in school. This performance, or score, on a vocabulary test is related to the pupil's performance in elementary school, high school, and college; and it is related to performance in foreign language, English, social studies, science, and mathematics. The general ability we infer from tests similar to vocabulary tests has been called academic aptitude, and we find that this ability is useful in predicting things other than academic success. For example, success on many jobs is related to the extent of a person's vocabulary.

Past experience and new statistical techniques have permitted us to restrict the number of abilities with which we must be concerned. A general ability seems to be related to success in many kinds of school work, although pupils differ in their ability to succeed in different kinds of courses. Through the use of a statistical refinement called *factor analysis* (Thurstone, 1947), a limited number of abilities have been identified that provide a comprehensive description of the entire ability and aptitude dimension of the pupil. At present we need not be concerned with more than thirty specific abilities, and most likely fewer than one-half of these are directly related to success in traditional academic and occupational programs. In this text, when we are concerned with the prediction of success in several more or less loosely related behaviors, we will call the ability a general ability. When we are concerned with an ability that predicts more specific behavior, we will label this a special ability.

Names we give to abilities and aptitudes can be misleading. When psychological tests are developed, the names of the aptitudes supposedly measured by these tests are selected according to the extent to which test scores are related to the behaviors the test authors were interested in predicting. If a personnel psychologist wishes to develop a test that will predict success in clerical jobs, he is likely to label his test a *clerical* test. When a test is to be used for predicting success in school, it is likely to be called an *academic* or a *scholastic aptitude* test. Sometimes, however, a test that has been developed for one purpose and given a name relevant to that purpose proves to do an equally effective or even better job of predicting another behavior. For example, the Minnesota Clerical Test was found in one study to predict success in machine shop courses more effectively than did a mechanical aptitude test. We must remember that the names given to tests primarily are useful for identification purposes, and that if one is to understand the concepts underlying the test and the nature of the behavior with which the test is concerned, one must look beyond the name of the test and study the information obtained through research and use.

ACADEMIC OR SCHOLASTIC APTITUDE

The school counselor most frequently is asked to help pupils make judgments about their abilities to succeed academically. The appropriateness of courses, curricula, schools, and training programs depends on judgments about pupils' abilities. Academic ability is a concept used as a convenience in predicting how well a pupil will succeed in academic tasks typical of those found in most schools.

School success is partly, but not completely, a general behavior. By this we mean that most pupils who do well in one subject tend to do well in others, and pupils who do well in one school tend to do well in other schools. Most A students tend to earn above average grades in all courses, and most C students tend to earn average or below average grades in most courses. In spite of this generality, many pupils do well in some courses and poorly in others. We know there are certain clusterings. For example, most students who do well in mathematics do well in science, social studies, and English; but many pupils, particularly in the elementary grades, do well in arithmetic but poorly in spelling, or vice versa. Many students learn easily in music and with difficulty in physics, or many are good in French and poor in mechanical drawing. Nevertheless, when one considers the traditional academic courses, some justification is found for accepting a concept of academic success, and this in turn is related to a concept called academic ability. By academic aptitude we refer to a type of ability that underlies and is a prerequisite for the pupil's success in school.

Several different observations help us make inferences about a pupil's academic aptitude, and many behaviors allow us to predict academic success. Usually the single best predictor or how well a pupil will do in school is how well he already has done. Nothing predicts future behavior as well as previous behavior on a similar task. How well a pupil has done during the first eight years of school provides the best prediction of how well he will do during the final eight years. We can make inferences about the scholastic aptitude of a pupil by observing his past academic behavior.

The academic record, however, does not provide a sufficient means, even though it may be the best single means, for predicting how well a student will do. This less than perfect validity is due to several things. The previous academic behavior of the pupil may be different from that demanded by subsequent education. He may have been required to do little reading in the past, and his academic achievement might have been evaluated from his participation in class discussions. A later school may require more reading, and his progress there might be evaluated from the results of his reading. A student with a reading disability might do well during the early schooling and have trouble later on.

Previous records of success are fallible also because changes occur within the pupil. These changes are relevant when we are predicting not only from previous success, but also when we are predicting from other types of records, including test scores. During his early years in school, a pupil may be well motivated, satisfied with his home and friends, and perform well in school. His motivation may change, his family situation may deteriorate, or other factors may shift for the better or for the worse. His future academic behavior as a result of these changes might be quite different from his previous behavior. Some students, called "late bloomers" (McClelland, 1958), develop later intellectually than others. Some students mature intellectually at an early age and then "peter out." These pupils have been called "morning glories." For these two groups of students, predictions of future academic behavior based on previous behavior or test scores will be filled with error.

The relationships between school marks in the early grades and those obtained years later are high (Berdie, 1955), but some students do change and counselors must have means available for identifying these changes when they occur. This provides one of the main reasons for having systematic cumulative records and continuing testing programs throughout the entire school career of the pupil. School grades and test scores should be examined each year for every pupil so that the changes can be detected and explained.

A pupil described in the lower elementary grades as low-average may plan a noncollege course. Later work in school and test scores may reveal that he has developed intellectually to the point where he is an above-average student and eventually he may want to attend college. Similarly, a pupil who at first appeared to be a good college risk and then did not develop the necessary skills and ability should know this so his plans can be changed. The school can attend properly to these pupils with ephemeral abilities only if it provides a continuous and cumulative counseling service.

In addition to records of past behavior, ratings by teachers and counselors provide a means for appraising a pupil's academic aptitude. When pupils apply for admission to college, teachers and counselors are asked to make such ratings. Usually these ratings are based on the previous school records of the pupil, his scores on achievement tests, and his performance on tests of academic ability. In general, the ratings made by trained counselors and teachers add little to the accuracy of prediction of academic success if one already has available school records and test scores. When such records and scores are not available, then predictions based on teacher and counselor observations may be useful; but always one must remember the many kinds of errors found in these observations and ratings (Bingham, Moore, & Gustad, 1959).

Psychological tests are among the most frequently used means for making inferences about academic aptitude. Many of these tests are available, and the behaviors they elicit, or the items used, vary greatly. In general, however, these tests have one thing in common. All of them tend to place great emphasis on the ability of the pupil to understand and to use words meaningfully. Most school work is done through the means of language, and verbal behavior is important not only in English, foreign languages, and social studies, but also in mathematics, the natural sciences, and even such courses as drafting and shop.

Students who know the meaning of many words, who can find similarities and differences between words, and who can correctly read words in meaningful context are the ones who tend to do well in school. Most academic aptitude tests are to a great extent verbal.

Many academic aptitude tests also include quantitative or mathematical items. The ability of students to think quantitatively, to work with numbers, and to reason mathematically is essential in many types of school programs. Although verbal ability and numerical ability are related to one another (Berdie, Dressel, & Kelso, 1951), nevertheless this relationship is far from perfect, and some pupils have a deficiency of one and a sufficiency of the other.

The sources of these variations in academic abilities still are not clearly understood. We know that to some extent the genetic, anatomical, and physiological constitution of the individual is related to his ability to do schoolwork, but we also know that this ability is influenced by certain kinds of experiences, particularly those in childhood. We do not know to what extent this ability can be modified by special training or carefully controlled experiences, but the best evidence now suggests that, within broad limits, most abilities and aptitudes, particularly academic aptitudes, are determined genetically (Woodworth, 1941). Within these limits, experiences can modify abilities, and we need not regard ability as something rigidly fixed for a person's lifetime. In some cases changes in environment can produce extreme changes in demonstrated ability, but we cannot be overly optimistic about the extent to which abilities can be changed for most persons. Case studies have shown that some persons who early in life are described as mentally defective can later in life develop into normal, or perhaps even somewhat above normal, individuals. The overwhelming evidence, however, forces us to conclude that our efforts are best directed toward helping persons use most efficiently the abilities and aptitudes they possess. An improved environment, particularly within the home and the school, can allow a person to perform at a level for which we previously thought he lacked the requisite ability, but the task of the school is best defined as helping the individual use to the maximum those abilities and aptitudes he possesses.

Tests of academic ability are used throughout the entire educational career of the pupil. They are given to determine whether pupils are intellectually mature enough to begin school, to indicate the readiness of pupils to begin certain kinds of training, particularly reading, to help teachers determine the speed with which pupils may be expected to learn and the complexity of the materials that they can master, and to help determine the kind of secondary school training pupils should have. These academic ability tests, along with other information, provide a basis for deciding whether pupils should go to vocational schools or general high schools, whether they should take commercial courses, college preparatory courses, or other specialized courses in school. These tests aid students and their counselors in selecting such courses as shorthand, foreign language, or mathematics.

After high school, these tests aid in decisions concerning college attendance and other post-high school training, selection of occupations, and selection of jobs. A sound school program for the individual must be based in part on information obtained periodically from tests of academic ability. However, the inferences concerning academic aptitude must never be based solely on tests, but always must take into consideration other kinds of information.

In later chapters the descriptions of available academic aptitude tests will demonstrate how counselors use these tests and what cautions must be observed if they are to be used wisely. These tests constitute a basis for school testing programs, as well as for testing individual counselees, and the information they provide influences many important decisions.

AN ILLUSTRATIVE CASE

Alfred Johnson was born on January 10. In the late summer of his fourth year, his parents discovered that if he were to enter school before his fifth birthday, his readiness for school would have to be evaluated by the school psychologist. This was Alfred's first experience with an intelligence test. The psychologist gave him a Stanford-Binet Intelligence Test and reported that Alfred's intelligence quotient was 124. A test of reading readiness showed him to be advanced, and his physical development and motor coordination suggested he would be able to compete successfully with other children beginning school. Consequently, he was allowed to begin school before his birthday.

His next experience with an intelligence test came in the second grade when he was given a Kuhlmann-Anderson test which provided him with an intelligence quotient of 118. His record of test scores, along with his quick learning in school, encouraged his teachers to expect much of him and to provide him with many stimulating school experiences. Another intelligence test was administered to Alfred in grade 5, and he was tested again in grade 7. The latter test score was lower than the scores on earlier tests and suggested that he was only slightly above average when compared with other students in his school, a school drawing a relatively representative group of American children having an average IQ of about 103.

In junior high school, Alfred had some difficulty with his first-year algebra course; and when he registered for his tenth-grade courses, the suggestion was made that he take a noncollege preparatory mathematics course. His parents questioned this, and he was given a college aptitude test which showed that, when compared with other ninth-grade students, he had a percentile score of 56 and thus fell in the upper 44 per cent.

By the time he graduated from high school, he had a grade average of slightly above C. His parents and teachers considered him a conscientious young man who worked hard, but who simply had trouble with his studies. His reading skills were not good, but he never had been considered a reading problem needing special remedial help.

Just prior to his graduation from high school, he, with the help of his counselors and parents, decided to attend college; but rather than attend the local state university, he selected a junior college which would provide him with some of the basic general educational courses he wanted and at the same time give him experience with college work and further information about his ability to succeed in college. A college aptitude test at that time showed that he was about average when compared with the students entering the junior college; whereas, when compared with entering university students, he was in the lower 20 per cent. Throughout his school career, Alfred's decision had been influenced by the information provided to him, to his parents, and to his counselors by the various academic aptitude tests he had taken.

DIFFERENTIAL ABILITIES

Recognizing that the number of tasks which comprise the world of work is practically unlimited, we are fortunate that the number of abilities and aptitudes with which counselors must be concerned is restricted. If it were necessary to use one special mechanical aptitude test to help a person decide whether or not to become a machinist and another to help him decide whether to be a machinist working with a turret lathe or a grinder, or if we had to use one special aptitude test to determine whether a person should become a refrigerator repairman and another to determine his probable success in repairing other appliances, the job of the counselor would indeed be a formidable one.

Psychologists recognized at a relatively early date that certain general categories of tasks could be grouped together according to the behaviors necessary for success in them. These behaviors in varying degrees were related to different aptitudes. For example, clerical aptitude tests were found to be related to success in learning accounting, bookkeeping, and filing. Mechanical aptitude tests were related to success in appliance repairing and certain kinds of production jobs. Another test related to the ability of a person to perceive visual spatial relationships was also related to success in drafting, drawing, and working with blueprints.

Today most special or differential aptitude tests are not designed to predict success in a specific job, but rather to provide information that helps the counselor and the student generalize about the probabilities of success in several jobs as they are grouped in related families.

At first these tests were developed separately by different psychologists and were made available for counseling use. Thus came into being the battery of Minnesota mechanical aptitude tests, the Minnesota Clerical Test, the Bennett Mechanical Comprehension Tests, the Purdue Pegboard, and the O'Connor Finger and Tweezer Dexterity Tests. Because these tests were developed at different times by different persons using different standardization populations, difficulties were encountered when counselors wished to make comparisons among the various abilities of an individual. For example, if a student asked whether his clerical or his mechanical aptitudes were best, good tests of these abilities were available; but the tests used different scoring systems, provided percentile scores from different norm groups, and had different difficulty levels.

To facilitate the job of the counselor, batteries of differential or multiple aptitude tests were developed. One of the first of these batteries, the Primary Mental Abilities Tests, was developed primarily for research purposes by Thurstone. His method of test development later was used by the United States Employment Service, which developed and now uses the General Aptitude Test Battery (GATB). The first group of differential aptitude tests especially developed for use in schools was the Differential Aptitude Tests by Bennett, Seashore, and Wesman. These tests include tests of verbal ability, number ability, abstract reasoning, space ability, mechanical comprehension, clerical speed and accuracy, knowledge of sentence structure, and spelling.

Tests such as these can be combined in a variety of ways. Already we have suggested that academic aptitude consists of a number of more specific abilities. The ability of a student to succeed in schoolwork depends on his verbal ability, that is, his ability to work with ideas expressed in words, and also on his number ability, or his ability to think quantitatively. Scientific aptitude consists of a combination of these along with other abilities.

The concept of specific aptitude is useful only when we have defined the behavior or performance with which we are concerned. When we have arrived at this definition, then we can identify the behaviors related to the success we are predicting. If, for example, we were to study ability to learn typing, we first would define the performance with which we were concerned, and we might say that successful typing consists of producing fifty words per minute with no more than three errors.

Then we would observe the antecedent behavior that is related to success in typing. We might give a vocabulary test, an eye-finger coordination test, and a number and name checking speed and accuracy test. If all of these tests were related to success in typing, we then would group them together and say that when we are studying these aspects of the individual, we are studying his typewriting aptitude.

Differential aptitudes are a step removed from specific aptitudes and can be inferred in a variety of ways. When a person succeeds on a job, we can assume that he possesses the specific aptitude for that job. If he succeeds on a job closely related to the one with which we were concerned, we sometimes can generalize that he possesses the kind of aptitude which now concerns us. Here, however, we must be careful. A student might learn French easily and quickly, and we might conclude that he has aptitude for learning French and generalize that he has aptitude for learning German. Ability to learn foreign languages depends somewhat on a person's academic aptitude, and a person who learns one foreign language is more likely to learn a second langauge than the person who has trouble learning the first language. We also know, however, that many specifics are involved and that some persons who can learn one foreign language will have trouble learning a second.

When a battery of tests is given to a student, the scores can be combined in different ways to provide predictions of success. On the General Aptitude Test Battery, for example, a person whose pattern of scores is analyzed and labeled as N-S-P-M (numerical aptitude, spatial aptitude, form perception, manual dexterity) may have the aptitudes judged necessary for an airplane mechanic, but not for a typesetter; whereas the person who has a pattern of scores labeled V-Q-K-F (verbal aptitude, clerical perception, motor coordination, finger dexterity) looks like a promising typesetter, but a poor mechanic.

The counselor's and teacher's use of information about special aptitudes is obvious. Selection of special academic training, of courses, of vocations, of jobs—all depends in part on judgments of a person's aptitudes. Although knowledge of his own aptitudes does not guarantee that a person will make a wise and satisfying educational and vocational choice, he has smaller chance of making such a choice without this knowledge.

AN ILLUSTRATIVE CASE

Melba Colby was a tenth-grade student with a mediocre academic record. During her early elementary grades she was a good student, but as she progressed in school and as the work became more abstract, her school marks declined. In spite of her perseverance and serious attitude in school, her efforts resulted in little progress.

In the ninth grade she was given the Differential Aptitude Tests, and on these tests her percentile scores were:

Verbal Reasoning................... 12
Number Ability.................... 19
Abstract Reasoning................ 8
Space Relations................... 49
Mechanical Reasoning.............. 61
Clerical Speed and Accuracy........ 24
Spelling.......................... 21
Sentences......................... 19

These percentile scores were derived from a large group of ninth-grade pupils tested in Melba's school during previous years, and they provided a norm group closely similar to the national norms published in the test manual.

Before the Differential Aptitude Test scores were obtained, the school counselor had reluctantly faced the forthcoming interviews with Melba and her parents. Melba's school marks were poor; her scores on the Kuhlmann-Anderson and the Otis Intelligence Tests were low, IQs varying between 70 and 90; and the counselor had little positive evidence on which to build. The new information, however, showed that Melba had some attributes stronger than others, and that these might provide a basis for realistic planning.

During the interviews, the counselor discussed the vocational school program for preparing seamstresses. Melba's pattern of scores was compared with the pattern of scores typical of girls who had succeeded in the seamstress course, and a similarity was noted. With this encouragement, Melba entered the course and succeeded. A comparison of her scores with scores of girls who had succeeded or failed in courses such as typing, bookkeeping, cooking, or practical nursing suggested that if she had entered any of these, she most probably would have failed.

Knowledge about Melba's special aptitudes helped her and the counselor find a future which promised some success.

ACHIEVEMENT AND INFORMATION BACKGROUND

Every teacher recognizes the need for information about the pupil's previously acquired skills and knowledge. No one would think of asking a pupil to take the second course in French if he did not have the knowledge included in the first course. No one would expect a pupil to do well in a second-year course in algebra unless he had mastered the content of the first course. Almost everything taught in school is dependent upon what the pupil already has learned. A teacher would not expect an eleventh-grade boy to read *Hamlet* unless his reading comprehension were adequate to allow him to read at that level. All learning is based on previous learning, and the person responsible for directing learning must be aware of the existing foundation.

Just as the teacher must evaluate and understand the academic status of the pupil, so must the counselor. The counselor uses this type of information in several ways. First, as we have said, the best predictor of future behavior is past behavior. Usually the pupil who has done well in high school will do well in college. Correlations between high school and college grade averages are about .50. The pupil who has done well in his ninth-grade algebra usually will do well in his future mathematics courses. The applicant for a selling job who has had successful selling experience is a better risk than the applicant whose previous experiences have been unsuccessful.

The behavior of the individual is a result of combined aptitude, opportunity, and motivation. Indexes of aptitude can be used to judge what a person is capable of doing, but having the capacity for a certain performance is quite different from actually performing. If a person has sold successfully in the past, we can infer the probable presence of aptitude for selling; and the fact that he has sold suggests that, in addition to this aptitude for selling, some of the other requisites are present also. Similarly, the pupil whose aptitudes in mathematics are high and who has done well in mathematics courses has demonstrated both ability and performance. When the counselor predicts future academic or occupational success, he should take into consideration evidence as to how the pupil has done in previously related tasks.

The counselor also can use information about the past achievement of the pupil to learn of needs for remedial work. The pupil who reads slowly or lacks spelling skills must be given special assistance to overcome these deficiencies so that he can profit from further training. Schools expect all pupils to attain certain minimum standards, but these standards are not and should not be rigidly fixed. Nevertheless, pupils who are to live in our society must possess certain information and skills; and for this reason, counselors must know about the competencies of their pupils.

We will not discuss here the use of tests made in schools by teachers and by administrators for purposes of evaluating instruction and other aspects of the school program. Other texts on tests in education provide adequate discussion of this use (Lindquist, 1951).

ESTIMATING ACHIEVEMENT

Estimates of a pupil's information and skills can be obtained in a variety of ways. Direct observation of a pupil in a learning situation is one way. Teachers can identify during the first few hours of class some pupils who have good backgrounds in their subjects and some who do not. Teachers frequently make erroneous judgments, however, and tests of achievement may be necessary to supplement other information.

Several types of achievement tests have been made. Traditionally, achievement has been seen as a mastery of a body of facts or the acquisition of certain information or specific skills. More comprehensively, achievement is not only the acquisition of facts, but also the development of skills fundamental to advanced learning and everyday living. Not only should a pupil know something about the history of his country, but he should know how to find desired historical information in a library and know the implications of this information. He should know something about Ohm's law and how to construct and interpret a graph based on it. Education consists in both building a store of meaningful information and acquiring basic skills, and tests can measure progress toward both of these objectives.

Many different achievement tests and batteries of achievement tests have been published. Some of these have been constructed, frequently by teachers, for specific purposes; almost every teacher has constructed tests to determine the extent to which his own individual purposes are being achieved. All teachers are concerned with the question, "Are my pupils learning what I hope they will?"

STANDARDIZED ACHIEVEMENT TESTS

Constructing a good comprehensive achievement test is a long and arduous task. Consequently, many persons specialize in the construction of tests which they then make available to other teachers. These tests are called *standardized tests*, and much information about them usually is made available by their authors.

Good standardized tests are accompanied by manuals or booklets which describe the purposes for which the tests were developed, the qualifications of the persons developing the tests, the problems with which the tests will help the teacher, suggestions for using the tests, the pupils used in the original development of the tests, the extent to which the tests provide consistent scores, and the general difficulty level of the tests. Information is included about methods for administering the test, how much time should be allotted, how the test is scored, and how different groups of pupils perform on the test (APA, 1954; NEA, 1955).

Standardized achievement tests are available to measure progress toward both specific and more general objectives. Spelling tests show how well pupils spell words commonly taught in each grade and provide information about errors pupils make. Mathematics tests show how much pupils know about elementary algebra and specific functions taught in algebra. Tests in English and in other languages reveal information about a pupil's vocabulary, his understanding of grammar and language usage, and his appreciation of style.

General achievement test batteries provide us with information about a pupil's relative standing in many subjects, usually including science, communication skills, mathematics, and the social studies. Some achievement test batteries are strongly oriented in the direction of finding out how much information a student knows. The early editions of the Stanford Achievement Test and the Cooperative Achievement Tests were examples of this kind of test. Other general achievement batteries are more concerned with the skills a pupil has developed. In these the pupil is not asked to recall from his fund of information; but rather the information required to answer a problem is presented in the test, and the pupil is asked to read that information, understand it, and apply it in answering the question. The tests from Dr. Lindquist's laboratory in Iowa emphasize this kind of testing. The Iowa Tests of Educational Development and the Iowa Tests of Basic Skills are well known to educators.

Most tests today attempt to combine these two purposes and, as a result, modern achievement tests require a pupil to supply and to use information and to demonstrate his skills in handling newly presented information. Nevertheless, most modern tests, even though they combine these two objectives, tend to emphasize either one or the other. The teacher and the counselor must study each test to determine the extent to which it measures the objectives which immediately concern the school.

INTERESTS AND VALUES

When young people make their decisions about schools and jobs, they consider not only what they will be able to do, but what they will like to do. A job selected on the basis of what a person can do might or might not be one the person would enjoy; a school selected on the basis of what the person would enjoy might or might not be one in which the person could succeed. What a person can do is determined in large part by a conglomerate we call abilities or aptitudes. What he will like to do is determined in large part by what we call interests and values. What he actually does is determined by abilities, interests, and opportunity.

ESTIMATING INTERESTS

Just as many methods are available for estimating a person's abilities, many ways are found for estimating his interests. Observation of what a pupil has chosen to do in the past when he has had free choice and equal opportunity to choose from many things provides one indication of his interests. When a boy in school can choose between music and athletics and year after year chooses athletics, one infers that his interest in athletics exceeds his interest in music. Actually, this inference is not without error; for the interest in music may be greater than the interest in athletics, but the choice may be influenced by the boy's parents, his friends, his fear of failure, or his inability to acquire an instrument. Recognizing these limitations, however, the previous behavior of an individual does provide clues to his interests.

Some attempts have been made to evaluate interests on the basis of success (Fryer, 1931). The assumption has been made that the activities in which the student is most interested are the ones in which he will persist longest and, consequently, obtain most practice and success. The difficulty of using success as a criterion of interest comes from, first, the dependency of success on ability, and secondly, the difficulty of determining equality of opportunity. Two pupils may succeed in mathematics; one may succeed because he has a great interest in mathematics which overcomes the effect of a poor teacher, and the second may succeed with little interest in mathematics but a teacher who overcomes this handicap.

One of the simplest methods for identifying a pupil's interests is to ask him what they are. Most pupils know how they have liked past activities and, consequently, can provide information about their interests. When these expressions of interest are considered in light of the extent of the pupil's experience, his opportunities, the variety of experiences that have been made available, and the social settings in which these experiences occurred, further inferences can be made.

Examination of a pupil's record, direct observation of his behavior, and personal inquiry concerning his interests all provide information useful in helping students make occupational and educational decisions, but increasingly counselors are using interest inventories which are based on pupils' expressions of more specific interests. Unlike a reply to a direct question concerning interests, these inventories sample a great variety of interests that are related. They allow pupils' interests to be described on the basis of many responses of interests or aversions, rather than on the basis of one answer to a single question.

One type of interest inventory provides scores which show the extent to which the pupil is interested in outdoor activity, clerical work, or working with machines. Another type of interest inventory provides scores that lead to inferences concerning the extent to which a pupil's interests resemble the interests of men or women successful in different occupations. On the basis of the latter inventories, we can say such things as, "Jane Smith's interests resemble the interests of women who are successful nurses, but are dissimilar to the interests of successful social workers." The interest inventory is the only method of determining interests that has been subjected to careful study and validation over a long period of time. Scores on some of these inventories are related to the extent to which a person continues in an occupation, the extent to which he succeeds in some occupations, and the extent to which he is satisfied with his occupation (Strong, 1943, 1955).

The successful person does his job well and derives satisfaction and happiness from it. Success defined in these terms is dependent on both abilities and interests; and before a person can make satisfactory decisions concerning educational programs or occupational choices, he must have information about both his aptitudes and his interests.

VALUES

Values are closely related to interests, but more directly reflect the ideas, activities, and persons an individual considers most important to himself. Two boys may be interested in engineering and both may have vocational interests similar to those of engineers. One, however, may consider most important in his life religious, aesthetic, and artistic experiences, while the other may consider most important making money and impressing others.

A person's values determine less what he does and what occupation he enters and more how he does it, his style of working in his occupation. Values, perhaps more than any other concept used by psychologists, refer to the life philosophy of the person—his style of life, his attitudes toward the world about him.

One of the most frequently used systems for categorizing values, based on the work of Spranger, was proposed by Allport, Vernon, and Lindzey and served as a basis for a test or scale of values they published (1951). The six values they propose are:

1. The Theoretical. The dominant interest of the theoretical man is the discovery of *truth*. In the pursuit of this goal he characteristically takes a "cognitive" attitude, one that looks for identities and differences; one that divests itself of judgments regarding the beauty or utility of objects, and seeks only to observe and to reason.
2. The Economic. The economic man is characteristically interested in what is *useful*. Based originally on the satisfaction of bodily needs (self-preservation), the interest in utility develops to embrace the practical affairs of the business world—the production, marketing, and consumption of goods, the elaboration of credit, and the accumulation of tangible wealth.
3. The Aesthetic. The aesthetic man sees his highest value in *form* and *harmony*. Each single experience is judged from the standpoint of grace, symmetry, or fitness. He regards life as a procession of events; each single impression is enjoyed for its own sake.
4. The Social. The highest value for this type is *love* of people. . . . The social man prizes other persons as ends and is therefore himself kind, sympathetic, and unselfish. He is likely to find theoretical, economic, and aesthetic attitudes cold and inhuman.

5. The Political. The political man is interested primarily in *power*. His activities are not necessarily within the narrow field of politics; but whatever his vocation, he betrays himself as a *Machtmensch*. Leaders in any field generally have high-power value.
6. The Religious. The highest value of the religious man may be called *unity*. He is mystical, and seeks to comprehend the cosmos as a whole, to relate himself to its embracing totality.

PERSONALITY AND TEMPERAMENT

In order to understand adequately many types of behavior, we must make use of concepts other than those of ability, achievement, and interest. These other concepts have been studied less, and we know less about them than we do about ability; but for the counselor and the teacher they are equally important. We do not even agree very well on the names or labels used when we talk about these concepts. Frequently, such words are applied as emotionality, sociability, emotional maturity, personal adjustment, stability, interpersonal relationships, feelings of inferiority, self-confidence, emotional control, introvert and extrovert, conforming tendencies, psychopathic behaviors. Regardless of this confusion, counselors and teachers must have much understanding of the organization of emotional behavior in general and much skill in applying this understanding as they work with individual pupils.[1]

INTERPERSONAL RELATIONS

One general behavior with which we should be concerned is how a pupil gets along with others. How much does he like other people, how much do they like him, how well can he cooperate with them, how well does he play the role of a leader or of a follower, how productive is he in group situations, and what skills does he have to help him achieve his social purposes? This aspect of behavior will be discussed more extensively in Chapter 4.

Every teacher has an opportunity to make judgments about these aspects of behavior, basing his judgments on the relationships the pupils have with the teacher and with other pupils. Teachers often know which pupils will be cooperative, which ones are pleasant to associate with, which ones have many friends, and which ones are placed in positions of leadership. Many schools systematically ask teachers to rate pupils on a number of traits. These ratings are then summarized on the cumulative record. Standardized forms are available for this purpose. As with many

[1] A review of the current status of the theory of personality will provide an understanding of why this confusion prevails. An excellent summary of personality theories is found in Hall and Lindzey (1957).

kinds of observation, however, we must be aware that these observations are fallible and are influenced by the observer's prejudices and biases, his limited opportunity to observe adequately, and the pupils' lack of opportunity to demonstrate the behavior in which we are interested.

Examination of the pupil's record, particularly if a school system has good cumulative and anecdotal records, provides a basis for making judgments. Judgments made over a long period of time tend to be more reliable than those made within a shorter period. However, agreement of two or three judges does not necessarily mean that a judgment is valid. We all have known pupils who behave in a certain way in the classroom and school and who behave quite differently in their home and neighborhood.

Another measurement technique frequently used to identify individual differences in behavior in groups is sociometric rating. Pupils are asked to choose from among their associates those with whom they would like to work, or to have as a leader. The variations in this technique are many, and the counselor can adapt it to meet his own needs for identification of pupils with varying traits.

Some psychological inventories or personality tests can help make these judgments. These tests are becoming more dependable and are demonstrating their usefulness. They provide information about the extent to which pupils like to be with other pupils, the extent to which they feel acceptance of other persons, the relationships pupils have with their families, and the extent to which they possess leadership tendencies.

EMOTIONAL STABILITY

Apart somewhat from these behaviors involving social relationships is another type of behavior that we might appropriately label "emotionality," or behavior that directly concerns the way a person feels about himself, the amount of his emotional control, the moods he experiences, his tendencies toward psychoneurotic or perhaps even psychotic behavior, and the general satisfaction he derives from his everyday experiences. Again direct observation provides the teacher with one means for making judgments about these aspects of behavior. Pupils who cry easily in the classroom, who lose their temper easily, who appear unhappy and depressed can be readily identified.

Observation alone, however, usually is not a sufficient means for identifying these characteristics. Frequently, a discrepancy exists between the way a person acts and the way he feels. Often only certain situations arouse significant behaviors, and these situations may not be related to the school. As has been noted many times, the unhappy child often is the quiet and unobtrusive child, and this kind of behavior usually does not call much attention from the teacher.

As with social behaviors, personality inventories can be used to provide additional information about the emotional behavior of the pupil. These personality measures may provide information about the emotional stability of the child, his mood, and how he feels about himself.

RESPONSIBILITY

Finally, in this rather vague group of concepts, we must include those related to dependability, character, and aspects of behavior which determine how predictable the pupil is. Again, teachers are in a position to observe the consistency of a pupil's behavior. Psychological inventories and personality tests can provide additional information about the child's tendency to become a delinquent or the extent to which a pupil conforms to the mores of his group. Admittedly, however, the task of making a judgment here is more difficult than in any other area so far discussed (Hathaway & Monachesi, 1953).

BEHAVIOR DEVIATIONS IN ADOLESCENCE

When we learn about pupils, inevitably we identify some whose behavior presents special problems; and then we must seek to understand children who may be considered abnormal by their peers, their parents, or themselves. Traditionally, behavior deviations have been categorized according to psychiatric nomenclature (Noyes & Kolb, 1958) or according to the customary classification of psychological mechanisms (Shaffer & Shoben, 1956). Insofar as our attempt here is not to present a comprehensive picture of adolescent psychopathology, but rather to suggest some of the implications of behavior deviations for the counselor, let us approach these deviations from the point of view of the social values which characterize our culture.

THE PUPIL AND HIS SOCIETY

The first value centers about the relationship between the individual and his society. Many of the problems of adolescence, as well as problems at other ages, result from the ambiguous nature of the relationship between the self and society. The child from early experience is taught to regard himself as a functioning member of a variety of groups—his family, his play groups, and his school groups. As a group member, he is encouraged to assume responsibility for the group's welfare, to sacrifice at times his own welfare for the group's advantage, and to integrate his needs and activities with those of the group. At the same time, he is encouraged to be independent of these groups, to be self-sufficient, to identify his own personal goals and values and work toward these, and to grant to others the right to behave in the same way. Many problems involving relationships between pupils and their peers, their families, and their teachers can be viewed as expressions of the conflict between striving for independence and developing suitable dependency relationships.

A psychologically mature person must modify his attitudes of dependency and independency from situation to situation and from person to person. If he veers too much toward excessive dependency, he is indecisive, unable to cope with solitude and privacy, and intolerant of the rights of others to seek their own individuality. On the other hand, if he fails to develop proper dependency relationships, he feels isolated and frequently is excluded from groups in which he desires membership, introduces conflict into the groups to which he does belong to the detriment of both himself and the group, and is unable to satisfy some of his basic needs which require that he establish close and intimate relationships with others. When the counselor views this particular aspect of adolescent development as an attempt to attain appropriate dependency relationships, rather than as an attempt to attain independence, then he will be able to provide greater assistance as the pupil attempts to establish new types of relationships with others, particularly with his family.

IDEALISM AND MATERIALISM

The second set of values concerning the behavior of the adolescent centers around materialism and spiritualism. Reinforcements arrive from a variety of sources to strengthen the child's conviction that fine homes, good clothing, expensive cars, and elaborate appliances are useful and desirable. Prolonged familial attempts to acquire such things, in addition to incessant bombardments from advertisers and salesmen, constantly remind the child that the material world, the "real" world, is good.

On the other hand, much of our literary and cultural heritage constantly reminds pupils of the greater importance of the transcendental. As he reads the Bible, as he is introduced to Shakespeare and Thoreau, as he is exposed to the writings of Hawthorne or Emerson, he acquires an ambivalent feeling toward things considered desirable by his peers. Many high school and university students apologize to counselors when they explain that one reason for their selecting an occupation is to "make more money." The attitudes people have toward property, both their own and that of others, are not results of simple experiences and learnings; rather these attitudes result from a complex of experiences which may present almost unresolvable paradoxes. Often these conflicts are expressed as problems of religion or belief.

THE PUPIL'S PLACE IN TIME

The time orientation of our society is the third value that helps us understand some of the behavior deviations and conflicts of the adolescent. Major educational and vocational decisions require proper evaluation of the relative importance of (1) delaying satisfaction of immediate gains to obtain future reward and (2) obtaining sufficient immediate satisfaction. The adolescent's ambitions not always are in accord with the ambitions of his parents, and he himself frequently has goals which are mutually noncompatible. Educational and vocational decisions are not the only ones related to the time orientation of the pupil. An increasing number of students are facing decisions involving early marriage and parenthood. These problems frequently are related to current economic conditions. When the individual is more able to provide for his immediate needs in the manner he desires, he may have less reason to anticipate with pleasure the rewards promised by lengthy and difficult endeavor.

ACCEPTANCE

Many problems demonstrated by adolescents result from the need for acceptance. When the child does not obtain recognition from his family and friends because of his performance and when he feels unworthy as a person, compensatory attempts will be made to obtain this recognition, and these attempts may be either constructive or destructive. When the child who feels unloved at home works hard to obtain the acceptance of others at school through constructive leadership activities, the existence of a problem may be masked; but when the child turns upon a rejecting society, the problem becomes quite explicit.

AUTHORITY

Finally, many adolescent problems spring directly from the attitude of the pupil toward authority. This attitude is closely related to and actually may be a part of the complex of attitudes mentioned earlier involving the relationship of the individual with society, but here we will concern ourselves with the problems presented as the child struggles to learn the appropriate use of authority relationships. Each child must learn how to live at both ends of the authority relationship; he must learn how to be the authority and he must learn how to accept others as authorities. At an early age, the child is faced with the conflict involving the authority roles of the parent and the teacher. When the parent and the teacher express opposing opinions or present conflicting information, the child must learn to evaluate the authority role of each person. As others come to the child for information or advice, he must learn how to evaluate his own competencies and how to use them with the greatest skill. If he fails to develop these judgments, he may tend to reject all authority, in which case we may have the rebel with or without a cause; or equally bad, he may accept any claim made to authority and consequently forfeit the right to his own judgment.

We see that many of the behavioral problems presented by youths of junior and senior high school age can be viewed as expressions of the students' attempt to incorporate the important values of society into their daily behavior. For no pupil is this an easy task, but for many this incorporation takes place with relatively little conflict and pain. For many others, however, the process is an extremely difficult one and may result in overt signs of distress, as expressed by conflict with friends, parents, and teachers, by rebellion against society and its representatives, and by attempts to aggressively fight against society; or the confusion may be expressed more implicitly by emotional distress and discomfort as shown by moodiness, depression, unhappiness, and dissatisfaction with one's self and one's world.

SUMMARY

The counselor must know a great deal about the pupils he counsels if he is to do an effective job. Several dimensions of personality must be studied—abilities and aptitudes, acquired information and skills, interests and values, personality, temperament, and character. Many methods are available for learning about pupils—direct observation in or out of the classroom, interviews, school records and reports, ratings, and psychological and educational tests.

Acquiring this information about pupils is a necessary step in counseling but not a sufficient one. Only with relevant information can the counselor work effectively, but just having the information does not imply the counselor's efforts will be successful. Just as the bricklayer must have both the bricks and the knowledge and the skill with which to use them, so must the counselor have not only the data about the pupil, but also the skill and the understanding to use them to aid the pupil.

QUESTIONS FOR STUDY

1. How is ability related to achievement? What other variables must be considered? Why are high school grades usually better predictors of college success than test scores?
2. Why do most comprehensive testing programs include tests of both general abilities and of differential abilities?
3. What various means are available for inferring vocational interests?
4. Why are the pupil's values of concern to the counselor?

5. Several dimensions of personality have been discussed in this chapter. Can you rank these dimensions in their order of importance to the counselor? To the classroom teacher?
6. What problems can you anticipate in integrating the many kinds of information described in this chapter into a meaningful description of the pupil?

REFERENCES

Allport, G. W., Vernon, P. E., & Lindzey, G. *Study of values—a scale for measuring the dominant interests in personality.* Boston: Houghton Mifflin, 1951.

American Psychological Association. *Technical recommendations for psychological tests and diagnostic techniques.* Washington, D.C., 1954.

Berdie, R. F. Aptitude, achievement, interest, and personality tests: a longitudinal comparison. *J. appl. Psychol.,* 1955, 39, 103–114.

Berdie, R. F., Dressel, P., & Kelso, P. Relative validity of the Q and L scores of the ACE Psychological Examination. *Educ. psychol. Measmt.,* 1951, 11, 803–812.

Bingham, W. V. *Aptitudes and aptitude testing.* New York: Harper, 1937.

Bingham, W. V., Moore, B. V., & Gustad, J. W. *How to interview.* New York: Harper & Row, 1959.

Committee on Measurement and Evaluation of the American Council on Education. *College testing: a guide to practices and programs.* Washington: American Council on Education, 1959.

Fryer, D. *The measurement of interests.* New York: Henry Holt, 1931.

Guilford, J. P. Three faces of intellect. *Amer. Psychologist,* 1959, 14, 469–479.

Hall, C. S., & Lindzey, G. *Theories of personality.* New York: Wiley, 1957.

Hathaway, S. R., & Monachesi, E. D. *Analyzing and predicting juvenile delinquency with the MMPI.* Minneapolis: University of Minnesota Press, 1953.

Lindquist, E. F. (Ed.) *Educational measurement.* Washington, D.C.: American Council on Education, 1951.

McClelland, D. C. *Talent and society.* Princeton, N.J.: Van Nostrand, 1958.

National Education Association. *Technical recommendations for achievement tests.* Washington, D.C., 1955.

Noyes, A. P., & Kolb, L. C. *Modern clinical psychiatry.* (5th ed.) Philadelphia: Saunders, 1958.

Shaffer, L. F., & Shoben, E. J., Jr. *The psychology of adjustment: a dynamic and experimental approach to personality and mental hygiene.* Boston: Houghton Mifflin, 1956.

Strong, E. K., Jr. *Vocational interests of men and women.* Stanford, Calif.: Stanford, 1943.

Strong, E. K., Jr. *Vocational interests 18 years after college.* Minneapolis: University of Minnesota Press, 1955.

Thurstone, L. L. *Multiple-factor analysis.* Chicago: University of Chicago Press, 1947.

Woodworth, R. S. *Heredity and environment: a critical survey of recently published material on twins and foster children.* New York: Social Science Research Council, 1941.

CHAPTER 4

Learning about the Social Development of Pupils

With the advent of adolescence, boys and girls become acutely aware of social pressures and, consequently, many of the adjustment problems of adolescents involve social relationships. Adolescents are sensitive to the opinions and attitudes of others and usually consider possible reactions of the group to everything they do.

Adolescence is a period of transition from the preadolescent pattern of friendships with members of one's own sex to friendships with those of the opposite sex. Thus, we find a shift from predominantly same-sex to mixed-sex interests. The single sex gang of preadolescent days becomes a crowd of boys and girls. As did the gang, the crowd usually has objectives which are determined and sought by its members; however, the objectives of the crowd are different from those of the gang. The primary function of the crowd is to provide social experience of a heterosexual nature for its membership. The crowd may participate in some organized social functions such as dances or parties, but to an even greater extent in informal social gatherings. In a middle-class culture, the crowd may gather at someone's house to listen to records or to lounge on a patio for endless discussion. These informal gatherings at home seemingly are most often concerned with raiding the family refrigerator. The locale, activities, and style of these gatherings vary with local customs and cultural mores. They may occur on a street corner, in a church parlor, or in a car. They may be organized or disorganized, supervised or unsupervised, lawful or unlawful, but the purpose for the individual remains relatively constant.

The crowd provides a necessary learning situation for adolescents. It is here that they are able to experiment with their own and others' social behavior. It provides an opportunity to sharpen one's skill at perceiving and conceptualizing other persons, and perhaps even more importantly it provides an opportunity to experiment with members of the opposite sex. An adolescent who is not a member of a crowd is handicapped in later life because he has not had the learning experiences possible only in a group. Being an accepted member of a crowd is important to adolescents, even to those youths who, rejected by the group, claim their own superiority and deprecate the conforming behavior so typical of adolescents.

During adolescence the pupil strives to break away from complete dependency on his parents and attempts to develop into a relatively independent and mature adult who will assume responsibility for himself and who will occupy a defined position in society. Social interaction during adolescence gives the pupil an opportunity to learn social behavior, to learn about himself, and to gradually become aware of what his societal role will be.

Because group membership is very important to the adolescent, a school counselor must know about the patterns of group relationships, so that he will be aware of the effects of the group on each student. The counselor will help isolates become members of groups and will be concerned with students who make inappropriate use of groups. Experience in social relations during adolescence can lead to acceptance of responsibility as citizens and to participation in community life in later years.

Pupils who are not accepted in a group often worry considerably about this, and their maladaptive behavior interferes with studying and the acquisition of knowledge; they cannot concentrate because of their strong awareness of the group.

SOCIAL NEEDS

A need[1] is a requirement of an individual which, when unsatisfied, motivates him to action and which is experienced as a desire. The requirement, when met, tends to further the welfare of the individual or to facilitate his usual behavior. English and English (1958), Maslow (1954), and Murray (1938) are psychologists who have written and researched extensively about needs and their assessment.

Some people have stronger social needs than others. Not everyone needs constant companionship or, contrariwise, needs to be isolated. Probably the norm is somewhere in between. As is the case with all physical and mental development, a large range of individual differ-

---

[1] Throughout this book we shall use the concept of need or needs. Usually an adjective will precede the noun so as to make specific the type of need being discussed.

ences exists among pupils in a class with regard to need for socialization. The child growing older learns techniques for satisfying his desire for socializing. He learns to smile at others, to help them, to avoid hostile, aggressive acts, and learns in other ways to facilitate successful social experiences. Early frustration of these desires for social relationships may lead to emotional maladjustment which many times is identifiable through the bashfulness or shyness of the individual. However, some people who are socially maladjusted aggressively seek friendships by bizarre behavior or by aggressive nonconforming. Some of them act idiotically in order to gain the center of attention. These pupils may achieve superficial acceptance but actual rejection by the group. Other pupils react to isolation by withdrawal and a rejection of their need for others.

ASSESSING SOCIAL RELATIONSHIPS

The counselor must have objective and reliable information about the social relationships of pupils in his school just as he must have objective information about physical and mental abilities and achievement. Through the use of adequate diagnostic procedures for social behaviors, the counselor can determine appropriate treatment. Incidental observation by the counselor and teachers in halls and at school functions can provide important information to the counselor. Through observation and reports of others, he often can become aware of scapegoats, that is, the targets for expression of hostile feelings by the group. He can at times be aware of the social isolate. However, this casual observation may be an unreliable and invalid measure of the social relationships which actually exist. Reliable and valid techniques other than personal observation are available for the use of the counselor. Personality or adjustment inventories and sociometric devices are two measurements that are widely used in schools to study social behavior and adjustment.

SOCIOMETRICS

Moreno (1934) was responsible for developing the technique now called sociometrics. In his book published in 1934, he reported a series of studies of groups in public schools and other institutions. He used many data-gathering techniques including that of sociometrics.

A sociometric device is a technique for assessing social relationships in groups by mapping the attractions and repulsions of the group members toward each other. It enables one to determine whether individuals are accepted or are rejected by the group. Sociometry makes use of a questionnaire which asks each member of a group to indicate with which group members he would prefer to engage in a certain kind of activity, such as working on a committee planning a school function. The questionnaire may ask him to list those individuals whom he would not want to be on his committee. Activities other than participation in a committee can be used as the criterion for the individual to consider as he indicates his choices or his rejections.

Rejections sometimes are not solicited because of their negative implications, for the act of listing negative choices might crystallize hostile feelings on the part of the group toward the individual rejected. Sometimes the respondent is asked to name only a given number of choices such as three or five and at other times he is called on to make unlimited choices.

In general, the basic principles to be observed in planning a sociometric study are:

1. The limits of the group membership from which choices are to be made should be outlined to the subjects.

2. The number of choices permitted should be indicated.

3. The specific criteria to be used in making a choice should be carefully outlined to the group. More specifically, the group should be told that they are to choose members, say, to serve on a committee with them, or to share a table in the classroom, or to work as a team during a laboratory experiment.

4. The group members should be allowed to make their choices in private. Usually this involves a paper and pencil technique and the members should be assured that their choices will remain confidential.

5. The mechanism for obtaining sociometric data should be a naturally structured group situation. For example, a class may be periodically subdivided into discussion groups or work groups of some kind. The students can be told this is the way the class will operate, and after the sociometric choices have been made and analyzed, the results can be used in forming the actual work groups.

The sociometric data usually are summarized graphically and a sociogram prepared. In the sociogram each person is represented by a symbol such as a square or circle, and the choices made or received by the individual are indicated by lines or arrows connecting the symbols. The pattern of choices reflects the group structure. Particularly important for group structure is the identification of the often chosen. This is the individual who receives a disproportionate number of choices by other members of the group. The isolate receives few and makes few choices. The rejected pupil is the individual who receives a large number of rejections. The mutual pairs are the individuals making reciprocal choices, and the triangles are the trios of mutual choices, and so forth. Below is an illustration of a simple sociogram.

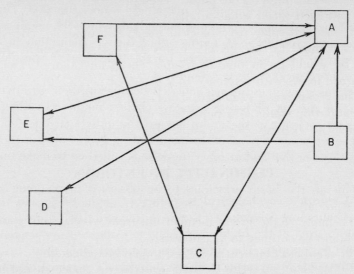

A was the child preferred by F, B, and C, while C was preferred by A and F. A preferred D, and A and E shared a mutual preference. B was an isolate, preferred by no other, but choosing A and E, and F and C were mutual choices.

As indicated earlier, group structure can be determined in part by direct observation of the formal organization of a group or through associations of pupils in the classroom or at social and school functions, but the sociometric technique adds to the reliability and validity of the analysis of group structure.

The periodic reformation or shifting of group members may be used to give individuals social experiences that can be therapeutic. Shoobs (1947) has demonstrated that continuous sociometric testing combined with "assignment therapy" and individual counseling for the poorly adjusted over a six-month period resulted in improvement in both scholastic standing and social behavior.

Sociometry has been used for research in leadership, minority group prejudice, social adjustment, social sensitivity, social status, and morals, as well as group structure. The chapter by Lindzey and Borgatta (1954) in the *Handbook of Social Psychology* summarizes well the sociometric technique. Jennings (1959) has prepared a helpful manual for those interested in sociometry.

SOCIOMETRIC SCALES

Gardner and Thompson (1959) have developed the Syracuse Scales of Social Relations which are a variation on the sociometric device pioneered by Moreno. These scales are for use with elementary, junior high, and senior high school pupils. They present social situations to the pupil, and each social situation elicits responses calling for the satisfaction of one particular psychological need. For example, one situation requires a pupil to rate his classmates as kind, sympathetic friends to whom he would go in time of trouble (need-succorance). The pupil's ratings are made with reference to a group of persons that extends beyond the group being evaluated. Thus, it is possible to compare the social relationship status of a pupil with others in a number of subgroups to which he belongs, for example, the classroom, clubs, or athletic groups.

PERSONALITY INVENTORIES

The California Psychological Inventory (Gough, 1957) and the Minnesota Counseling Inventory (Berdie & Layton, 1957) are personality inventories used at the high school level to evaluate the personality and adjustment of pupils. The information obtained from these inventories is multifaceted. Many aspects of the individual's personality other than his social behavior are analyzed. However, in this chapter we are concerned only with social behavior.

The California Psychological Inventory has 480 true-false items, about half of which were drawn from the Minnesota Multiphasic Personality Inventory (Hathaway & McKinley, 1951). The remainder of the items were written to assess social and personal interests and attitudes. "I hate entering by myself a room where other people have already been talking" is a paraphrased item.

The inventory yields eighteen scores: dominance, capacity for status, sociability, social presence, self-acceptance, sense of well-being, responsibility, socialization, self-control, tolerance, good impression, communality, achievement via conformance, achievement via independence, intellectual efficiency, psychological mindedness, flexibility, and femininity. Of these, dominance, capacity for status, sociability, social presence, and socialization are most important for an understanding of the pupil's social behavior. However, all traits measured by the inventory probably interact to determine the social activity of the pupil.

The manual for the inventory (Gough, 1957) presents the following purposes for the five scales listed above:

Do (dominance)   To assess factors of leadership ability, dominance, persistence, and social initiative.

Cs (capacity for status)   To serve as an index of an individual's capacity for status (not his actual or achieved status). The scale attempts to measure the personal qualities and attributes which underlie and lead to status.

Sy (sociability)   To identify persons of outgoing, sociable, participative temperament.

Sp (social presence) To assess factors such as poise, spontaneity, and self-confidence in personal and social interaction.

So (socialization) To indicate the degree of social maturity, integrity, and rectitude which the individual has attained.

These listed purposes show that scores from the Gough inventory have direct relevance to the study of pupils' social behavior. This assumes, of course, that the inventory scales do measure what they purport to measure. The inventory manual and critical reviews in *The Fifth Mental Measurements Yearbook* (Buros, 1959) should be consulted for information on this point.

The Minnesota Counseling Inventory (Berdie & Layton, 1957) has 355 true-false items, approximately one-half of which were drawn from the Minnesota Multiphasic Personality Inventory (Hathaway & McKinley, 1951) and one-half from the Minnesota Personality Scale (Darley & McNamara, 1946). The inventory was specifically devised for use at the high school level and was extensively standardized on high school pupils. Twenty-five thousand pupils were tested in the initial phase of the standardization process. The inventory yields nine scores which are descriptive of the high school pupil: question, validity, family relationships, social relationships, emotional stability, conformity, adjustment to reality, mood, and leadership. The social relationships and leadership scales are especially pertinent to the present discussion.

In the standardization process, teachers were asked to nominate pupils who fit behavior descriptions written by the inventory authors. Pupils described by positive and negative descriptions were nominated and used as criterion groups on which the items and scales were validated. Following are the nominating forms used for the nomination of pupils exhibiting good and poor social relationships.

STUDENT EVALUATION FORM
(Good Social Relationships)
What *boy* in your school that you know conforms best to this description?
He appears to be thoroughly happy and comfortable when he is with groups of students or adults. He has good social skills—talks easily and well, knows what to do and when to do it, has acceptable manners and is reasonably courteous, and appears to have a genuine liking for others and is well liked by them. For example, this student may:
1. Usually be found with other people.
2. Be the one who introduces people at social gatherings.
3. Appear to enjoy talking with others—be interested in what they say.

(Boy)
1. _____ (first choice)

What *girl* in your school that you know conforms best to this description?

(Girl)
1. _____ (first choice)

STUDENT EVALUATION FORM
(Poor Social Relationships)

What *boy* in your school that you know conforms best to this description?

He is unhappy and uncomfortable when he is with groups of students or adults. His social skills are poor, he doesn't enjoy talking with others, he appears to be awkward and doesn't make a good impression on others. He doesn't appear to enjoy being with others, and they in turn derive no great satisfaction from being with him. For example, this student may:

1. Refuse to attend class or school functions.
2. Usually be alone.
3. Not answer questions in class when called upon even if he knows the answers.
4. Be restless and uncomfortable when talking with others.

(Boy)

1. _____ (first choice)

What *girl* in your school that you know conforms best to this description?

(Girl)

1. _____ (first choice)

The leadership description, as taken from the evaluation form, is as follows:

He has outstanding leadership skills and knows how to work well with others. He is willing to and often assumes responsibilities in groups of which he is a member and shows initiative in developing and carrying out ideas. Others recognize these qualities, and he is frequently placed in positions where he is enabled to exercise them.

The inventory authors could not construct a behavior description opposite to the one above. Consequently, in the standardization process, pupils nominated as leaders were contrasted with those not nominated as leaders, i.e., the remainder of the group.

Pupils who score high (compared to their appropriate sex and grade norm group) on the social relationships scale tend to behave like pupils described as having poor social relationships. Pupils scoring average or below on the social relationships scale tend to have average to excellent success in social relationships. On the leadership scale a low score indicates leadership potential, whereas a high score indicates its lack.

The leadership and social relationships scales are positively correlated as one might predict from a general knowledge of behavior and from general observation. However, each of the scales is reliable enough to ensure reliably significant differences in scores between them for some pupils. Pupils who have very discrepant scores are ones who should be of especial interest to a counselor. A boy who scores in the high direction on the social relationships scale but low on the leader end of the leadership scale may have leadership ability but may be using his leadership roles to satisfy social needs which he cannot satisfy outside the leadership position. Another pupil with good social relationships may be only an average to below average leader; yet his popularity may cause others to place him in a leadership position in which he may fail. If the counselor is alert to discrepancy scores like these, he should be able to counsel more effectively.

USE OF SOCIAL INFORMATION

Knowledge of the social structure of the school and of the social characteristics of individual pupils can be a powerful tool in the hands of the counselor and his colleagues.

Some schools organize classwork and cocurricular activities around pupil committees. Social relationship or group structure information is helpful to the administrator, counselor, and teacher in forming these committees to facilitate pupil adjustment. The sociometric devices and inventories can be used as pre- and postmeasures on the pupils to make objective observations about pupils' growth in social relationships. Social data should be obtained early in the pupil's school career to take advantage of the opportunity for formation of groups to facilitate adequate social relationships. A counselor working with an individual with poor social relationships can actively attempt to bring together pupils of similar backgrounds and interests and, through knowledge of the social structure of the school, can ensure their having frequent contact.

SUMMARY

Adolescence is a period of development of social and heterosexual relationships. The adolescent is much concerned with the adequacy of his social behavior especially as he anticipates his transition from dependence on his parents to his relative independence from them. This independence carries with it the need and responsibility to assume one's mature role in society. Social interaction and experimentation during adolescence provide the pupil an opportunity to learn and gradually develop into a mature adult.

Sociometric devices and personality inventories integrated with sensitive observation can provide the counselor with knowledge of the group structures and social relationships existing in his school and with knowledge of the social behavior of individual pupils. The counselor can use this knowledge to facilitate social development of his counselees through active but subtle manipulation of the group structure.

QUESTIONS FOR STUDY

1. Can a pupil be an effective leader and not have good social relationships?
2. How might the counselor work with the homeroom and classroom teachers to identify and socialize social isolates?
3. List three activities other than choosing persons to participate with on a committee which might be used in determining sociometric patterns.
4. Would one expect sociometric choices to be the same regardless of the activity selected from Question 3?
5. How might a counselor determine what are the out-of-school social activities of pupils?
6. Should the counselor concern himself with or "interfere" in out-of-school social activities of pupils?

REFERENCES

Berdie, R. F., & Layton, W. L. *The Minnesota Counseling Inventory.* New York: Psychological Corporation, 1957.

Buros, O. K. (Ed.) *The fifth mental measurements yearbook.* Highland Park, N.J.: Gryphon Press, 1959.

Campbell, E. H. The social-sexual development of children. *Genet. Psychol. Monogr.,* 1939, **21,** 461–552.

Cole, Luella. *Psychology of adolescence.* New York: Holt, 1959. (In association with Irma N. Hall.)

Crist, J. R. High school dating as a behavior system. *Marriage Fam. Living,* 1953, **15,** 13–28.

Darley, J. G., & McNamara, W. J. *Manual of directions: Minnesota personality scale.* New York: Psychological Corporation, 1946.

Ehrmann, W. W. Influence of comparative social class of the companion upon premarital heterosexual behavior. *Marriage Fam. Living,* 1955, **17,** 48–53.

English, H. B., & English, Ava C. *A comprehensive dictionary of psychological and psychoanalytical terms.* New York: McKay, 1958.

Erickson, E. H. *Childhood and society.* New York: Norton, 1950.

Gardner, E. F., & Thompson, G. G. *Social relations and morale in small groups.* New York: Appleton-Century-Crofts, 1956.

Gardner, E. F., & Thompson, G. G. *The Syracuse Scales of Social Relations.* New York: Harcourt, Brace & World, 1959.

Gough, H. *The California Psychological Inventory.* Palo Alto, Calif.: Consulting Psychologists Press, 1957.

Hathaway, S. R., & McKinley, J. C. *Manual, Minnesota Multiphasic Personality Inventory.* New York: Psychological Corporation, 1951.

Havighurst, R. J. *Human development and education.* New York: McKay, 1953.

Hess, R. D., & Goldblatt, Irene. The status of adolescents in American society: a problem in social identity. *Child Develpm.,* 1957, **28,** 459–468.

Holman, M. Adolescent attitudes toward seeking help with personal problems. *Smith Coll. Stud. soc. Work,* 1955, **25,** 1–31.

Hurlock, Elizabeth B. *Developmental psychology.* (2nd ed.) New York: McGraw-Hill, 1959.

Jennings, Helen H. *Sociometry in group relations: a manual for teachers.* (2nd ed.) Washington, D.C.: American Council on Education, 1959.

Kinsey, A. C., Pomeroy, W. B., & Martin, C. E. *Sexual behavior in the human male.* Philadelphia: Saunders, 1948.

Kinsey, A. C., Pomeroy, W. B., Martin, C. E., & Gebhard, P. H. *Sexual behavior in the human female.* Philadelphia: Saunders, 1953.

Kuhlen, R. G. *The psychology of adolescent development.* New York: Harper & Row, 1952.

Lane, H., & Beauchamp, Mary. *Understanding human development.* Englewood Cliffs, N.J.: Prentice-Hall, 1959.

Lewis, O. Y. Problems of adolescents. *Calif. J. sec. Educ.,* 1949, **24**, 215–221.

Liccione, J. V. The changing family relationships of adolescent girls. *J. abnorm. soc. Psychol.,* 1955, **51**, 421–426.

Lindzey, G., & Borgatta, E. Sociometric measurement. In G. Lindzey (Ed.), *Handbook of social psychology.* Cambridge, Mass.: Addison-Wesley, 1954. Pp. 405–448.

Maslow, A. H. *Motivation and personality.* New York: Harper & Row, 1954.

Moreno, J. L. *Who shall survive? A new approach to the problem of human interrelations.* New York: Nervous and Mental Disease Publishing, 1934.

Murray, H. A., et al. *Explorations in personality.* New York: Oxford, 1938.

Pressey, S. L., & Kuhlen, R. G. *Psychological development through the life span.* New York: Harper & Row, 1957.

Shoobs, N. E. Sociometry in the classroom. *Sociometry,* 1947, **10**, 154–164.

Zeleny, L. D. Status: its measurement and control in education. *Sociometry,* 1941, **4**, 193–204.

CHAPTER 5

Tests

"What is he like?" and "What can he do?" are questions often asked by counselors about pupils. Tests provide partial answers to these questions and help the counselor build a picture in his mind about the pupil. In addition to this kind of conceptualization, we are concerned with prediction of future behavior, assessment of current behavior, and description of the characteristics of the pupil. We want to predict what the pupil will do in certain situations, assess his present status, and determine how well he has learned in the past. We are interested in obtaining an objective description of him.

Psychologists have used the term *measurement* to define certain operations which are utilized to assess and describe people. Though many concepts of psychological measurement are analogous to concepts used in measurement in the physicial sciences, the two should not be confused. Usually in physical measurement, the relevant characteristic of the measuring instrument corresponds directly with the characteristic of the object being measured, and direct measurement has been effective because the objects being measured obviously seem to have such characteristics as length, weight, and volume as do the appropriate measuring instruments. In psychology the measuring instruments do not correspond in this obvious way to the object of measurement. Psychologists often are concerned with objective descriptions of behavior which may appear chaotic to the casual observer. The problem is how to bring order from seeming disorder to construct an efficient framework within which to describe the behavior of an individual.

Many psychologists have proposed theories, usually called theories of personality, to help explain the behavior of human beings. The personality theory with which we are primarily concerned in testing and counseling is the *trait theory*. Traits are the inventions of psychologists and are postulated to help explain and understand the characteristics and behavior of people. A trait is considered to be a characteristic of an individual and is a dimension of behavior which can be used in describing, comparing, and contrasting individuals. Intelligence is one of the oldest psychological traits. Other examples of psychological trait names are emotional stability, verbal ability, mechanical aptitude, and curiosity. The English language contains thousands of possible trait names. Allport and Odbert (1936) categorized approximately 18,000 terms taken from an unabridged dictionary. These terms, descriptive of people's behavior, were classified as to whether they represented traits in personality, temporary states, or evaluative ideas.

Sir Francis Galton, sometimes called the "father of mental tests," was perhaps the first person to become interested in the systematic study of psychological traits and the subject of individual differences. He devised tests to reveal differences in ability between individuals and developed statistical methods for summarizing the large masses of quantitative data which resulted from testing. Karl Pearson, a student of Galton's, further advanced the theory of statistics and developed the product-moment formula for the coefficient of correlation, a statistic which is widely used in analyzing tests. In the early twentieth century, Binet, in France, with his development of an individual intelligence test, and Cattell, in the United States, with his concern with mental measurement, did much to stimulate the development of testing and the definition of psychological traits. This work was accelerated by successful attempts in World War I to classify military personnel into appropriate military jobs. Testing was carried on during the depression preceding World War II by organizations such as the Employment Stabilization Research Institute of the University of Minnesota, and military research during World War II further stimulated the development of testing.

Growth of the testing movement has been so great that the number of tests and psychological traits presumably being measured is staggering. *The Fifth Mental Measurements Yearbook* (Buros, 1959) lists 957 tests and 6,468 references on the construction, use, and limitations of specific tests. French's two monographs (1951, 1953) catalog several hundred psychological traits defined in factor analytic studies and which may be of interest to psychologists.

What traits should be defined by psychologists to enable them to most efficiently conceptualize individuals? This major question is still unanswered. However, traits are often classified into broader categories such as aptitudes, achievement, interests, values, and personality which help us in our attempt to conceptualize pupils' behavior.

In Chapter 3 we saw that aptitudes are characteristics of an individual which indicate potential for learning. Some specific aptitudes are termed verbal, numerical, spatial relations, mechanical, and clerical. By *achievement* we mean the extent to which an individual has learned or accomplished something. In counseling, we usually are concerned with achievement in specific subject matters such as reading, writing, arith-metic, science, social studies, and mathematics. Interests reflect to some extent the motivation of a person and most often are expressed in terms of the likes or preferences of the individual. The values of an individual are attitudes indicative of the things he prizes. In the personality domain are included traits which seem to be typical of the person or which give the individual a particular flavor or quality, such as sociability, gre-gariousness, anxiety, leadership, or conformity.

Psychological trait theory assumes that responses which are correlated with one another can be elicited from an individual to form a response constellation which defines a trait. In testing, we present a standard stimulus to the subject to call forth what we hope are standard responses and response constellations. Individuals differ in their capacity to respond to stimuli. The differences in responses elicited by a standard stimulus are the result of learning mediated by heredity and the psychological and physiological state of the individual at the time of response. Response capabilities are of complex origin, and though in large part determined by heredity, they are shaped by the individual's environment through his learning experiences. Heredity determines developmental limits to re-sponse capability. In testing, we are often concerned with predicting future behavior by measuring the results of previous learning as they are expressed at the present moment. The individual's responses at a given moment are used to infer characteristics of the individual. Through adequate experimentation, we can identify the behavioral correlates of an individual's response constellations.

Every high school pupil has an enormous response potential. Some parts of this response potential are more adequately developed than others and easier to call forth in a response constellation. Research has shown that for high school pupils certain traits such as verbal and nu-merical abilities are easier to "measure" than are traits in the interest, value, and personality domains. This may be because, in our culture, the educational system provides opportunity for systematic and intensive practice in making responses of a verbal or numerical nature, whereas there is no culturally determined systematic practice in directly calling forth emotional and personality responses.

WHAT THEN ARE TESTS?

Tests are collections of standard stimuli (test items) used to evoke responses. These responses are usually scored, i.e., compared to a standard response and classified in terms of item scores such as right or wrong, true or false, or other indexes. These scored responses to stand-ardized tests have certain known statistical characteristics. Adequately standardized tests are associated with reference data which enable one to interpret the responses.

As we indicated earlier, one of the basic assumptions in testing is that behavioral correlates can be identified empirically with a response. This assumes that controlled observations of responses which are evoked by standard stimuli are made. The field of psychometrics, or testing, has developed observational techniques yielding controlled observations. The implications of the responses must be the subject of further experimentation in order to determine their exact meaning and consistency.

VALIDITY

Tests were described earlier as procedures that allow us to sample behaviors. A spelling test of relatively few words can provide a representative sampling of the pupil's entire spelling skills. Similarly, a vocabulary test consisting of 100 words can be constructed to give us a good sample of the pupil's total vocabulary, perhaps one consisting of 75,000 words. The value of a test depends in part on how adequate a sampling it provides. If a spelling test consisted only of four-letter words beginning with "a," we might know a great deal about the pupil's ability to spell these words, but relatively little about his ability to spell words consisting of more letters or of different letter combinations. If we were interested in a person's arithmetic skills, we could provide him with all possible combinations of numbers and problems involving multiplication, division, addition, and subtraction. This would be too long and arduous a task, so we would select the most representative from all of these combinations and use a shorter test. If the problems selected are not representative—for instance, if we have no problems requiring multiplication by odd numbers, or by even numbers, or if we omit the digit 3 from all problems—we shall have a biased sampling, and our information about the arithmetic skills of the child will be incomplete.

To evaluate a test, particularly an achievement test, we can examine its content to determine to what extent it deals with the information which concerns us. This evidence is relevant to *content validity*.

We can examine a test to see how well it predicts what we wish to predict (*predictive validity*). We might give a college aptitude test to high school seniors to predict how well they will do in college. This information would be useful in advising pupils regarding college attendance and in helping them plan college courses. If the test actually predicts success in college efficiently, then we have a valid test. If it does not predict success in college, then the test's value is questionable.

To evaluate a test in a third way, we can compare the behavior of an individual on one test with his behavior on other tests in other situations. If all the pupils in a group have been given several general ability tests, the agreement we find among these various tests will provide us with some information concerning their value. Such evidence is relevant to *concurrent validity*. If three of four short, highly verbal group tests of general intelligence provide similar results, but scores on the fourth are different from those on the other three, we must carefully examine each test, for the fourth may really be the best. If a test provides results consistently disagreeing with information obtained from other sources, say from observations of classroom behavior, we must examine both the tests and the other observations carefully to learn more about reasons for the differences. Frequently, examination of the discrepancies among several observations leads to fruitful explanations of an individual's behavior. Observation of a pupil with a high intelligence test score but with poor academic achievement may lead us to examine the pupil's motivation or the adequacy of his adjustment.

These methods of determining the accuracy of a test provide us with information about *test validity*. The term validity indicates the extent to which a test measures what we intend it to measure. An intelligence test is valid if it relates directly to behavior independently observed as being intelligent. A vocational interest test is valid if it relates directly to other evidences of the vocational interests of a person.

Whether or not a test is valid always depends on the purpose for which we use it. If a number-checking test is called a clerical aptitude test and if the scores on it predict success in bookkeeping, the test is valid for this purpose. Even though typing is a clerical task, if scores on this test are not related to success in typing, then the test is not valid for this purpose. A test does not have *a* validity, but rather a test is or is not valid for a specified purpose within a given context.

How much evidence do we need before we decide that a test measures what the test author has defined as his objective? The meaning of a test is often mapped after the test is published, but, in general, two major types of data are important in determining the meaning of test scores. The first has to do with direct identification of what is being defined by the testing operation. What is being measured by the standard stimulus-response observation procedure? The concept of validity refers to the identification of the behavior being elicited by a test.

The technical recommendations for psychological tests and diagnostic techniques prepared by a committee of the American Psychological Association, the American Educational Research Association, and the National Council on Measurements Used in Education list four validities (APA, 1954). Three of these have been discussed in the preceding pages. The fourth, *construct validity*, is the extent to which certain psychological concepts explain or account for the performance on the test. The investigation of construct validity requires both logical and empirical operations. Evidence of many different kinds must be integrated in order to evaluate this validity, and its importance and meaning to the science of psychology still is being debated (Bechtoldt, 1959; Cronbach & Meehl, 1955; Loevinger, 1957).

RELIABILITY

We are also concerned with a second general characteristic of tests, i.e., how consistent is the information provided by the test? If we give the same test to a person on four successive days and each day obtain a widely different score, either the test does not measure consistently or the individual changes so much from day to day that we cannot measure consistently. To be useful, tests must provide relatively consistent results, and the trait being measured must be relatively stable. We should not expect all scores to be identical; but if we use an intelligence test at two different times, we should be able to make approximately the same inferences about the individual's ability, e.g., that he is in the upper 10 per cent, or in the lower 10 per cent of a reference group. This consistency is called *reliability*.

Many ways are used to determine how reliable a test is. The same test may be used with the same group of persons on two different occasions, and the scores of individuals in the group compared. Two forms of the same test can be developed (that is, two highly similar tests having different items), and the similar forms can be given to the same group and the scores of individuals compared. A given test can also be divided arbitrarily into two separate tests, for example, scoring the odd and even-numbered items in the test separately. If the two scores obtained for each individual are highly related, then we assume that the test gives us consistent measurement. Kuder and Richardson refined this internal consistency approach to one which does not require two different scorings but uses total score and item statistics (Gulliksen, 1950; Kuder and Richardson, 1937; see also Cronbach, 1947, 1951; Tryon, 1957). The lower the reliability of the test, the more skeptical we must be of its results and the more careful we must be in using it, since the resulting scores have a large error of measurement.

Tests provide us with one means, but not the only means and not necessarily the best means, for obtaining information about pupils. We must first determine whether tests are appropriate or whether other methods of observation should be used. Then we must determine which tests are most appropriate for our situation and evaluate the available tests in terms of both accuracy and consistency.

We also must evaluate tests in terms of their cost and the amount of information gained per unit cost. If we already have adequate intelligence test information about pupils, the administration of another intelligence test would produce little additional useful information about the pupils. The money for further testing would be better spent to gain increased information about interests or special aptitudes. Only after such careful evaluation can we be sure that the test we have is the best test for our purpose and that we are obtaining maximum information for the money spent (Cronbach & Gleser, 1957).

TEST SCORES

A test score results from scoring responses to test items and is a symbol used to communicate information about how a person has behaved in response to a test. People frequently regard test scores as "things" and sometimes endow them with almost magical qualities. Test scores, just as other symbols, should be used only for convenience in communication. When we find we are more concerned with the test score than with the behavior underlying the score, then we are misusing tests.

The intelligence quotient (IQ) has been widely used and more misused than any other test score. Originally, the concept of the IQ allowed psychologists to compare the intelligence of one individual with that of other persons of the same age. The IQ tells us whether a person of a given age behaves on a certain test more, less, or equally efficiently than other persons of the same age. It allows us to relate the test behavior of the individual to his future academic behavior and to make predictions about the quantity and quality of education from which the person can benefit.

This convenient symbol soon began to be used by teachers, parents, and even by some psychologists in a way that almost indicated that a person *had* an IQ. People argued whether the IQ was inherited, how stable it was, and how many different kinds of IQs there were. Often these arguments departed far from the behavior observed in the test situation. Some of the arguments could have been settled easily if more careful attention had been paid to the test observations.

Because of this misuse, many test specialists recommend that the IQ symbol no longer be used and that other means for communication be found. Today the IQ concept is used mainly with individual tests of intelligence like the Stanford-Binet or the Wechsler tests. The IQ is obtained by dividing the person's chronological age (CA) into his mental age (MA), which relates directly to the child's performance on the test expressed in terms of the ages of persons who on the average perform similarly; that is, $IQ = 100MA/CA$. When we say that an eight-year-old has an IQ of 125, we mean that his performance on the test is similar to that of the average ten-year-old.

A score is also a means for quantifying a person's behavior on a test. By weighting each response a person makes on a test, we are able to combine these weights and arrive at a total score. Usually we give a weight of 1 for each correct response. If a person makes 40 correct responses in a fifty-item spelling test, his *raw* score is 40. Sometimes we correct scores for the guessing a person has done and, for example, subtract one-half a unit for every error he makes. The person who had 40 items correct and 10 items wrong in the above spelling test would have a raw score of 35. We can give weights of 1 to relatively simple words and weights of 2 or more to difficult words. A person's ability to spell harder words would add more to his total score than his success with easy words. By weighting, we hope to improve the validity and the reliability of the test.

With the information about a person's behavior on a test quantified, we are able to record the information easily, to communicate it to others, to compare the performance of an individual with the performance of other persons, and to compare the performance at one stage of an individual's life to his performance at some other time.

Using the above spelling test, we can examine different levels of quantification. We can give the fifty-item spelling test to a person and report that he had hardly any correct or that he had almost all of them correct or that he had quite a few wrong and quite a few correct. This kind of report gives some information, but is of limited value. If we told a teacher that this person obtained a score of 39 on the spelling test, the score does not tell which words the person spelled correctly or incorrectly, but it does provide the teacher with more specific information concerning the person's spelling skills than the gross statements above. The teacher can then compare the spelling skills of this pupil with the spelling skills of persons in similar age ranges in similar grades. If this spelling test score is compared to a score on a similar test given a year earlier, inferences can be made concerning improvement or changes in the spelling skills of the pupil. Thus, the score provides us with a summary of the behavior of the person on the test and allows us to make inferences concerning the meaning of this behavior.

TEST NORMS

Scores are only approximations of the behavior of the person. A person with a score of 27 on a spelling test might receive a score of 26 or 28 if the test were given a day earlier or a day later. A score should be seen as falling in a range or zone indicative of the person's behavior.

One way of interpreting scores meaningfully is to compare them with the performance of individuals in an appropriate and well-identified group. For example, we can compare the raw score of a ninth-grade pupil on the spelling test with raw scores earned by a random sampling of all ninth graders in the state. He might also be compared with the other ninth graders in his school or his school system. One can summarize the performance of a group in the form of norms which facilitate individual versus group comparisons.

NORMS

A *norm group* is a specified group which supplies a standard of reference for evaluating the score of the individual. Raw scores for persons in the norm group are arranged in numerical order to form a *frequency distribution* of scores. Manipulations are then made on the frequency distribution to obtain derived or normalized scores possessing certain statistical properties which aid in interpretation of the raw scores. *Percentile ranks,* sometimes called *centile ranks,* are common derived scores. The table showing raw scores and their corresponding derived scores for a given group is known as a *norm table* or a set of *norms.*

To visualize the percentile rank of an individual, consider it as representing his standing in a group of 100 persons representative of the norm group and ranked according to their scores. The individual with a percentile rank of 15 would be 15th from the bottom; conversely, 85 of the 100 representatives of the norm group would have higher scores than this individual.

Our interpretation of a derived or normalized score depends directly upon what we know of the norm group. If we have given a Cooperative English Test to a ninth-grade pupil and he obtains a raw score of 145, using one norm group, this gives a percentile rank of 74, using another norm group, it gives a percentile rank of 27. Interpretation of this pupil's score is meaningful only when we know that the first norm group consists of pupils completing the ninth grade and the second group consists of high school juniors. Our interpretations would be even more meaningful if we also knew how the courses taken in English by the norm group compared with those taken by the pupil. The more relevant information we have about the norm group, the more meaningful is an individual's score. Norm groups drawn representatively from the local school or school system, and from the state, regional, or national levels all yield relevant and valuable interpretative information for the counselor.

Standard scores are other very commonly used derived scores with linear or area transformations of the raw score distribution to a new distribution which has a specified mean and standard deviation. Linear transformations are usually applied when the raw score distribution approximates that of the normal frequency distribution. Area transformations are utilized when the raw score frequency distribution does not have the shape (for example, normal curve) desired by the test author. Frequently, a mean of 50 and a standard deviation of 10 are used for distributions of standard scores. Another type of derived score is the predicted criterion score such as may be found in an expectancy table. Chapter 9 discusses these scores in greater detail. Thorndike and Hagen (1961) and Lindquist (1951) can be consulted further about norms and derived scores.

ADVANTAGES AND DISADVANTAGES OF TESTS

The discussion so far has suggested directly many of the advantages of tests and has implied some of the disadvantages. Eventually, perhaps, tests will be devised to assist in the observation of almost every type of behavior. If at the present time we attempted to develop tests directed at some behaviors, they would be so complex and so inefficient that they would not be worthwhile. Currently, tests of achievement and ability seem more efficient than tests of personality or interest. When we consider the advantages and disadvantages of tests, we must relate these to the personality dimension with which we are concerned and to the efficiency and convenience of other methods available for making observations.

In general, observations made with tests are more easily communicated than observations made through other means. Persons usually can be trained more easily to use tests wisely than they can be trained to use other methods of observation. Without training, many persons use other methods of observation such as rating scales, anecdotal records, and interviews, but it is actually more difficult and more complex to use these methods effectively than it is to use tests such as the Stanford Achievement Test or the Otis Intelligence Tests. We have less difficulty in determining the efficiency of tests than of other methods. Tests are subject to less bias than most other methods of observation. Although test information can be influenced by the prejudices of the test constructor or test administrator, we can control these biases to a great extent in tests. That is, a test situation can be more objective than a nontest situation, and the biases and prejudices of the observer are easier to control when the observer is making use of a standardized test.

Tests may be more expensive than other methods of observation, but if we consider expense in terms of accuracy and usefulness of information, the cost per unit of information obtained through tests might well be less than the per unit cost of information obtained with other means.

The chief danger in using tests is that tests and test scores easily can become the center of attention, displacing the individual with whom we should be concerned. A test score can accrue a reality of its own. Counselors and teachers sometimes use tests not much differently than fortune-tellers use cards or tea-leaf readers use teacups.

Tests are not to be interpreted to persons but rather should be used to help persons obtain better understanding about themselves. Consider the two different approaches used by the counselor in the interview excerpts below. A ninth-grade child during the past year has taken an intelligence test, the Differential Aptitude Tests, the Iowa Tests of Educational Development, and the Minnesota Counseling Inventory. This pupil is talking with a counselor who has on his desk the pupil's cumulative record, including test scores and other relevant background data. Preliminary remarks have been made by the counselor to indicate his hope that he can be of assistance to the pupil. Several courses are now open to the counselor, who might proceed as follows:

COUNSELOR: You've taken several tests during the past year or so. Would you like to discuss the results of these tests first?

PUPIL: Yes, I'd be interested in that.

COUNSELOR: Well, let's look at the general ability test first. This test tells us something about how well you should be able to do in school. It indicates you should be doing well in school. Are you?

PUPIL: I guess I've been between an A and a B student up to now, but I'm having more trouble now.

COUNSELOR: According to this test you have enough ability to do pretty well in high school and then, if you wish, you should be able to do successful work in almost any college. In other words, you're a pretty intelligent person and shouldn't be limited because you can't do the work. How does that strike you?

PUPIL: I guess I've known that I had enough ability to do better than I'm doing.

COUNSELOR: Now let's look at the achievement tests you've taken to see how they compare with the grades you've earned in school. You know as well as I do that grades depend not only on what you learn, but also on a lot of other things, such as how much a teacher likes you, how much trouble you cause in class, and so on. Sometimes these tests show that a person knows a lot more than his grades would indicate, and that is the case here.

The probable purpose of this interview is to help the student increase his self-understanding, but the counselor appears to be test-oriented rather than pupil-oriented. The needs of the pupil are in danger of being overlooked, but we have no research evidence that suggests this type of interview is not effective in imparting information.

Here, however, is another possible counseling approach and another way of using test information:

COUNSELOR: I'm glad to have this chance to talk over your schoolwork with you. How have you been getting along in school recently?

PUPIL: Oh, I've been managing to do a little better than satisfactory work, some A's and B's, but I'm having more trouble now.

COUNSELOR: You sound as if you're not quite satisfied with this condition.

PUPIL: I'm so busy with outside things that I don't have much time for schoolwork, but I should be able to do a lot better. I know I have enough ability to get better grades anyway.

COUNSELOR: Yes, the test of ability that you took earlier this year suggests that you should be able to have a good school record and later on get into college and do successful work there, if that's what you want. But do you feel your out-of-class activities interfere with your schoolwork?

PUPIL: Yes, I'm in a couple of clubs and I also play in the band. My father owns a grocery store, and I help him out a couple of hours every afternoon and on Saturday. I think that I learn a lot from these different things so I don't think the time is wasted, but I don't get as good grades as I could.

COUNSELOR: There are many ways to learn things, and the tests that you have taken here suggest that you have actually learned more than we would conclude from your grades alone. For instance, you haven't had very good grades in English, but you do very well on English and literature tests.

PUPIL: I haven't liked my English teachers very well for the last couple of years, and maybe that's why I haven't worked too hard there, but I do spend a lot of time reading.

The second approach concentrates counselor and pupil attention on the pupil and his status. The test information is introduced by the counselor to illuminate beliefs the pupil has about himself and to strengthen self-understanding. Tests are important, but tend not to be overemphasized in the mind of either the counselor or pupil. Pupils counseled in this manner are less apt to leave the counseling interview thinking "the tests said I should be a farmer," and hence the counselor avoids one of the pitfalls in using tests in counseling.

SUMMARY

Tests are collections of standard stimuli (test items) which enable us to observe behavior under controlled conditions. These standard observations enable us to assess the achievement of pupils, to describe their psychological traits, and to predict their future behavior.

Test scores are symbols summarizing, usually in quantitative terms, an individual's test behavior. Studies of test validity yield evidence about the meaning and significance of test scores. Content validity is evaluated by how adequately the test items represent the larger group of possible items from which they have been drawn. Predictive validity shows the utility of test scores to predict future behavior. Concurrent validity is evident when test scores bear a significant relation to other behavior evaluated at the same time. Construct validity is indicated by the extent to which certain explanatory psychological concepts explain performance on a test. The consistency with which a test measures is called reliability. Reliable tests are necessary for use in counseling since the greater the reliability of a test, the smaller the errors of measurement associated with it. Even with the very reliable tests available today, we should expect some variation in an individual's test performance.

Tests help counselors better understand pupils through assessing their aptitudes, achievement, interests, values, and personality. However, the counselor should be aware of the limitations of tests and make sure that in his work the importance of tests is not overemphasized.

QUESTIONS FOR STUDY

1. Compare achievement and interest testing in terms of relative importance of evidence of content, concurrent, predictive, and construct validity.
2. What are some psychological traits the measurement of which is important for counseling and guidance?
3. In your opinion, what are the three most important psychological traits that might be used in describing a person?
4. Compare the standard errors of measurement for several widely used intelligence tests, such as the California Test of Mental Maturity, the Lorge-Thorndike Intelligence Tests, and the Henmon-Nelson Tests of Mental Ability.

REFERENCES

Allport, G. W., & Odbert, H. S. Trait names: a psycho-lexical study. *Psychol. Monogr.,* 1936, **47,** No. 211.

American Psychological Association, Committee on Psychological Tests. *Technical recommendations for psychological tests and diagnostic techniques.* Washington, D.C.: APA, 1954.

Bechtoldt, H. P. Construct validity: a critique. *Amer. Psychologist,* 1959, **14,** 619–629.

Buros, O. K. (Ed.) *The fifth mental measurements yearbook.* Highland Park, N.J.: Gryphon Press, 1959.

Cronbach, L. J. Test "reliability"; its meaning and determination. *Psychometrika,* 1947, **12,** 1–16.

Cronbach, L. J. Coefficient alpha and the internal structure of tests. *Psychometrika,* 1951, **16,** 297–334.

Cronbach, L. J. & Gleser, Goldine C. *Psychological tests and personnel decisions.* Urbana, Ill.: University of Illinois Press, 1957.

Cronbach, L. J. & Meehl, P. E. Construct validity in psychological tests. *Psychol. Bull.,* 1955, **52,** 281–302.

French, J. W. The description of aptitude and achievement tests in terms of rotated factors. *Psychometric Monogr.,* 1951, No. 5.

French, J. W. *The description of personality measurements in terms of rotated factors.* Princeton, N.J.: Educational Testing Service, 1953.

Gulliksen, H. *Theory of mental tests.* New York: Wiley, 1950.

Kuder, G. F., & Richardson, M. W. The theory of the estimation of test reliability. *Psychometrika,* 1937, **2,** 151–160.

Lindquist, E. F. (Ed.) *Educational measurement,* Washington, D.C.: American Council on Education, 1951.

Loevinger, Jane. Objective tests as instruments of psychological theory. *Psychol. Rep.,* 1957, **3,** 635–694.

Thorndike, R. L., & Hagen, Elizabeth. *Measurement and evaluation in psychology and education,* second edition. New York: Wiley, 1961.

Tryon, R. C. Reliability and behavior domain validity: reformulation and historical critique. *Psychol. Bull.,* 1957, **54,** 229–240.

CHAPTER 6

The Organization of a Testing Program

The broad objectives of a testing program are the same as those of education in general. A school which has a system of testing designed to meet educational needs and to provide regularly information about specified groups of pupils has a testing program. The program may be a simple one consisting only of a group reading-readiness test in grade 1, or it may be a comprehensive program that includes testing all pupils in all grades each year and selective testing of groups and individuals as well. Before a school can have a program, it must determine what purposes testing can serve and decide which tests are to be given to what pupils at what times.

No single testing program will be suitable for all schools. Though common objectives of education and similar socioeconomic backgrounds of pupils permit similar testing programs, each school must build a testing program suitable for its own specific needs.

The term "testing program" also refers to the systematic use of certain tests by a number of institutions, perhaps throughout the country. In addition to school-wide programs, we have system-wide, city-wide, state-wide, regional, and national testing programs.

A teacher or a counselor may decide to use a test with a pupil or with a group of pupils on an irregular basis, that is, test persons when a special, nonrecurring need arises. Every experience may result in changes in the school's testing. This is the least systematic and least organized level of testing.

Some tests are used on a classroom basis. For example, a teacher or a counselor may decide that for a particular class or group, a certain test or group of tests should be used, and these tests then may be administered to that and similar groups. Frequently a school will decide that tests should be used on a school-wide basis.

The large city school system with many separate elementary, junior high, and senior high schools may organize a nearly autonomous testing program, developing some of its own tests and having its own centralized scoring and data-processing service.

On the other hand, certain schools may decide to use some tests and other schools may decide to use others. For example, a high school located in an industrial area of a large city may have relatively few graduates attending colleges and many students seeking work during the latter years of high school. This school may decide to place greater emphasis on vocational aptitude tests than on academic aptitude tests. A school in the same system which sends most of its graduates to college may find academic aptitude tests much more important for counseling purposes.

Most school systems will have tests that are used throughout the system at given grade levels. All kindergarten or first-grade children may be given the same reading-readiness test. Some schools may use other tests in addition. In order to provide continuous information about the students in the system and for purposes of research, evaluation, and comparison, usually some of the same tests will be used throughout a system.

Even in a system that has a comprehensive city-wide testing program, provisions should be made so that individual schools have the opportunity to select and use tests which meet their unique purposes and which may not be included in the city-wide program. We shall assume that the major objectives of schools in a given system are the same, but because of differences in both pupil populations and school staffs, some diversity of educational goals should be expected and encouraged. Similarly, provisions should be made for a diversity of tests used among the schools in a system.

Small schools in which the elementary, junior high, and senior high schools are all housed in one area may have a teacher serving part time as a counselor and may need to draw heavily on outside centralized testing agencies and consultative services to maintain an adequate counseling and testing program. Schools may range at every step of the continuum between two extremes, from the nearly autonomous testing program to nearly complete dependency on others for testing services.

A system-wide testing program should be approached with both courage and ambition. Ideally, the testing program in a school system should provide for each pupil a continuous and comparable record of educational growth and development starting in grade 1 and covering all educationally relevant areas of individual development. With this type of test record, a high school or college counselor could trace the development of a student's reading skills from the very beginning of the time he started to learn to read. The record would show which were the student's relatively strong and relatively weak educational areas at each stage of his educational development, and at each of these stages comparisons could be made not only among the student's various skills and knowledges, but also between the student and his peers. This kind of record would enable a counselor to tell when a student's special skills in mathematics began to develop, or when his timidity and fearfulness first appeared in school, or when his interests in science started.

Obviously, we are not yet ready to have such inclusive and comprehensive testing programs (Bloom et al., 1954). The educationally relevant areas have not yet been agreed upon, and the testing methods and the tests themselves are not yet available to allow us to measure adequately these developments, whatever they may be. With this goal in mind, however, we can look at what the testing program within a system might be.

Testing in all levels of the schools would be coordinated. Tests given during the elementary school years would be known by and useful to teachers and counselors in the junior and senior high schools. Testing would minimize duplication and would maximize efficient use of the students' testing time and the school's testing dollar. Tests with multiple uses would be selected as often as possible. When tests were needed for purposes of classification of pupils, evaluation of the individual's academic progress, and vocational counseling, whenever possible the same test would be selected to serve all of these purposes. Thus, we would not have in a school a separate testing program for counseling purposes, another for instructional purposes, and a third for research and evaluation. Rather, we would have a single testing program where the tests would be selected with all these purposes in mind. Whenever a single test could serve more than one purpose, this would be the test used (Berdie, 1954).

A system-wide testing program should provide tests of academic aptitude given periodically, at least twice in the elementary school, once in the junior high school, and once in the senior high school. Tests of academic achievement should be given annually or biannually, and these tests should be selected so that comparisons could be made from year to year in order to provide information about the student's educational growth. These achievement tests should include not only general academic achievement tests concerned with the broad fund of knowledge, but also more specific achievement tests that provide information about the pupil's background in such things as American history, beginning algebra, or introductory French. Tests of special or differential aptitudes should be given during junior high school or at the beginning of senior high school. During the senior high school years, tests of vocational interests and personality inventories would provide additional valuable information in schools which have adequate personnel to make use of such data. No tests should be used in a school unless personnel are available who understand the meaning of the information provided by the tests. Very few persons know all there is to know about any one test, or even about any one kind of test, but certain knowledges about testing are necessary if a counselor or a teacher is to be allowed to make use of test scores.

SOME ANCHOR POINTS FOR TESTING PROGRAMS

When a school seeks to develop a testing program or to modify a testing program already in existence, it must simultaneously keep in mind the society of which it is a part, the immediate community in which it exists, the physical plant it can afford, the teaching and counseling staff it can hire and retain, the pupils it receives as its raw product, and the changes that take place in them, physically and intellectually, as they progress through school. From these considerations a number of points emerge of which the school administrator and the counselor must be aware. It is within the context of these principles that a testing program is developed or evaluated.

1. *What is the philosophy of education under which the administration operates or wishes to operate?* This philosophy is characterized by varying degrees of traditionalism, authoritarianism, pragmatism, experimentalism, and progressivism. Ramifications of the question of basic philosophy are elaborated in subsequent points.

2. *What are the requirements of the State Office of Education?*

3. *What are the requirements of state, regional, or national accrediting agencies?* These agencies determine basic courses which must be taught. They may prescribe certain classroom methods or proscribe others. They determine training procedures and establish standards for certification of teachers and counselors. They may recommend, or even require, that certain tests be given. Societal demands for education find their expression through policies laid down by these agencies.

4. *What are the over-all educational objectives to be achieved?* The specific objectives include, of course, all the requirements of the agencies in points 2 and 3 above and may include additional objectives desired by the school administration itself or by the local community. These objectives are given expression in the curricula developed by teachers and specialists who work within the framework of policies and principles determined by the controlling and certifying agencies.

5. *What are the individual differences that exist among students?* The wide range of general intelligence, of abilities, and of specific achievements within a given school and within a given grade must be recognized.

6. *What is the general ability level of the students at a given grade?*

7. *What are the achievement levels of a given grade in various subject areas?* Points 6 and 7 are points in which a "feedback" process is at

work. Through knowledge about ability and achievement levels of students, decisions about testing programs are made. Test results themselves are, in turn, one of the most valuable sources of information about the levels of ability and achievement.

8. *What are the personality characteristics of the students in the school?* What resources do the school, community, and state have to which the school can turn for help with students who have severe personality problems?

9. *What is the socioeconomic background of the community?* What are its main industries? What are the occupations of its citizens? What are its major religious groups? Does it have a public library, and how active are its services? What leisure time activities does it afford?

10. *What are the future occupations and education of the graduates and dropouts in the school system?* How many of its students complete only eighth grade or graduate from high school? Do its students graduate and work within the community or mostly go elsewhere? How many go on to college and to what colleges? What other post-high school training do they receive?

11. *What are the requirements of the colleges and other post-high school institutions which most of the students obtaining further education will attend?* Points 9, 10, and 11 illustrate many of the things of which a counselor must be aware in order to properly guide the students throughout their school careers. Counseling and testing programs must be cognizant of the over-all needs and requirements of the community and of society at large. Again, this emphasizes how the activities of counseling and testing are an integral part of the over-all educational process.

Having considered the broad points of educational philosophy and societal needs which determine the basic educational policies, several more specific points need to be kept in mind which will influence the testing program.

12. *What is the specific school calendar and its schedule of classes?* These factors affect many administrative decisions about testing such as what time of the year and what days testing will be done.

13. *What special programs does the school sponsor or obtain special assistance for?* These may be such things as:

   a. Classes for exceptional children
   b. Remedial classes, e.g., special reading sections
   c. Enriched programs for the gifted
   d. Identification of students with special talents and development of accelerated programs for talented pupils

14. *What scholarship programs affect students about which the counselor should keep the students informed?*

15. *What are the special outside testing programs whose tests or serv-*

ices may be used? These may be statewide or regional programs, either required or voluntary, but which have an important bearing on the pupil's subsequent education. Examples of such programs are the College Entrance Examination Board and the American College Testing Program, the results of which are used by many colleges throughout the United States; the Educational Records Bureau program of New York, the results required by many private high schools in the Northeastern United States; and the statewide testing programs which are used by many colleges for admissions purposes.

The administrator and counselor aware of all the points above are still concerned with the actual procedures of conducting a testing program. Additional factors may influence the actual development of the testing program.

16. *What trained personnel are available to counsel students and to interpret test results adequately?*

17. *To what centralized scoring and consulting services can the school turn for aid?*

18. *What is the financial ability of the school to maintain and expand its counseling and testing programs?*

FOUR ILLUSTRATIVE SCHOOLS

Descriptions of four schools will illustrate how the points listed above influence the planning of and the decisions about testing programs. In reading them, one should contrast the decisions to be made about the testing programs and consider how the setting and characteristics of each school influence the counseling process.

HIGH SCHOOL A

This is a small private secondary school. It enrolls 25 to 30 freshmen boys each fall, and four years later 90 per cent or more of them graduate. Only occasionally does a graduate of School A fail to go to college; usually about one-third of the graduates go to Eastern schools. Families of these students are economically well-to-do or wealthy. There is rarely a question of economic inability to go to college. The headmaster is a retired army officer who believes in firm discipline. Parents who enroll students in School A, for the most part, do not maintain exceptionally high intellectual standards, yet demand that their children be able to enter the college of their choice. The educational program is rich with the classics and has rigorous courses in mathematics, science, and literature. The majority of graduates are adequately prepared and succeed in obtaining a college degree.

SCHOOL B

This is a public school organized in the 1920s as a combined elementary, junior high, and senior high school housed in one building. It is situated in an upper middle-class suburb of a large metropolitan area. Since the end of World War II, population growth has been unusually rapid. Because of strict zoning laws and building requirements and the unusually high price of land, the suburb has been able to enforce its economic selectivity. In 1950, the high school seniors numbered over 200, and a separate six-year high school was built. By 1955, the high school was graduating 300 seniors and the suburb built a second elementary school, converted the six-year high school into a junior high school, and built a separate new three-year senior high school. About 70 to 80 per cent of School B's seniors go to college. Half of the college-goers select the local state university; a quarter go to liberal arts colleges within the state; 10 to 15 per cent to "name" colleges; and the remaining to scattered colleges around the country. Of the 20 to 30 per cent not going to college, a number are girls who marry within a year of high school graduation, a sizable group seek post-high school education other than regular college, such as commercial or retailing training, and a few drift into jobs in the nearby metropolitan area.

The superintendent received his undergraduate training from a small liberal arts college and has a master's degree from the local state university. He served several years as a principal and several more years as superintendent of another moderate-sized school district. The local PTA is active and the members vocal. Many of the parents expressly encourage their children to compete scholastically and to vie for scholastic honors. The school competes in a strong athletic league and the superintendent, who was a college athlete, encourages a comprehensive sports program.

SCHOOL C

This is a four-year senior high school located in an old industrial area of a large city. The bulk of the working population are skilled tradesmen, semiskilled operators, and laborers. Population mobility is moderate, but in one section of the district it is unusually high. Since World War I, college going has been steadily on the decrease; by 1955 only about 20 per cent of the seniors were entering college. About one-half of the pupils take trade school courses in their last three years of high school. The drop-out rate from the freshman to senior year is 30 to 40 per cent. Many of the parents are indifferent to their children's continued education and few attend PTA. School C is only one of many schools under a city board of education headed by a city superintendent of schools. Its immediate head is a principal aided by an assistant principal. Many of the decisions about testing and counseling are made by the central office.

SCHOOL D

School D is located in a town of 2,000 persons, is surrounded entirely by a farm community, and is 100 miles away from the nearest metropolis. Farming conditions are good, but the region has severe dry spells every few years. Several rural school districts around the town provide about 20 per cent of the high school's entering freshman class. Many of the boys begin to farm immediately after high school graduation. Many of the girls marry within 1 to 3 years. From 15 to 25 per cent of the students go to college, most of them to junior and teachers colleges and nursing schools. Only one or two students from each graduating class become doctors, lawyers, or dentists, and in the history of the school, only four graduates eventually received the Ph.D. Many graduates receive from a few weeks to a year of training in trade school, business school, or some other proprietary school. A considerable number drift into local jobs as filling station attendants, waitresses, or store clerks. Many families, particularly among the farm families, could afford to, but do not send their children to college. Most of the pupils who go to college do not return to the home community. Within five years, from one-third to one-half of the graduating class leaves the community.

Four widely divergent schools have been quickly sketched. Their salient characteristics have been starkly protrayed deliberately to emphasize the disparate conditions which influence a testing program. If a high school counselor were asked to develop a testing program for each school, what would he recommend? The eighteen points enumerated earlier indicate the diversity of requirements the different programs would have to meet. Each school would have common elements to test in the achievement area as far as they worked under the same requirements of the State Department of Education and had the same societal demand to educate. But, School A would have rigid entrance requirements and would demand an excellent standard of performance throughout the four years of high school. School A's counseling and testing problems would center around the selection of students, appropriate achievement testing, and adequate measurement of scholastic aptitude for college work.

School B would have somewhat similar testing problems to School A, but would deal with a wider range of ability. With 20 to 30 per cent of its high school graduates not going to college, it might well consider some special aptitude tests in its program, and it would need a somewhat different achievement testing emphasis. It could afford trained counselors on its staff and probably could handle some of the testing problems itself as well as make use of outside testing agencies.

School C has an entirely different situation. It must provide the usual achievement and scholastic aptitude testing, since many of its students take the college preparatory program. Many test data are available about its entering freshmen, since most of them come from the same public school system which has a common testing program in the elementary grades. In addition to the usual tests given by all high schools in this public school system, this school needs a heavy emphasis on testing for special aptitudes and for interests in technical and trade occupations in order to adequately counsel the large number who enter the skilled and semiskilled trades.

School D presents still another set of problems. Indeed, its testing requirements run the gamut. It has the particular problem of determining the ability and achievement level of a large group of entering freshmen who have not come from its own school system. Whereas School C already has considerable information about its ninth graders with regard to their achievement and abilities and will select tests to supplement the existing information, School D must start with tests aimed at determining basic achievements of its ninth graders and from these develop its senior high school testing program.

These examples have been developed briefly to illustrate some of the situations and factors from which testing decisions must be made. The eighteen points cited and the illustrations given reemphasize the tenets repeated throughout this text—that the testing program must relate itself to the objectives of the school and that test data are *only one* of the kinds of information with which counselors work.

TESTING SERVICES AVAILABLE TO SCHOOLS

Services of outside testing agencies have become a vital part of the testing programs in schools. These services range from comprehensive testing programs which include the use of all necessary test material, the scoring of tests, and the reporting of results on specially designed forms, to a simple scoring service in which the number of right answers is written on the answer sheets and the answer sheets returned to the school. Some outside testing programs are part of local, state, regional, or national scholarship programs which provide many valuable grants of money to worthy and needy students each year. Counselors must be aware of the provisions and requirements of these programs so they may alert their eligible students to these opportunities for continuing their education.

Many schools incorporate into their own testing programs the services of more comprehensive testing programs. For example, in the state of

Iowa, the state university makes available to all schools a comprehensive program of achievement tests. In the state of Minnesota, the University of Minnesota and the Association of Minnesota Colleges make available to all schools in the state a complete testing service which provides for the testing of abilities, aptitudes, vocational interests, educational achievements, and personality characteristics. Such testing programs, some very comprehensive, some more limited, are found in every state.

These state and regional programs provide school counselors and teachers with a convenient and efficient way of obtaining test information about their pupils. In no case does one of these programs aim to provide the only means for obtaining counseling data, and certainly a school cannot claim to have a guidance service or a testing program just because it participates in one of these broad-scale programs. These programs assist schools to develop their own counseling and guidance work and supplement the individual efforts of the school so the counselors and teachers can do a more comprehensive and efficient job.

Broad-scale testing on a state or regional basis has several advantages to offer to the local school. It makes available extensive and relevant norms obtained from schools with which the local teachers and counselors are familiar. Teachers are interested in knowing not only how each pupil compares with the other pupils in his class, but also how each pupil compares with the other pupils in the school, in the system, and throughout the state. Schools and systems can develop their own local norms and obtain standards of reference in this way, but only through a statewide or regional program can broader norms be obtained.

Testing done on a broad-scale basis has the important advantage of economy. The careful screening and evaluation of tests included in a state or regional program remove this responsibility from the shoulders of the local school. Nevertheless, before any test is incorporated into a school's program, it should be carefully examined and evaluated in terms of the school's own needs. A school must compare the objectives measured by the test to its own objectives. The technical adequacy of the test, the efficiency of the test in terms of time and money, the acceptability of the test to teachers, counselors, and pupils all must be carefully considered. As many schools have neither staff nor time to make a careful and detailed technical evaluation of the test, a statewide or regional program saves the local school much time. Schools considering tests offered by the large testing programs assume the tests have met certain minimum basic requirements. This does not mean that a school should adopt carelessly or hastily any test provided in a statewide program, but that more attention can be given in the school to the objectives of the tests and less to the technical aspects.

Tests used in statewide and regional programs frequently are more economical to acquire, administer, and score. Usually the school does not purchase the test booklets, but rather purchases a testing service which includes the testing materials, the test booklets, answer sheets, the special pencils, test scoring, and reports of the scores. One of the principal savings for the schools is in the scoring, since large volumes of tests can be scored more efficiently and economically than an equal number of tests in small quantities.

Broad-scale programs tend to stimulate guidance and counseling by relieving schools of some of the more tedious chores involved in accumulating information about pupils. By taking from teachers and counselors some of the more unpleasant tasks of testing, time is left to them for more constructive activities. If a counselor can devote four hours a week less to testing, scoring, and reporting results and spend this time in talking to pupils and their parents, a real gain is made.

The counselor in each school, and other persons bearing responsibility for testing pupils, should become fully acquainted with the testing programs available in their state. Usually those responsible for these programs distribute descriptive literature about them and often make specimen sets of tests, test manuals, and other materials available for examination by the local schools. Frequently they distribute research bulletins and other training materials and conduct meetings and conferences to inform local schools about the programs. In every case when a local testing program is being planned or evaluated, information should be obtained concerning how these broad-scale programs can supplement local programs.

SUMMARY

A school that uses tests which meet its educational needs and regularly provides information about its pupils has a testing program. Before a school can have such a program, it must carefully determine what its needs are and which tests can best meet these needs. A school's needs are unique, and no single testing program will be suitable for all schools. Within a large school system individual schools should have freedom to select tests which are different from the tests required throughout the entire system. A testing program may vary from a completely autonomous program with its own testing center and counselors in each of its schools to a program making almost complete use of outside testing agencies and consulting services. An ideal program will provide cumulative information throughout the pupil's career and will give information about a pupil's academic achievement at different stages in his development. Whenever possible, multiple-purpose tests should be selected.

Testing and counseling are integral parts of the educational process. When a school is developing a testing program, it must carefully evaluate its role in society and the specific community in which it exists and be aware of how its role is determined by the requirements of various boards of control and accrediting agencies. Knowledge of pupils' abilities and achievements, of the education they receive after high school graduation, and of the occupations they are most likely to enter plays an important part in determining what testing program is developed. Descriptions of four quite dissimilar high schools illustrated how these various factors would influence the development of their testing programs.

Services of outside testing agencies can greatly facilitate the schools' work. Before selecting such test services the school should determine how well the agency's objectives meet its own objectives. Use of the outside service may free counselors and teachers of many detailed tasks and permit them more appropriate use of their time. Large testing agencies are in a much better position than the school to ensure technical adequacy of the tests and to provide interpretative materials.

QUESTIONS FOR STUDY

1. Outline a testing program for School A. Include tests that School A might specify for admissions testing.
2. You are the senior high school (grades 10 to 12) counselor for School B. Assume that in junior high school the Sequential Tests of Educational Progress—Reading, Writing, Listening, Mathematics, Science, and Social Studies, are administered each year, and the Differential Aptitude Tests are administered to the ninth grade. What testing program would you recommend for senior high school?
3. In the city system of which School C is a part, the city board of education requires the Otis Mental Abilities Test in grade 7, and the Differential Aptitude Tests in grade 9, and the Iowa Tests of Educational Development in grades 10 and 12. What additional testing would you outline for School C?
4. School D has not had a counselor up to this point. You are hired as the school counselor for junior and senior high school, and one of your duties is to develop a testing program for these grades. A couple of the school board members are vocal in their dislike of all this "newfangled" testing. Outline a program you would like to install and have going by the end of a three-year period. Consider tactics and arguments you might use to influence the parents, teachers, and school board members in getting the program started.
5. Consider either the high school from which you graduated or one in which you have taught or counseled. Then (a) describe this school in terms of the anchor points of Chapter 6, (b) outline the testing program it had in effect when you were there, and (c) indicate what changes you would make in the testing program and why. If you would not make any changes, why not?

REFERENCES

Berdie, R. F. Bringing national and regional testing programs into local schools. *Proceedings of the 1953 invitational conference on testing problems.* Princeton, N.J.: Educational Testing Service, 1954. Pp. 78–83.

Bloom, B. S., et al. *Taxonomy of educational objectives.* New York: McKay, 1954.

CHAPTER 7

The Administration of Tests

After the school counselor and administrator have agreed on what tests to use, they must make decisions about giving the tests. A test may be carefully devised and have maximum reliability and validity, but its results may be meaningless unless it is administered correctly.

STANDARD CONDITIONS

The most important policy in the administration of tests is to follow directions. The importance of exactly following directions can best be understood by considering the nature of a test. A test is a sampling, under standardized conditions, of a person's behavior in a specified situation or field. When a teacher gives an achievement test to a pupil in history, the specific behavior which interests the teacher is the pupil's knowledge of history. Mathematics or English test items would be inappropriate. In an intelligence test, the items often are verbal items or tasks requiring logical thinking. In a personality test the items may call for expression of attitudes, description of certain behaviors, or choice of alternative behaviors. Intelligence and personality tests, though not as delimited in scope as achievement tests, do include only items relevant to the theory of intelligence or personality held by the test constructor. Every test is a sample. Time and space would not permit asking for everything that a pupil should know about history, or for all verbal items in the intelligence test, or for all possible behavior agreements or disagreements in a personality test.

Standard conditions are essential for all types of testing. For example, time is critical in a clerical test, for we are interested in how many items of a given task a person can complete within a time limit. The task chosen usually is not difficult, but is one which requires quick recognition of relationships. If one test administrator allows exactly the time specified in the directions, if another allows a minute too long, and still another allows a minute too short, the three sets of scores cannot be compared.

An example in sports will help make the meaning of standardized conditions clear. Athlete X, on a given day, ran the 100-yard dash in 9.2 seconds in a track meet in California. A new world's record was claimed. Athlete Y, the current 100-yard dash record holder with a 9.3 record time, doubted the authenticity of the new record. Athlete Y had run his record time in a meet in Illinois. However, a subsequent check indicated that in the California track meet, the distance was exactly 100 yards long, that three qualified timekeepers with certified stopwatches agreed on the time, that the wind was only 3 miles per hour, and that the track was an inspected cinder track. The athletic commission then certified the record, and Athlete Y conceded that his world's record had been broken. Why can a new record time be accepted even though the two men did not race against each other on the same track? Simply because standard conditions had been observed at the separate track meets.

Even though psychological tests are given in different locations by different administrators, one test score can "compete" or be compared with another test score when standard conditions have been observed. The further the deviation from the standard conditions specified by the test manual, the greater the difficulty of interpreting the score correctly.

To interpret a test score correctly, directions must be followed exactly as specified by the test publisher in his test manual. Achievement tests frequently are used to assign grades. They may be used to measure growth of knowledge, to compare the same pupil's knowledge at the beginning and end of the course. They may be used to compare the performance of the same class (e.g., sophomores) in the same school system from one year to the next. Many psychological tests, particularly those of scholastic aptitude, are used by colleges in their admissions procedure. Appointments to preferred positions or scholarships are based on examination results. If a test administrator, either inadvertently or deliberately, has given too much time to his pupils, he has handicapped his students by giving them an unrealistic picture of their ability. If inadvertently he allows too little time for a test, his pupils will be at a disadvantage when their scores are compared to the norm group being used by the admitting college.

When test scores are used in counseling, unless standardized conditions have been met, the scores will not accurately represent the true performance of the person taking the test and both the counselor and the counselee will obtain a false picture of the counselee's aptitudes, achievements, and interests. Thus they may arrive at a wrong decision as to the course of action that the counselee should pursue.

MOTIVATION

Differences of motivation may create unstandardized conditions even under the best administrative arrangements where the pupils have been seated properly, the time limits have been rigorously observed, the handling of test material has been as specified, and directions have been read word for word as given in the manual. Test publishers do spend time in discussing motivation in their manuals; however, frequently they assume that motivation is going to be constant from one test administration to another. Experience and observation indicate a wide variation of students' motivation in different testing situations.

Motivation, for the purpose of this discussion, may be defined as the pupil's desire to do the best he possibly can on a test. Achieving motivation consists of properly preparing pupils for the administration of the test.

Motivation is related closely to the general attitude and feeling that pupils have for school and for the school staff. Obviously, a good healthy attitude among pupils toward the school administration and toward school in general will enhance the entire program of the school and not just ensure good test conditions.

The superintendent, principal, or person who is to administer the test should tell the pupils about the test well in advance of the time it is given. The administrator should bear in mind that some of his pupils may not have had any experience with standard intelligence or achievement tests. He should prepare these pupils with particular care, taking pains well before the day of the actual test administration to acquaint pupils with this type of test. He should stress the reason for taking the test and let the pupils know for what purposes the test results will be used. He should answer as honestly and as completely as he can all questions pupils raise. If he does not know the answer to a question, he should frankly say that he doesn't know and that he will do his best to find the answer. When he does find the answer, he will see that the information is given to the pupil raising the question.

The superintendent or principal can greatly influence motivation by selecting as the administrator some person whom the pupils know well, whom they respect, and with whom their relations are cordial. No one thing will ruin a test administration more, even when all other standardized conditions have been met, than an unruly, undisciplined group of pupils. Where they are noisy and laugh and talk, the morale of the whole group can be lowered. A counselor or teacher whom the pupils respect can do much to prevent such situations before they arise.

SCHEDULING TESTING DATES

Once a testing program has been planned, the testing dates must be set. Shall the tests be given in the beginning, in the middle, or toward the end of the year? The purposes for which the test results are used should help to answer this question. If the tests are to be used for counseling and guidance, they should be given early in the year, so that as much as possible of the school year remains during which the counselor may use the results in counseling. If tests, particularly achievement tests, are given for purposes of evaluating the standing of a given class from one year to the next, the tests should be given at the same time, preferably the same month, each year. The pupils then will have been exposed to the same amount of teaching and the same experiences in the school curriculum. When pupils' scores are going to be compared with their scores on the same test given previously, the testing dates should be selected according to the experiences the pupils should have had before they are retested.

After the school administrator and the counselor have answered the question of what they wish to use the test for and have decided upon the approximate testing dates, they should next look at their school program and see what other activities will be scheduled about that time. To use an extreme case, it would be a poor policy to schedule a test session the day of the football game with the traditional rival. Students may be highly motivated, but it is unlikely that their motivation would be for taking a test. Is any other testing taking place in the school program? Will the date selected for a standardized achievement test or a scholastic aptitude test coincide with the six-weeks or semester finals? The wise administrator will select specific dates which minimize conflicts with other activities.

Where long testing sessions are being scheduled, timing should be such that rest periods are provided. Natural breaks such as those between test sections should be utilized. Especially for younger pupils, longer rest periods or scheduling over several days may be necessary to avoid fatigue or boredom.

SELECTION OF THE TESTING ROOM

Many schools will find it impossible to provide an "ideal" testing room, particularly for large group testing sessions. However, the administrator should be aware of how deviations from an ideal may interfere with good testing procedure so he can do everything possible to avoid a poor or "unstandardized" testing situation.

The room should be large enough to permit only alternate seats to be filled. This is the simplest and easiest way to prevent cheating and unnecessary talking between students. Should the school be unable to provide this seating arrangement, additional proctors should be available to help the examiner. When a suitable room is available, a proctor for each fifty students is sufficient. Under less favorable conditions, one proctor for each twenty-five students should be provided. Lunchrooms and auditoriums frequently are used by schools for large testing sessions. Auditoriums usually are large enough, but often do not have seats with writing surfaces. Lapboards of adequate size must be provided in this case. Lunchrooms where students face each other around a table are generally poor, but if used, can be satisfactory if provided with additional proctors and if groups of troublemaking students are not permitted to sit together. The fewer students who sit at each table the better. Whatever room is used, adequate provision should be made for left-handed persons so their writing position does not offer an undue opportunity for cheating by others.

Use of a public address system with a central examiner to read directions and keep time and individual examiners to distribute materials and answer questions in each of a number of small rooms has proved to be a feasible method of group test administration. However, this method needs even more advance preparation than usual, and a trial run of test conditions must be provided. The central examiner and the individual examiners will need to discuss carefully their plan of action.

Lighting, heating, and ventilation must be adequate. The examiner should know in advance what he must do should a fuse blow or some other emergency occur during a test session. The rooms chosen should be free from outside disturbances, e.g., noise of passing classes, band rehearsals, or other pupils entering the room. A notice should be posted outside the door of the testing room and a proctor should stand outside the door while classes are passing. A check several days beforehand with the maintenance staff may provide happy dividends in avoiding a conflict with repairmen hammering in nearby rooms or even attempting to paint or wire in the test room itself.

CHECKING TEST MATERIALS

Nothing can disconcert a test administrator more than to find himself on the day of testing without enough materials. The simple precaution of ordering supplies early and counting all the material as soon as it is received by the school should preclude any need for emergency orders on the day before or on the day of the test itself. Changes from anticipated enrollments and errors by test publishers and test centers can all be corrected well in advance if material is counted as soon as it is received. When material has been received and is being held until the testing date, it should be stored in a vault or in some place where tests cannot be obtained for "advance study."

READING DIRECTIONS BEFOREHAND

The examiner should study the directions for administration well ahead of time. He should know who his proctors are going to be and should meet with them and brief them thoroughly on their duties. If, as was suggested, a central public address system is used, each homeroom teacher is an examiner and needs to study the material thoroughly.

TIMING OF TEST SESSIONS

Tests vary widely as to time limits. When time limits are specified, they should be followed exactly. On many aptitude tests where the count of the number of items completed is the student's score, the correct amount of time is absolutely essential. Some scholastic aptitude tests are closely timed, and deviations by a few seconds from the specified time limits can alter the students' scores considerably. A special interval timer is ideal, but a school need not provide a costly timepiece. A stopwatch, such as most schools' athletic departments have, is an excellent timepiece, and the examiner would do well to arrange to borrow one from the athletic department. An electric wall clock or wristwatch with sweep second hand can be used in lieu of a timer or stopwatch. If a timepiece with a sweep second hand is used, the examiner should write down the starting time, add the working time, and write down the time at which he will call "stop." Timepieces such as housewives buy for kitchen use usually are not accurate enough for timing tests.

For tests that do not have a time limit (e.g., personality and interest tests), the examiner needs to know what he will do with pupils who do not complete the test in the regularly scheduled period. If only a few do not finish, they can be brought into the examiner's office and allowed to complete the test there. For a larger number a small classroom may be needed. If at all possible, the unfinished tests should be completed in the next class period following the regular administration. Again the examiner must remember the requirement of standardized conditions.

PROBLEMS OCCURRING IN THE TESTING SESSION

When the day of the testing session arrives, even when the examiner is prepared thoroughly, several problems still may arise which the examiner should anticipate. Suppose the local paper has heard that a college admissions test is to be given and wants to write a story about the testing and include some pictures. This matter should be discussed with the superintendent. In no case should pictures be permitted while actual work is in progress. A photographer moving about and flashbulbs popping are hardly standard conditions of testing.

The test administrator always must report any unusual circumstance which may affect an individual pupil's score. Several such circumstances are cited below, along with suggestions for handling the situation as it arises. Usually a notation on the answer sheet is sufficient to explain the occurrence, but the examiner should attach a longer explanation on a separate sheet of paper should he feel it necessary. The central testing agency and whoever uses the test score are then in a position to judge the accuracy of the score and make a fair decision on whether a retest of the pupil is warranted.

In spite of careful advance preparation of pupils and repeated announcements on date and time, some will arrive late. On timed tests the tardy pupils should start with the rest of the group at the beginning of an independently timed section. The part or parts they miss should be individually made up as soon as possible before the tardy pupils have had a chance to discuss the test with their friends. The examiner should note such irregularities on the answer sheet. For untimed tests the examiner should start tardy pupils as they come in. If they are not finished by the end of the period, he then simply treats them like others who have not completed the test.

A pupil may ask for permission to leave the room temporarily while a test is in progress. Some test directions specifically state what to do in such cases. As a general rule, warn the person that he gets no adjustment in time, collect his test material and hold it until he returns, and permit *only one* person to be gone at the same time. Appropriate time breaks during long testing sessions will practically eliminate such requests.

Cheating will seldom occur under good testing conditions, especially when the seating arrangement is adequate and when enough proctors are *actively present*. Pupils should be told to place books, notebooks, and handbags on the floor. When a proctor is suspicious of an irregularity, he should warn the pupil quietly, but emphatically. For instance, he might write on a sheet of paper, "Your eyes are straying too much. Stop it," and show it only to the specific pupil. Even if a pupil is caught cheating red-handed, he should not be summarily ejected from the testing session. The examiner or proctor should remember the general rules for standardized conditions and handle any such irregularity with as little disturbance as possible.

A few pupils may fail to comprehend the directions and completely ruin their answers or spend valuable time in fumbling around getting started. These instances should be carefully noted. Not only can the pupil's performance be reevaluated, but the school, the central testing agency, or the publisher can revise their directions to eliminate as many ambiguities in the directions as possible.

COMPLETING THE TESTING SESSION

A wide variation exists in the speed with which pupils complete a test. Some may complete the test in half or two-thirds the allotted time. In the last ten or five minutes of the examination period, a large number are likely to be finished. The examiner should pay particular attention to what the specific test manual says should be done, whether early finishers should be allowed to leave as they complete the test or whether the entire group should be retained for the entire period.

In the absence of any specific instructions, the examiner should retain the entire group for the whole period. Pupils leaving intermittently throughout the examination period will disturb those working. Retention of the entire group will permit easier collection of material and enable the examiner to ensure that all material is collected. Many tests have high security attached to them and the loss of one test booklet is a most serious matter.

As soon as "stop" has been called to terminate the examination period, the examiner and his proctors should move swiftly to collect and check all test materials. The group should not be dismissed until all material is accounted for. Material should be passed to the end of the row at a given aisle and each row checked as the material is collected to see that all pupils in each row have returned their material. The different test materials should be collected separately. First have the special pencils passed to the aisle and collect them, then have the booklets passed to the aisle and collect them, and then the answer sheets. By following the plan of collecting the test materials separately and checking them at each row as they are collected, the examiner can reduce the amount of time and trouble it takes to complete the testing session.

RETURNING MATERIAL

Test materials from a central testing agency or publisher should be returned as soon as possible after the testing session. In cases when the material can be held to permit testing absentees, security precautions should be taken in storing the material. In packaging and mailing test material, post office regulations must be observed. The postal law, Public

Law No. 426, passed by the Eighty-fifth Congress and effective August 1, 1958, provides preferential rates for test materials. Although Congress raised rates for all postal classifications, testing materials were reclassified as eligible for postal rates for books. The pertinent section of Public Law No. 426, Section 206-d, is reproduced below. We have put the part specifically mentioning tests in italics.

Section 206. (d) The following materials when in parcels not exceeding seventy pounds in weight may be sent at the postage rate of 9 cents for the first pound and 5 cents for each additional pound or fraction thereof, and this rate shall continue until otherwise provided by Congress: (1) books permanently bound for preservation consisting wholly of reading matter or scholarly bibliography or reading matter with incidental blank spaces for students' notations and containing no advertising matter other than incidental announcements of books; (2) sixteen-millimeter films and sixteen-millimeter film catalogs except when sent to commercial theaters; (3) *printed objective test materials and accessories thereto used by or in behalf of educational institutions in the testing of ability, aptitude, achievement, interests, and other mental and personal qualities with or without answers, test scores, or identifying information recorded thereon in writing or by mark;* (5) phonograph recordings; and (6) manuscripts for books, periodical articles and music.

Used answer sheets and the schedule sheets need not be mailed first class, but may be returned in the same package as the other test materials, including pencils. This change means both a saving in postage and more convenient packaging of test materials. The packages containing test materials should be stamped "Educational Material." If there is any question about the postal regulations, be sure to consult the local postmaster.

The administrator should be especially careful to note where the various test materials are to be sent. Frequently today, test publishers, central testing agencies, and large commercial scoring centers have contractual agreements under which used answer sheets go directly to the scoring center and the other materials go either to the central agency or to the publisher.

When special answer sheets are used, great care must be exercised in handling and packing them, since they are usually scored by machine. Avoid folding, tearing, or bending the edges of the answer sheets, since this will affect their ability to be handled by the scoring machine.

SUMMARY

The need for providing standardized conditions of testing has been shown. Not only can efficiency be achieved, but more important, a well-planned program, scheduled and publicized in advance, can help maximize the student's motivation. Selection of appropriate test examiners will help to achieve motivation and will preclude some obvious disciplinary problems. Testing dates must be carefully selected to avoid undue competition with other school or community events. Appropriate physical surroundings are an important part of the testing procedure. The administrator must be prepared for any "surprise" changes in the physical environment. Checking in the test materials, studying the directions, and reviewing the procedures carefully with school administrators and proctors before the actual day of the test will do much to simplify the problems and to ensure standardized conditions. The examiner must be alert to specific problems which may occur in the test room. A few general suggestions were given about handling some problem situations, but the specific test manual should always be consulted for different procedures. All irregularities should be noted and reported so that the school administration, the test agency, or the scholarship commission can make a wise decision about using a pupil's test result or obtaining a retest score. The most important thing is to provide and maintain standardized conditions of testing.

QUESTIONS FOR STUDY

1. By now you have taken many tests yourself or you may have administered them or have served as a proctor. List a number of things you have observed which caused failure in meeting standard conditions of testing. How could these things have been avoided?
2. As a high school counselor you have been asked by your school superintendent to talk to the seventh-grade students about the Lorge-Thorndike Intelligence Tests, both Verbal and Nonverbal, a week before they are to be administered. Special IBM machine-scorable answer sheets will be used. Outline a half-hour talk you would give. Keep in mind this chapter's discussion of motivation and assume the students have had no experience with machine-scored tests.
3. What would you do if, when administering a test,
   a. A student became ill during the work period and could not continue?
   b. Two students persisted in talking to each other?
   c. You noticed a student had quit working halfway through the test and was only staring out the window?
   d. You noticed a student had started marking his answers in the wrong spaces on the answer sheet?
   e. You found out that many of the pencils included with the test supplies did not have the appropriate electrographic lead in them?

CHAPTER 8

National Testing Programs

Space limitations make it impossible to describe all the large testing programs which are available to schools, but some will be described. The advent of new tests or testing programs and the rapid changes occurring in the nature of the services offered due to electronic scoring and data-processing equipment may make some of the information about these programs obsolete even while this text is in the process of publication. Nevertheless, the information about the programs outlined in this text is of direct relevance to high school counselors and can be considered a model by which counselors may summarize services of other testing programs. At all times the counselor must consult the most recent manual of any testing program whose services he desires to use.

Since World War II many testing programs have appeared. We have selected those testing programs for discussion which, in our judgment, either are of most historical importance (but still current) or have the greatest impact on testing on a national scale. Described are two college admissions programs, three scholarship programs, and three programs whose test services counselors can incorporate directly into their own high school guidance programs.

THE COUNSELOR'S ROLE IN COLLEGE ADMISSIONS AND SCHOLARSHIP TESTING PROGRAMS

The high school counselor will play an active role in assisting his students with various testing programs. One of the most important functions a counselor can perform is to help his students understand that test scores alone do not determine college admissions and scholarships. He must point out to them throughout their school careers that their achievement in high school is one of the most important evidences of scholastic promise they can present to the college to which they apply.

104

The main purposes of education should not become subordinated to test scores.

When the test scores for a program are reported to the school, the responsibility of interpreting the results to the student and his parents will fall upon the counselor. The student and his parents may be staking much on the outcome of tests given to help determine admissions to college or to grant scholarships.

Careful preparation beforehand and anticipation of student and parental anxieties may pay handsome dividends in easing tensions aroused by examinations. Knowledge of the odds against receiving a scholarship will prevent unrealistic financial planning by the student and his parents. Alternative courses of action, or choosing other than the preferred college, may be much easier for the student and the parent to accept when they have been well briefed ahead of time. The counselor, working with his superintendent and principal, may organize meetings at which he can explain to interested students and their parents the main features of testing programs most likely to affect the future education of the student. The testing programs can be publicized in advance through stories in local newspapers, bulletin-board displays, and announcements at appropriate assemblies and group meetings. Students and their parents can be encouraged to explore the various problems involved in choosing a college and gaining admission to it.

When the student and his parents insist on a certain college, but the counselor feels certain the student cannot qualify for this college, the counselor must not assume the role of the admissions officer and tell the student he won't be admitted. He may point out to the student the improbability of being accepted at that college and suggest alternate courses of action. By avoiding outright rejections of the student's plans, the counselor may maintain his role of being seen as one who gives sympathetic assistance.

COLLEGE ENTRANCE EXAMINATION BOARD

The first comprehensive national testing program was the College Entrance Examination Board (CEEB). This board, organized by a group of Eastern colleges about the beginning of the twentieth century, was concerned exclusively with the examining of college applicants. The tests given at first were the traditional essay-type examinations. Students were placed in standardized situations and asked to write answers to a number of common questions related to the subjects taught in the colleges. After several years the increasing number of people to be examined and the demonstrated weaknesses of this type of examination led to the board's adoption of objective-type examinations. Increasing emphasis was placed upon academic aptitude tests, although objective achievement tests also were kept in the program.

CEEB is a group of colleges whose purpose is the better selection of students for college admissions. By using College Board scores as part of their admissions procedures, member colleges hope to obtain a more precise description of the college applicant's ability and to increase the accuracy with which his performance in college courses can be predicted. The College Board tests are primarily concerned with determining whether or not the applicant has the intellectual ability to cope with the academic work of the college to which he is applying.

Most colleges belonging to the board are privately endowed liberal arts colleges concentrated in the eastern part of the country, but member colleges include publicly supported universities and colleges distributed throughout the United States. As the membership list changes from year to year, the high school counselor must keep abreast of the published list of member colleges. When a student expresses interest in a specific college, the counselor can then inform him if the College Boards are required. Each year the board publishes a Bulletin of Information which gives detailed information about the tests, how to register, fees, dates of testing, testing centers, how results are reported, and a list of tests each member college requires. Any questions not covered in the bulletin should be referred to the appropriate regional CEEB office given below. All states east of the Mississippi, as well as North and South Dakota, Nebraska, Kansas, Oklahoma, and Texas, should use the address:

> College Entrance Examination Board
> Box 592
> Princeton, New Jersey

The Western states should use:

> College Entrance Examination Board
> Box 27,896
> Los Angeles 27, California

The CEEB consists of a three-hour Scholastic Aptitude Test (SAT), a series of one-hour achievement tests in various subjects prepared by College Board committees of school and college teachers with the assistance of the professional staff of the Educational Testing Service, and a writing sample test. A student pays a fee when he registers, the amount depending on the tests he will take. The registration fee entitles the student applying for College Boards to receive booklets describing the tests for which he registers. Counselors should make sure students obtain this information and should discourage students from buying books, correspondence courses, or tutorial courses which purport to prepare students for these examinations. *The College Handbook,* published by CEEB, is a valuable aid in determining the requirements of colleges, since it contains information about the member colleges and their admission requirements. The counselor would do well to have one or more copies available in the counseling library rather than expect each student to buy one.

After studying the Bulletin of Information, the student must apply for *each* date he wishes to be tested, using the application form in the bulletin. He may take both the SAT and the achievement test(s) in one day or he may take SAT on one date and the achievement test(s) on another date. In the latter case he must register twice, once for each date. Saturdays are selected as testing dates, but for special circumstances a Sunday date can be established. A letter explaining the circumstances of such a request must accompany the application. The SAT dates (mornings only) are in the months of December through May, with one date set in August. The achievement test dates (afternoons only) parallel the SAT dates. Usually six dates are established for SAT and four dates for the achievement tests. Deadlines for registering for a given testing date usually fall about one month in advance of the testing date, with about a two-week period of grace *within which period a late fee must be paid.* A closing date is also listed for each testing date after which registrations are not guaranteed. The counselor should urge interested students to apply for College Boards as early as possible. If a considerable number of students from his school apply for College Boards each year, it would be well to publicize and hold a briefing session, outlining carefully the College Board requirements. The counselor should assist students who are applying to complete their applications properly.

Scores are reported automatically to the college designated by the student about five weeks after the testing date. Reports are sent without charge to the first three colleges indicated on the application blank. Reports can be sent to additional colleges listed on the application blank, but a fee is charged for each additional college listed. After applications have been filed, reports also can be sent to additional colleges, but a fee is assessed for each extra report. Information about a student's admission status should be addressed to the college to which he applied, not to the College Board. Scores are *not* reported to the student or to his parents. but are reported routinely to the student's high school about five weeks after the testing dates. The counselor will probably be the person designated to give this information to the student.

THE PRELIMINARY SCHOLASTIC APTITUDE TEST

In addition to the examination just described, CEEB sponsors the Preliminary Scholastic Aptitude Test (PSAT). All correspondence or inquiries about it should be addressed to:

> CEEB Guidance Service
> c/o Educational Testing Service
> Box 589
> Princeton, New Jersey

The purposes of PSAT are twofold: (1) PSAT aids in the high school's own guidance program; and (2) PSAT aids in the preliminary selection of secondary school candidates for a large number of scholarship programs—national, regional, and local. As the high school junior year is more and more becoming the year of decision in college planning, CEEB has provided PSAT for junior-year testing. It is similar to the Scholastic Aptitude Test, being a two-hour version of the three-hour SAT. The two PSAT scores, Verbal and Mathematical, are reported on a scale ranging from 20 to 80 points which parallels the 200- to 800-point scale of SAT.

CEEB research has shown that the grades of the first three years of high school plus a junior-year test of scholastic aptitude predict college academic performance almost as well as senior-year grades and test results. Though many College Board members will continue to use SAT as an admissions test, some will consider PSAT results in early counseling if schools give them scores of interested students. High schools sending a number of students to colleges requiring CEEB-SAT for admissions may find PSAT useful in their own counseling programs. The students will obtain an inexpensive prediction of their SAT scores and will gain experience in taking tests of this nature.

The test is administered to students through the cooperation of the principal at their own secondary school. The specific date is set by the Educational Testing Service and usually is in October. Principals who wish to administer the test at their schools must register the *number of interested* students by the specified date in advance of the actual testing date (about three weeks). The principal registers by submitting the appropriate registration form in the PSAT Bulletin of Information to the address given above. The fee is collected by the principal and forwarded to the Educational Testing Service after the test administration. Like the bulletin for the College Board examinations, the PSAT Bulletin of Information gives detailed information about the test.

PSAT scores are reported to the secondary school principal with a booklet describing the interpretation and use of the scores. Principals may release the scores of either juniors or seniors to the students, sponsors, or colleges. Each scholarship sponsor routinely receives the scores for students who have indicated their eligibility for his particular program on the back of their answer sheets. Descriptions of the scholarship programs using PSAT are given in the bulletin. These descriptions indicate the number of the scholarships, the eligibility requirements, the amount of the scholarships, and the colleges to which the scholarships apply.

THE AMERICAN COLLEGE TESTING PROGRAM

The American College Testing Program (ACT) is similar in some ways to the College Entrance Examination Board program. It was first offered in 1959 to high school seniors who might possibly attend college, and participating colleges tended to be in Midwestern and Western states. In 1960–1961 ACT was offered in all states. Its address is:

American College Testing Program
P.O. Box 168
Iowa City, Iowa

Since it is a new program, it will be particularly important to refer to the ACT Student Information Bulletin published each year; undoubtedly procedures will change and new member colleges will be added each year.

ACT presents an admissions, scholarship, guidance, and placement test battery designed to provide helpful information and service to colleges, to high schools, and to students at a time when this information will be most helpful. ACT has four tests, each forty-five minutes in length, representing the fields of English, mathematics, social studies, and natural sciences. The tests in English and mathematics are designed particularly for use in placing students in college English and mathematics classes so that they have the greatest chance for success in these fields. The total score of the four tests provides an over-all estimate of the student's general ability to succeed in college. Scores are reported to the three colleges designated by the student on his application form and to the student's high school. A set of scores in a specially designed booklet of interpretive information goes to the high school counselor to give to the student. The counselor should urge and assist students interested in a particular ACT college to determine how that college will use ACT's test results.

To apply to colleges associated with ACT, the procedure outlined in the manual must be followed carefully. Determine whether the college actually requires the ACT tests. Institutions which require ACT are listed in the Student Information Bulletin alphabetically by state. The application, completed as specified, should be sent to:

ACT Central Regis Unit
104 Pearl Street
McHenry, Illinois

The fee for ACT must accompany the application. Testing centers will be located within each state to minimize the amount of travel for students who take the tests.

ACT specified Saturday testing dates in November, 1960, and February and April, 1961, with scores to be reported five to six weeks after the testing dates. The deadline date for applying preceded the testing date by three weeks.

NATIONAL MERIT SCHOLARSHIP QUALIFYING TEST

The National Merit Scholarship Qualifying Test (NMSQT) is a nationally administered test the results of which are used for awarding scholarships. The program is conducted under the auspices of the National Merit Scholarship Corporation, 1580 Sherman Avenue, Evanston, Illinois. However, the agency which administers the test is:

Science Research Associates
27 West Grand Avenue
Chicago 10, Illinois

NMSQT requires three hours of testing and provides five subtest scores and a total score which are reported to the school, the National Merit Scholarship Corporation, other scholarship agencies, and, on request, to other agencies who wish to use the data. The scores are:

1. English Usage: Ability to understand and use the English language
2. Mathematics Usage: Ability to use arithmetic and mathematical principles in the solution of practical problems
3. Social Studies Reading: Ability to read, evaluate, and draw significant inferences from material in social studies
4. Natural Sciences Reading: Ability to locate and critically evaluate the important facts presented in discussions of scientific matter
5. Word Usage Test: Ability to understand the meaning of words

NMSQT is the initial step in the selection of scholarship recipients. It is the screening examination in the selection of finalists who then must take an additional examination. Approximately 10,000 finalists are named after the second examination and each finalist receives a "Certificate of Merit." Finalists are later identified to colleges, universities, and other scholarship granting agencies. A large percentage of finalists who do not receive Merit Scholarships receive scholarships from other agencies who make use of the list of finalists. The National Merit Scholarship Corporation reports that in 1957–1958, for example, two-thirds of the finalists who did not receive Merit Scholarships did receive some other scholarship.

Currently, second-semester juniors and first-semester seniors from any secondary school located in the fifty states, the District of Columbia, Canal Zone, Puerto Rico, and the iVrgin Islands are eligible to take NMSQT. The fee is payable on the day of the examination. A limited number of students of unusual ability are tested free if they are unable to pay the fee. Principals should write directly to the National Merit Scholarship Corporation if they have students in this category. In 1960 two possible testing dates were available, March 8 or March 19, the school selecting the best date in terms of its own schedule. Test results are reported to the high schools in August. Students qualifying as semi-finalists take the second examination in November or December of the same year. Formal offers of actual scholarships are sent to students in March and April of their senior year in high school. In 1957–1958, stipends ranged from $150 to $1,500 per year, and the average was $750.

Application for the test is made through the school principal, and the school is the administrative center. The current bulletin should always be consulted for specific information about dates and application procedures, since these may change from year to year.

The timing of the NMSQT administration and reporting of scores permit the counselor adequate time in which to help his students integrate this new information with other information about themselves and with plans they may have for further education. As finalists do not receive actual scholarship offers until March and April, the wise counselor will not permit a student to depend on this source of support, but will help him make alternative plans should he not actually receive a scholarship offer. The National Merit Scholarship Corporation considers need in determining the size of the scholarship.

SELECTIVE SERVICE COLLEGE QUALIFICATION TEST

Our nation operates under Universal Military Training (UMT) which requires males within five days of reaching age 18 to register for military service. Recognizing the importance of college and university training, UMT has provisions for deferment of military service. One of the evidences of college ability that the Selective Service System provides to local draft boards is the results of the nationally administered Selective Service College Qualification Test (SSCQT). Since high school graduates and candidates for admission to college *are not eligible until they have entered upon their first year of college work,* SSCQT will not be described as fully as the previous examinations. However, the counselor should be aware of the salient features of SSCQT and how the Selective Service System grants deferments.

In 1961 the administrative agency was the Educational Testing Service, Princeton, New Jersey. It served as the testing and reporting agency for the Selective Service System. The Selective Service System alone made all decisions regarding an examinee's selective service classification. A student should address inquiries regarding his classification to his local board of jurisdiction. To be eligible to take SSCQT, an applicant, on the testing date, (1) must be a selective service registrant who intends to request student deferment; (2) must be satisfactorily pursuing a full-time college course, undergraduate or graduate, leading to a degree (the applicant need not be in a four-year college, but his entire course of study must be satisfactory for transfer of credits to a degree-granting institution); and (3) must not previously have taken the test.

As the student makes plans for college, the counselor should make sure the student is aware of the service requirement and alert him to seek specific information about the first SSCQT he will be eligible to take. Generally it comes in the spring of the year. The counselor can publicize the SSCQT by including descriptions of it in orientation materials, discussing it with parents and students, and having its bulletin readily available for prospective college-goers.

The test presupposes no schooling beyond the ordinary high school preparation for college. Scores on the test will not themselves determine eligibility for deferment, but will be used by the Selective Service local boards in considering the eligibility of registrants for student deferment.

NAVAL RESERVE OFFICER TRAINING CORPS

The Naval Reserve Officer Training Corps (NROTC) program is also related to the Selective Service System. The NROTC program offers remarkable career opportunities for pupils interested in the Naval Service as a career.

The steps leading to NROTC appointment are:

1. A student must apply for and take the Navy College Aptitude Test, usually administered in December.

2. If the student attains a qualifying score on the Navy College Aptitude Test, he will be requested to report to the Navy Recruiting Station designated by him at the time of the test. There he will be given a

physical examination, will be interviewed by at least two Naval officers, and will complete the necessary forms and applications required to provide a standard application file for use by the State Selection Committee.

3. From the candidates found qualified, State and Territorial Selection Committees will make the final selection of candidates.

4. Selected candidates will be nominated for admission to NROTC colleges.

5. The candidates selected by the colleges for admission within the NROTC quota allotted to a particular institution will be ordered to report to the Commanding Officer, NROTC Unit, at their college.

6. The competition within each state or territory is restricted to candidates who maintain legal residence within that state or territory.

The NROTC Bulletin of Information is extensive and detailed. As new naval regulations or directions from the Department of Defense may be issued each year, it is important for the counselor to have the latest edition in his library. The Navy College Aptitude Test is administered by:

> Naval Examining Section
> Science Research Associates
> 104 Pearl Street
> McHenry, Illinois

As to who should apply, the following quotation is pertinent:

The answer to this important question is in two parts and should be understood by every young man who applies for this program. Firstly, the Regular NROTC is maintained for one purpose—to train and educate young men for ultimate commissioning as career officers in the Navy and Marine Corps. This and the Naval Academy are the two most highly competitive officer candidate programs in the Navy. Secondly, only men reasonably disposed to making the Navy a career should plan to enter into the Regular NROTC program, and in any case no man should plan to enter this Regular NROTC program who is certain he will not make the Navy a career (NROTC Bulletin of Information, 1960, p. 3).

To be eligible for regular NROTC Student Status, the student must:

1. Be a male citizen of the United States.

2. Have reached the seventeenth anniversary of his birth, and not have passed the twenty-first anniversary of his birth on July 1, unless contemplating a college course which takes five years to complete, in which case he must not have passed the twentieth anniversary of his birth on July 1.

3. Be unmarried and never have been married.

4. Be physically qualified in accordance with the standards prescribed for Midshipmen as described in the NROTC Bulletin.

5. Be a high school graduate or possess an equivalent certificate. High school students who will graduate by the end of the current academic

year may apply. High school juniors and students who will not be ready in all respects to enter college in September *are not eligible and should not apply.*

6. Have no moral or personal convictions which will prevent him from conscientiously bearing arms and supporting and defending the Constitution of the United States against all enemies, foreign or domestic.

7. Be prepared to enter into an appropriate contract with the Secretary of the Navy providing for the obligations set forth in the NROTC Bulletin. (Minors must obtain an agreement to the contract signed by their parent or guardian.)

Further, to meet eligibility requirements the students must accept certain contractual obligations:

1. To remain unmarried until commissioned.

2. To complete such naval science courses, drills, and cruises as may be prescribed.

3. To accept a commission in the Regular Navy or Marine Corps if offered. Officers of the United States Navy and United States Marine Corps serve at the pleasure of the President, and no terminal dates are established for their commissions. The Secretary of the Navy, by virtue of his authority, establishes such criteria for the voluntary termination of an officer's status as are deemed necessary for the maintenance of a sound officer corps. The minimum active duty requirement is presently four years.

4. To serve a minimum of six years in an active and inactive status from the date of acceptance of the original commission.

Normally, a student will attend college for four years and may take any course leading to a baccalaureate or higher degree. However, candidates for specialized degrees in medicine, dentistry, agriculture, and theology are not accepted. Again, the manual should be referred to.

The physical requirements of the Regular NROTC are so exacting that it is well to quote them in detail.

The physical requirements for the Regular NROTC are the same as those required of candidates for entry into the U.S. Naval Academy. These standards, necessarily exacting, have been determined after proper evaluation of requirements peculiar to the Naval Service. They are especially appropriate inasmuch as those men who are tendered commissions must have a reasonable expectancy of withstanding the high pressures and strenuous demands of the young naval officers aboard ship. Therefore, *these requirements are inflexible and cannot be waived.* . . . The importance of understanding these physical standards cannot be overemphasized. Almost 30 per cent of the candidates who have successfully passed the Navy College Aptitude Test in previous years have subsequently been rejected for physical deficiencies. This has resulted in great disappointment as well as needless expenditure of time and money by the candidate.

You are reminded that the physical requirements . . . are inflexible. The slightest deviation will be cause for rejection. For that reason you are urged to discuss the requirements with your parents so that they may assist you in obtaining any remedial treatment. You should schedule early appointments with your family physician and dentist to review your qualifications for this program. A copy of this booklet should be submitted to your physician and dentist for review of the standards prescribed for this program. Applicants who undergo expensive corrective procedures solely for the purpose of qualifying for the program, are advised that the quota of selected candidates is limited and based on many factors. Each year many candidates are rejected for defects which could be determined in advance through careful examination by their family physician or dentist (NROTC Bulletin of Information, 1960, p. 10).

Application for the Naval College Aptitude Test is considered an application for NROTC. However, *a student is under no obligation until such time as he is selected and appointed Midshipman, Naval Reserve.*

As NROTC offers an entire career for the student, the counselor must make sure the obligation of NROTC is well understood. The stringent physical requirements may preclude many interested and otherwise qualified candidates from winning NROTC appointments. The counselor should discuss the physical requirements with the student's parents and refer them to a physician or dentist on any question related to the requirements and the possibility of correcting any physical defects.

USE OF NATIONAL AND REGIONAL PROGRAMS IN THE SCHOOL'S OWN TESTING PROGRAM

The national and regional testing programs discussed here are primarily concerned with college admissions and selection of scholarship recipients. The counselor should integrate the admissions and scholarship test results with other data and make as much use of the results as he can in his counseling. Further, by being alert to scholarship offerings and encouraging scholastically able students to apply for scholarships, he may help some students go to college who otherwise would not be financially able to go. However, the school and the counselor cannot control many aspects of these tests. Objectives of the test, dates of the testing, and use of the test results are under the control of outside agencies and pose limitations in the use of the results.

Several other regional and national programs offer similar testing services, but the interests and purposes of these programs usually are to assist the schools in their teaching and counseling. These programs generally offer reliable and valid tests that can be fitted into the school's own program. The publisher or the central testing agency frequently provides all the routine services connected with scoring and reporting and makes a variety of interpretative aids available with the test results. The advantages of using such programs already has been discussed. The most important advantage which merits repeating is that the use of such services frees the school's administrative and counseling staff from routine clerical tasks involved in test scoring, norming of results, and recording of scores and permits this time to be spent in teaching and counseling students.

Many reputable test publishers and agencies offer reliable and valid tests. Selection of the tests and of the services of a test agency must begin with the school's own objectives. When the purposes of the tests offered by the agency coincide with the school's own objectives, it may be wise to use the agency's services.

IOWA TEST OF EDUCATIONAL DEVELOPMENT

One of the oldest and best developed test services provides the Iowa Tests of Educational Development (ITED). Developed at the University of Iowa for use in Iowa secondary schools, they are available to schools outside of Iowa through:

> Science Research Associates
> 57 West Grand Avenue
> Chicago 10, Illinois

The ITED's provide nine subtest scores and a composite score based on tests 1 to 8. The tests give a comprehensive and dependable description of the general educational development of the high school pupil. They are designed for annual administration to all students within grades 9 to 13 regardless of course registration.

The nine tests of the ITED are:

1. Understanding of Basic Social Concepts: General knowledge and understanding of contemporary social institutions and practices

2. General Background in the Natural Sciences: General knowledge and understanding of scientific terms and principles, of common natural phenomena and industrial applications, and of the place of science in modern civilization

3. Correctness and Appropriateness of Expression: Basic elements of correct and effective writing, punctuation, usage, capitalization, spelling, diction, phraseology, and organization

4. Quanitative Thinking: General mathematics involving practical problems every high school graduate should be able to solve

5. Interpretation of Reading Materials in the Social Studies: Understanding, interpreting, and evaluating materials from social studies textbooks and magazines and newspaper articles on social problems

6. Interpretation of Reading Materials in the Natural Sciences: Understanding, interpreting, and evaluating materials from textbooks and magazine and newspaper articles in the field of natural sciences

7. Interpretation—Literature: Appreciation and comprehension of selections from the major types of world literature

8. General Vocabulary: Measuring not only the student's ability to handle words, but also his "index of intelligence"—his general aptitude for learning

9. Use of Sources of Information: Utilizing standard references and current literature for answers to specific problems

The school orders the tests directly from Science Research Associates at the address given above. All necessary supplies are furnished by Science Research Associates, and all supplies are returned to them once the tests are administered (except the answer sheets). The answer sheets are sent to the Measurement Research Center at Iowa City, Iowa, where they are scored on specially developed electronic scoring equipment. The school is billed for the number of students tested. Results are reported to the schools on individual report forms, class rosters, frequency distributions for local norms, and confidential reports of the school's standing as compared to other schools. In addition, considerable interpretative material is included which aids the counselor and teacher to make optimum use of the results.

THE NATIONAL GUIDANCE TESTING PROGRAM

The National Guidance Testing Program (NGTP) offers a combination of achievement tests and a scholastic aptitude test. The program is sponsored by:

> Cooperative Test Division
> Educational Testing Service
> Princeton, New Jersey

The agency also has an office at Los Angeles 27, California. NGTP aims to provide tests broad in their coverage and integrated in their testing approach from grades 4 to 14. The tests offer measures of critical skills and applications of learning rather than retention or memorized information.

NGTP offers a scholastic aptitude test, the School and College Aptitude Test (SCAT), and six achievement tests, the Sequential Tests of Educational Progress (STEP) for Reading, Writing, Listening Comprehension, Mathematics, Science, and Social Studies. One score is reported for each STEP test, and two subscores (Verbal and Quantitative) and a total score for SCAT. Each test requires 70 minutes of working time, about 85 minutes for total administration time. SCAT has five levels available with two forms at each level. These are:

SCAT 5A, 5B for grades 4 to 6
SCAT 4A, 4B for grades 6 to 8
SCAT 3A, 3B for grades 8 to 10
SCAT 2A, 2B for grades 10 to 12
SCAT 1A, 1B for grades 13 and 14

Each STEP test has four levels available with two forms for each. These are:

STEP 4A, 4B for grades 4 to 6
STEP 3A, 3B for grades 7 to 9
STEP 2A, 2B for grades 10 to 12
STEP 1A, 1B for grades 13 and 14

The school can order several combinations of STEP tests with SCAT. When the school uses the National Guidance Testing Program service, it buys its own test booklets and manuals. It then registers for the service for either fall or spring administration, indicating how many students will be tested, and when. For the winter semester of 1961 two program scoring periods were provided, January 31 to March 14, and April 4 to May 23. Before the specified test date, the school receives all the necessary test materials. After the tests are administered, the school mails the answer sheets to the Educational Testing Service, Princeton, New Jersey, for scoring on electronic scoring equipment. Reports are sent directly to the schools from Princeton, New Jersey. Scores are reported on list reports, a gummed label which can be mounted on the student's permanent record folder, a report card, and a student report form. Schools that have IBM equipment can obtain IBM cards with the results punched in them. A flat rate per student tested is charged to the school for the scoring and reporting service, whether one test or all seven are administered. This charge includes the cost of the answer sheets. In calculating the cost of this program, the counselor must include the cost of booklets, manuals, and interpretative aids he will need and desire.

THE EDUCATIONAL RECORDS BUREAU

The testing program of the Educational Records Bureau (ERB) is wide enough in geographic scope and broad enough in tests used and services offered to merit an extended discussion. ERB is a central testing agency offering many different tests to elementary and secondary schools, providing a variety of scoring and reporting services, and conducting research for and with member schools. ERB could be characterized geographically as Northeast United States and Central Atlantic, but schools throughout the United States are members. Its membership consists largely of independent (private) schools, but a number of public schools belong. It has a regular testing program with certain tests offered as a program service to member schools, but in addition it provides central scoring to members on out-of-program tests. It also does much scoring for nonmember public schools and colleges.

The tests used in ERB are so numerous that no attempt will be made to describe them individually. ERB does some of its own test development, but usually uses tests from several different publishers. Further information may be obtained from:

> Educational Records Bureau
> 21 Audubon Avenue
> New York 32, New York

ERB is a good illustration of how the services of a central testing agency can provide many advantages to a school. Tests selected are from reputable publishers and have adequate reliability and validity. Enough different tests are offered to enable an individual school to select tests which meet its own specific objectives. Norms are tailor-made for the schools using the tests, and research conducted is specific to the problems of member schools. In addition to the regular scoring and reporting services, ERB offers advisory and statistical analysis services.

STATEWIDE PROGRAMS

No attempt will be made to describe the many statewide programs in existence (Berdie, 1954). The counselor should be aware of the state or local services that are available and use them when he profitably can. Services generally are provided by state departments of education, state universities, or colleges of education. Local private testing agencies may offer limited service.

OTHER FEATURES OF TESTING PROGRAMS

An important feature of most of the testing programs is the interpretative data they provide for and the research they conduct on their tests. National, regional, and institutional norms usually are available. Correlations of test scores with school and college grades are furnished. Ample case history material is provided giving illustrative uses of a particular test. Increasingly, expectancy tables, some of them for individual colleges, show the chances a student has of obtaining passing grades when his test score falls in a given score range. Profiles, graphs, and other visual aids make it easier to obtain the general meaning of test scores and help to explain them to the students, teachers, and parents. Again a caveat must be entered—the very wealth of norms, research reports, case histories, and visual aids may seduce the counselor into the false acceptance of test results as the be-all and end-all of counseling or of education itself. The authors urge that testing and counseling be perceived as part of the educational process and that the educational process itself be seen as part of the larger social structure in which it exists and in which it finds its *raison d'être*. The counselor must interpret a student's test score as one bit of data, among myriad bits of data, trying his best to determine what importance the test score really has.

QUESTIONS FOR STUDY

1. Using the most recent manuals or descriptive materials for the scholarship programs discussed in this chapter, make a testing schedule for the coming school year for the seniors in a high school of your state. Assume also that in your state, the state university is offering a number of scholarships to be decided by an examination to be given in January and February of the senior year and administered by the local schools.
2. If you were a counselor in a high school from which a number of students went to colleges requiring CEEB scores, would you recommend to your principal and superintendent that PSAT be given to juniors? Support your answer whether yes or no.
3. You are a high school counselor and one of your students became ill the day before the date of the CEEB examination for which he was registered. His mother calls you and is anxious about his not taking the examination, since the college the pupil desires to attend requires CEEB. What do you tell the mother?
4. An able senior who had decided not to go to college changes his mind in May of his senior year and decides he wants to go. The college of his choice requires the ACT battery for admission. What do you advise him about taking it?
5. From the descriptive materials for the Iowa Tests of Educational Development and the complete National Guidance Testing Program battery draw up a chart comparing test content, reliabilities and validities, administration time, per student cost, format of test, reports and additional services available.
6. As a counselor in a high school, you have been asked to give a twenty-minute talk to the local PTA and answer questions about the tests being used in your high school. Outline a talk on one of the scholarship or other testing programs discussed in this chapter. Anticipate questions such as: Why is this particular test being used? What does it tell me (a parent) about how well my son or daughter is doing in school? Does this test tell me how well he or she should be doing? Will this testing tell me about my child's success in college? What occupation should he enter?

REFERENCE

Berdie, R. F. The state-wide testing program. *Personnel Guid. J.*, 1954, 32, 454–459.

CHAPTER 9

The Use of Information in Counseling

Although no experimental evidence at present justifies the assumption that *effective counseling depends on the counselor's knowledge about his counselee,* this is an opinion to which many counselors subscribe on the basis of years of counseling experience and one which underlies the entire discussion in this volume.

As we have seen, information about pupils is required for many purposes in the school. Administrators and boards must know about pupils in order to decide where schools are required and what kinds of schools are needed. Curriculum planners and teachers must know about pupils in order to make decisions about the content of the school program and to plan appropriate teaching and instructional programs. Classroom teachers must possess this information in order to individualize their instruction so that each pupil can best benefit from the available opportunities and so that progress can be evaluated and learning experiences properly timed. Much information is needed to help administrators and teachers evaluate what they have done and to study educational goals and objectives and means for attaining these objectives. The purpose of this chapter, however, is not to discuss these uses of information in the school, since entire volumes have been devoted to each of the above educational goals (Lindquist, 1951; Remmers & Gage, 1955; Ross, 1954). Here we shall concern ourselves with the problem of using information about pupils for purposes of counseling.

ASSESSMENT OF PUPIL NEEDS

Counseling is provided for pupils in response to their needs, and the needs for counseling vary from pupil to pupil and from day to day. The organization of a counseling program not only should be based on the predictable appearance of these needs, but also should take into consideration the variations with which these needs appear.

In many schools counselors routinely schedule appointments with

121

certain groups of students. For example, one counselor is responsible for interviewing all graduating senior men during the months of November and December, because many seniors at this time of the year are faced with problems concerning their future educational and vocational plans. The earlier counseling and other experiences of these students frequently have provided a basis for planning, and many seniors by this time have arrived at satisfactory decisions about their future. Nevertheless, the senior year is an exceptionally good time to systematically review plans that have been made and to consider again points where indecision remains.

Even when interviews are systematically scheduled with selected pupils for specific purposes, the counselor must determine how each interview can best serve each person. In other words, when the decision has been made that most seniors can benefit from counseling because of the questions many of them face, the counselor cannot generalize and for each pupil say, "This is the time for us to talk about your college plans" or "This is the time for us to discuss the job you will take."

Some pupils' needs for counseling do center about their indecision about jobs. Others can benefit from counseling about higher education. Still others are thinking about leaving home, marriage, military service, changing church affiliations, and relationships with friends and family. During the first part of an interview, the counselor often can sense how counseling can best serve the student, and information already at hand about the pupil aids in this judgment.

Sometimes the needs of students can be regarded as being related to problems, and information about pupils provides a means for helping counselors and teachers identify which persons have which types of problems. For the teacher, this can be described as finding the characteristics of each pupil so that he can be taught what he is ready to learn. A test of reading skill for children at the beginning of the third grade helps the teacher decide what kinds of books the children should read. An arithmetic test in the sixth grade helps a teacher decide about appropriate instruction for each pupil. When these tests used in the classroom reveal that certain pupils are not ready for the instruction planned for most pupils, then a problem is present for the student and for the teacher, and remedial work may be necessary.

The use of a personality inventory in high school also illustrates how tests can help identify pupils with problems. When pupils come from different junior high schools to a senior high school, they move into a new and strange environment, and little is known about these pupils by the new school. In school systems which have good coordination of records, accurate and complete information accompanies the student from junior to senior high school, and these records help new counselors and teachers understand their pupils. In many schools, however, complete records are not available, and the school frequently has to obtain, as soon as possible, as much relevant information as will be needed about new pupils.

Most schools include in the records of new pupils information about personal and family backgrounds, parental education and occupation, hobbies and recreations, work experience, occupational goals, educational plans, and health and medical status. Often information is obtained about the pupils' achievement backgrounds through the systematic use of achievement tests or batteries.

As many entering high school pupils have trouble because of personal difficulties as because of academic difficulties. Sometimes pupils with personal problems can be identified only after they have been in a school long enough to allow teachers and counselors to become well acquainted with them. In order to shorten the time a pupil must be in a school before his needs are known, and consequently to increase the time during which help can be offered, personality inventories can help identify pupils who have problems of personal adjustment. Some of these inventories help find pupils who have problems with their families, their relationships with their fellow students, or who have various kinds of emotional disturbances. This kind of inventory does not provide information that allows a counselor to say, "These students have problems and these others do not," but rather, "The scores on these inventories identify students who are most likely to have problems and in turn, force us to look at these pupils with particular care and attention in order to find those who most need help" (Darley, 1937).

We often make inferences about the needs of students on the basis of the knowledge we have of the groups to which students belong (Meehl & Rosen, 1955). For example, we know that practically all pupils in the ninth grade can spell relatively simple three-letter words, and we don't include such words as "the" or "and" in their spelling tests. Should a ninth-grade pupil appear who could not spell these simple words, we would regard him as an unusual occurrence. Our everyday experiences, sometimes backed by systematic research, show that all or most persons belonging to a given group behave in certain ways. As we learn about groups, we discover that the behaviors of the individuals in the group fall within defined limits. Thus, when we work with a group of university freshmen we are not concerned with identifying mental defectives, since persons with IQs below 70 are not found among college freshmen. We do have much important knowledge about persons which is based not on direct observation of the individual, but rather on our general knowledge of the group from which the individual comes. We know the general needs of high school pupils and use this knowledge to help us decide what kinds of counseling and testing programs are needed in schools, though we do not use it to decide about the needs of individual pupils. The counselor in his day-to-day work is most concerned with understanding how one individual in a group differs from others in the same group. He is not concerned with identifying mentally defective pupils, but rather with how each pupil compares intellectually with others in his high school. Information about individual pupils is needed by counselors in order to provide this type of understanding.

INFORMATION USED TO DEFINE PROBLEMS

The counselor must learn how to identify problems and how to understand better the problems he does identify. Often many persons in a school may be aware that a pupil has a problem and is having difficulty, but usually more must be known about the nature of the problem before anything can be done. A reading test can be used to identify people who have reading problems. If a reading test given to an eleventh-grade pupil shows that his skills are about equivalent to those of a fifth-grade pupil, and if his teacher's observations substantiate these test scores, the counselor then must learn more about the nature of the problem. More careful observations are made of the pupil's reading, and a diagnostic reading test is given. As additional information is obtained, the problem becomes better defined and the nature of needed remediation is clarified.

THE CASE OF KATHRYN

Kathryn Smith always had been a good student and earned high grades. Her scores on academic aptitude tests consistently showed that she was about average when compared with other pupils in her high school, but her grade records showed that she always had achieved better than would have been predicted on the basis of her test scores. During her junior year, however, one teacher who knew Kathryn well noted that she had become more seclusive and appeared to be unhappy and depressed. She spent less and less time with her friends and in the student organizations in which she previously had been active.

The teacher and her counselor discussed this and the counselor then talked with Kathryn about the observed change. She was unable to elicit any helpful information. The interview did support the teacher's impression that Kathryn was not a happy girl, but nothing was learned regarding the nature of her problem.

About this time all the eleventh-grade pupils were given a personality test, the Minnesota Counseling Inventory. The counselor noted that some of Kathryn's scores were different from the scores of other pupils. The score on the section related to family adjustment suggested that considerable conflict might be present between Kathryn and others in her family. Other scores related to social behavior and to mood were high enough to suggest the probability of further problems.

The counselor again talked with Kathryn, but this time focused her attention on the relationships between Kathryn and her family. Kathryn quickly started to discuss the problems she faced as a result of pressure from her parents to maintain the academic record she earlier had acquired without much difficulty. Now, however, she was finding increasing difficulty in achieving because of the increased competition in senior high school.

In this case no test was required to determine the existence of a problem. Many symptoms or indications of problems were obvious to the counselor and the teacher, but none of the information seemed to fall into place; no pattern was formed. After the test scores were incorporated with the other information about the pupil, hypotheses then could be derived by the counselor from the patterns formed by the previous information. The counselor was able to test out these hypotheses in a tentative fashion and select the one that offered most promise for productive counseling with Kathryn.

We must regard each bit of information as it is related to all other information about the pupil. Each item of information slightly changes our point of view when we look at a person. No one bit of information tells us all about a pupil; rather each bit added to all the other available information helps us create for ourselves and for the pupil a more consistent and meaningful picture of the individual as he currently is.

THE CASE OF BRYON

Another example of how to use information in defining a problem is found in the case of Bryon Kelly, a high school senior with a moderately good school record, who came to his counselor during the middle of the year for assistance in making plans. Bryon did not know whether he should go to college, go to a trade school, join the Army, or get a job. He thought he would like to be a lawyer, but knew little about the profession. His father, an expert automobile mechanic, did not want Bryon to follow in his steps. Bryon had worked on a highway crew and thought he would like civil engineering, but he did not like mathematics. His mathematics grades had been poor. Some of his friends told him he should be a salesman. When he took typing in high school, he liked it and did well.

The counselor carefully reviewed Bryon's record with him and noted that he had taken the Differential Aptitude Tests in the ninth grade. He suggested that Bryon take the Mechanical Comprehension Test, the

Minnesota Clerical Test, the Ohio Psychological Examination, and the Strong Vocational Interest Blank. Scores on other academic aptitude and achievement tests were available. The counselor and Bryon then reviewed all this information and quickly were able to reject certain broad occupations from consideration and to concentrate on a few that looked most appropriate. They quickly agreed that rejecting engineering was justified because of low scores related to mathematics. Bryon's high mechanical aptitude test scores, his hobbies, and some of his work experiences suggested that certain skilled trades would be appropriate. The interest scores provided additional evidence and suggested that some consideration should be given to jobs in business, particularly bookkeeping and office work. The academic aptitude test and the interest blank lent no support to the choice of law, and the counselor and Bryon agreed that work requiring much verbal skill and a high degree of academic aptitude would not be appropriate.

In this way, Bryon was able to select from the entire gamut of occupations a few that seemed most appropriate for him, and then to investigate these more carefully to learn which would provide him the best probability for success. Opportunities for training provided by the Army were carefully reviewed. During the entire counseling process, the counselor and the pupil continually used information about the pupil, jobs, and schools to identify and evaluate alternatives and plan accordingly.

The test scores were not used in isolation; neither was the counseling done in the absence of test scores. Considered in counseling was information about Bryon's family, his work experience, his reactions to school, his hobbies and recreations, his relationships with others, and his test scores. Any one kind of information omitted from consideration might have resulted in a different outcome, and the counselor had no way of determining before the interview what information would be relevant and what would not. Consequently, all possible information had to be reviewed and considered.

SYSTEMATIZING PREDICTIVE INFORMATION

The validity of the counselor's information about a pupil and the sophistication of its use determine the accuracy of his predictions. In some instances a counselor will have relatively little information, know little of its relevancy, and little of its use. A pupil previously unknown to the counselor and for whom there is no personnel record may come to the counselor for a ten-minute discussion about whether he should apply for admission to a school about which the counselor knows nothing. The deadline for applying for admission may fall on the day of the brief interview. The counselor may be able to help the pupil, but any predictions of success based on the available data will not be much different from predictions based on chance alone.

Let us assume the counselor has more information. He knows that success in the school being considered depends largely on mathematical ability. When the pupil tells him of his high school record in mathematics, the accuracy of the counselor's predictions should increase. If the high school record including actual mathematics grades is available, even greater accuracy should be obtained. If the counselor knows what special mathematical competencies are demanded by the school being contemplated, greater accuracy may be possible. Scores on aptitude and achievement tests of mathematics should further increase accuracy.

Up to this point we have assumed that the counselor's knowledge of the relationship between mathematical competency and school success has not been quantified. He knows that "much mathematical ability helps." When this knowledge is quantified, however, he may be able to make better predictions. For example, one school of engineering found that students who obtained scores of less than 27 on a mathematics test it used had less than 1 chance in 100 of doing satisfactory work during the first semester. To help counselors and pupils predict success, the school prepared tables such as those in Figure 9.1 demonstrating the

FIGURE 9.1

SPECIAL EXPECTANCY TABLE FOR THE UNIVERSITY OF MINNESOTA
INSTITUTE OF TECHNOLOGY BASED ON MATHEMATICS ADMISSIONS TEST

Expectancy for first-year grade point average based on freshmen entering college the fall of 1959. Sex: Male. Size of group: over 300.

Quintile group* (percentiles)	Chances in 100 of a freshman obtaining an average grade of			Size of group
	D or higher	C or higher	B or higher	
80–	97	75	22	Over 50
60–79	95	50	5	Over 50
40–59	83	30	8	Over 50
20–39	55	11	. . .	Over 50
–19	35	3	. . .	From 20 to 50

* These percentiles are based on entering freshmen to the Institute of Technology. These groups are based on the IT Mathematics Test, form Y. However, as forms X, Y, and Z are very similar, it is reasonably accurate to enter the percentile obtained from any one of these forms.

relationship between scores and success. The table in Figure 9.2 presents similar information about the relationship between high school grades (or percentile rank in class) and college aptitude test scores and college success in the same school.

FIGURE 9.2
EXPECTANCY TABLE FOR THE UNIVERSITY OF MINNESOTA INSTITUTE OF TECHNOLOGY

Expectancy for first-year grade point average based on freshmen entering college the fall of 1959. Sex: Male and Female.* Size of total group: over 300.

Predictions based on high school rank

High school rank quintile group	Chances in 100 of a freshman obtaining an average grade of			Size of group
	D or higher	C or higher	B or higher	
80–	95	65	15	Over 50
60–79	71	28	3	Over 50
40–59	72	19	…	Over 50
20–39	88	42	…	Less than 10
–19				

Predictions based on MSAT

MSAT quintile group	Chances in 100 of a freshman obtaining an average grade of			Size of group
	D or higher	C or higher	B or higher	
Raw score 51–78 Percentile 80–	94	71	19	Over 50
Raw score 42–50 Percentile 60–79	88	47	6	Over 50
Raw score 34–41 Percentile 40–59	82	42	8	Over 50
Raw score 27–33 Percentile 20–39	70	26	1	Over 50
Raw score 1–26 Percentile –19	70	18	2	From 20 to 50

* Seven women enrolled in this entering freshman group.

These tables are called prediction or expectancy tables and are one of several methods used to quantify predictive information for counselors. The idea of such tables is not new (Bingham & Freyd, 1926; Johnston, 1930; Wesman, 1949), but only since 1958 have many been made available to counselors. Figure 9.3 shows some tables used by counselors to predict success in Georgia colleges and universities. Figure 9.4 shows similar ones for another Minnesota institution.

The formats of these tables differ, but the basic idea is the same. Pupils for whom predictive information, such as test scores, high school grades, or work experience, is available are divided into groups according to categories of this information. For each group the proportion of pupils attaining various levels of success is observed, and the tables reflect these proportions.

For example, in Figure 9.1, the several hundreds of freshmen admitted to engineering school were classified in five groups (quintile groups) on the basis of their scores on the mathematics test. The first group contained the students in about the upper 20 per cent of the class according to their test scores. The second group contained the next 20 per cent, etc.

At the end of the first quarter in college, each of these five subgroups was further divided into three groups: students with grade averages of B or higher, of C or higher (including those in the first group), and of D or higher (including those in the other two groups). The remainder of the students received grade averages of less than D and are not directly represented in the table.

In each cell is presented the proportion of students in each test score category who were in each grade-average group. For example, of all the students with test scores of 80 and above, 97 per cent had grade averages of D or better. Considering D as a passing grade, only 3 per cent of students with high test scores failed their first quarter. In this high-test-score group, 75 per cent earned grade averages of at least C, and 22 per cent of at least B.

Of students with scores from 20 to 34, 45 per cent failed, 55 per cent had averages of D or better, only 11 per cent averaged C or better, and none did B work or better.

With this table a counselor can talk with a pupil about his test score and relate the score meaningfully to the decision being faced. Most pupils easily can grasp the probability concept underlying predictions and understand that all predictions are fallible. They can understand that pupils with a broad range of abilities can succeed and also fail. Some very bright pupils receive poor grades; some mediocre pupils earn high grades. They see the need to balance their desires and motivations with their probabilities for success and realize that within limits theirs is the responsibility for determining what odds they wish to risk, how big a

FIGURE 9.3

EXPECTANCY TABLE FOR GEORGIA INSTITUTE OF TECHNOLOGY

Proportions of students with various index scores (based on formulas using college board scores and high school average) who will make an average college grade of C or better, B or better, and A their first year. Sex: Male.

All students, N = 1,744

Index V + 2 M + 33 HSA	Student will get average of		
	C	B	A
3,800	...	.74	.09
3,600	.99	.58	.04
3,400	.96	.41	.01
3,200	.91	.25	
3,000	.81	.13	
2,800	.67	.06	
2,600	.50	.02	
2,400	.33	.01	
2,200	.19		
2,000	.09		
1,800	.04		
1,600	.01		

Aeronautical engineering, N = 286

Index V + M + 23 HSA	Student will get average of		
	C	B	A
2,600	...	.86	.20
2,500	...	.77	.12
2,400	.99	.66	.07
2,300	.98	.54	.04
2,200	.95	.41	.02
2,100	.91	.29	.01
2,000	.85	.19	
1,900	.77	.12	
1,800	.66	.07	
1,700	.54	.03	
1,600	.41	.02	
1,500	.29	.01	
1,400	.19		
1,300	.12		
1,200	.06		
1,100	.03		
1,000	.02		
900	.01		

Architecture, N = 130

Index V + M + 20 HSA	Student will get average of		
	C	B	A
2,500	.99	.44	.01
2,400	.97	.33	
2,300	.95	.23	
2,200	.91	.15	
2,100	.85	.10	
2,000	.78	.06	
1,900	.68	.03	
1,800	.58	.02	
1,700	.46	.01	
1,600	.35		
1,500	.25		
1,400	.17		
1,300	.11		
1,200	.06		
1,100	.03		
1,000	.02		
900	.01		

FIGURE 9.4

EXPECTANCY TABLE FOR THE UNIVERSITY OF MINNESOTA COLLEGE OF SCIENCE, LITERATURE, AND THE ARTS

Expectancy for first-year grade point average based on freshmen entering college the fall of 1959. Sex: Male. Size of total group: over 300.

Predictions based on high school rank

High school rank quintile group	Chances in 100 of a freshman obtaining an average grade of			Size of group
	D or higher	C or higher	B or higher	
80–	96	70	22	Over 50
60–79	92	46	5	Over 50
40–59	87	27	1	Over 50
20–39	79	21	1	Over 50
–19	55	9	...	From 10 to 20

Predictions based on MSAT

MSAT quintile group	Chances in 100 of a freshman obtaining an average grade of			Size of group
	D or higher	C or higher	B or higher	
Raw score 51–78 / Percentile 80–	95	61	17	Over 50
Raw score 42–50 / Percentile 60–79	89	42	7	Over 50
Raw score 34–41 / Percentile 40–59	88	37	4	Over 50
Raw score 27–33 / Percentile 20–39	81	27	3	Over 50
Raw score 1–26 / Percentile –19	99	54	...	From 10 to 20

gambler each is. In this sense, the counselor's task is to help the student understand the relative probabilities and consider their implications.

The probabilities vary even when predicting the same criterion depending on the predictors used. In Figure 9.4, a boy with a high school percentile rank of 75 would have a probability of 92 out of 100 of earning at least a D average, 46 of earning a C average, and 5 of earning a B average. If his percentile score on the college aptitude test (MSAT) was 50, his probabilities of earning D, C, or B, would be 88, 37, or 4, or slightly lower than those based on high school rank. These probabilities are not different enough to have much practical implication, but in some cases differences do occur, and in these instances, the counselor must consider the relative accuracy of the predictions, i.e., what are the correlations between predictors and grades and what are the standard errors of estimate.

In Figure 9.3 the tables present probabilities based on a combination of two test scores, V (verbal) and M (mathematics), and high school average. The formula at the top of the table shows how an index is obtained for each pupil. In the left-hand table the score of the verbal test is added to twice the score of the mathematics test and to 33 times the high school rank. Thus, a pupil with a V of 450, M of 500, and high school average of 35, would have an index of

$$450 + 2(500) + 33(35) = 2,605$$

His probability of earning at least a C average during his first college year would be .50, but he would have a probability of only 0.2 of earning a B average. Obviously the lack of an entry for earning an A average does not mean the probability is zero. It does mean that in the group of students on whom this table is based, none with an index of 2,600 earned an A average.

This figure demonstrates the need for different expectancy tables for different colleges and curricula. To determine the probable success of the student mentioned above if he entered aeronautical engineering, we would use the formula

$$450 + 500 + 23(35) = 1,755$$

Using the index 1,755, we would see that this student's probability of earning a C average lay between .54 and .66, only slightly better than the probabilities obtained when we compared him to all students entering the institute.

If the student were planning to enter architecture at the school, our formula would be

$$450 + 500 + 20(35) = 1,650$$

and the probability of earning at least a C average would be about .40, somewhat lower than the corresponding probability in aeronautical engineering.

Other ways have been used to aid counselors in predicting success, and the multiple regression equation is the method most often used with test scores. This is a method based on an analysis of the correlations between each of the predictors and the criterion (the correlation is computed between each test score and grade average) and between each of the predictors and every other predictor. This method provides a prediction formula similar to this

$$\bar{y}_1 = 12.95x_2 + .2438x_3 + 44.18$$

where $\bar{y}_1$ = fall quarter grade point average for freshmen in law school

x_2 = percentile score on American Council on Education Psychological Examination

x_3 = prelaw grade point average

The counselor inserts the appropriate test score into the formula, performs the necessary arithmetic, and produces a figure which is the student's most probable grade average.

This method has some advantages and some disadvantages, but regardless of these, or perhaps because of some of them, counselors have been reluctant to use predictions made with multiple correlation or regression equations. The accuracy of the obtained prediction depends of course on the size of the correlations, and this accuracy can be estimated through use of the standard error of estimate, which is a fairly complex statistic, however, and is difficult to interpret in a counseling interview. The ease of accurate interpretation makes the empirical prediction table more attractive to counselors.

IMPROVING STATISTICAL PREDICTIONS

Our thesis has been that test scores and other counseling information are used to help the counselor and the counselee originate and study hypotheses concerning the counselee's future behavior. The predictions about which we have been talking are in a sense hypotheses of this sort. When a counselor has a student take a college aptitude test and then through the use of a prediction table or prediction equation arrives at an estimate of the student's probable success, he is formulating a hypothesis about the pupil's future behavior. He could originate or review the hypothesis without the test data or without other pertinent data, but the more relevant and accurate the available data, the greater the probability that the hypothesis will correspond to the actual outcome.

Most of the hypotheses and most of the predictions made by counselors are not quantified. Seldom does a counselor make use of statistical methods of prediction; usually his predictions are formulated in a more intuitive or subjective manner. A counselor may use a statistical prediction when he is attempting to help a student understand his probability of success in a given college. When he is attempting to help a student understand his possibility of success in an occupation or his probability of liking that occupation, he is less likely to use a statistical prediction and more likely to use the intuitive, or what has been called a clinical, prediction.

The relative accuracy of clinical and statistical predictions has been carefully studied. Traditionally counselors have assumed that the best conclusions can be attained through careful consideration of whatever statistical predictions are available, manipulation and correction of these predictions on the basis of information that cannot be or is not included in the statistical prediction, and use of the statistical prediction as adjusted for other conditions. For example, a counselor working with a pupil considering college attendance has a series of test scores and a prediction table indicating that this particular pupil has 84 chances out of 100 of achieving at least a C average during his freshman year in college. The counselor knows, however, that the pupil will live at home while attending college and will have to commute to the campus and that the student will have to work on an outside job to help meet his expenses. He considers the ten hours a week the student will spend traveling back and forth between home and school and the twenty hours a week the student will spend on his job and decides that, in light of these considerations, the pupil's true probability for success in college is not 80 out of 100, but closer to 50 out of 100. Consequently, the counselor has adjusted the statistical prediction to account for information not included in the prediction tables.

This approach seems so reasonable that for decades nobody questioned its validity. Sarbin (1944) was the first person to study the accuracy of predictions derived statistically and predictions derived from clinical manipulation of statistical predictions. He studied a number of college freshmen who had taken college aptitude tests and using regression equations, predicted the probable grade averages of these freshmen. He also had the college counselors who had access to the statistical predictions make clinical predictions as to the academic success of their counselees, and he compared the statistical predictions and the clinical predictions to the actual success of the student. Consistently the statistical predictions were somewhat superior to the clinical predictions, even though the latter were based in part on the statistical predictions.

The problem of statistical versus clinical prediction and the research related to this problem have been reviewed by Meehl (1954), and in general Meehl's conclusions tend to confirm and expand on Sarbin's results.

In the case of the pupil cited above, the kind of information the counselor incorporated into the prediction, information about commuting and working, well might have been incorporated into a prediction table, and separate prediction tables could be prepared on the basis of test scores for students who live at home and who live on campus and for students who work varied numbers of hours a week. By using such tables, predictions most likely would be more accurate than those based on test scores alone or those made without access to prediction tables. The need for more comprehensive means of arriving at statistical predictions is obvious.

Ideally, the counselor would have before him tables presenting the probability for all events for all categories of students in all situations. These probabilities would be based on observations of actual outcomes. A counselor and a pupil would be able to look at such a table and to observe that of all pupils similar to this one who entered a certain curriculum in a given school, a given proportion succeeded, a given proportion failed. Little of the counselor's or pupil's time would have to be spent finding out the probability of success, and more time could be spent counseling and helping the student use the new information. Such probability figures are not available now and perhaps will not be for a long time. Counselors and pupils will have to continue to use whatever probability information is available and "semiprobability" information arrived at experientially, subjectively, intuitively, and vicariously.

The conscientious counselor constantly and systematically will strive to gather and organize observations in order to provide bases for making probability predictions. For example, a counselor in a high school which sends large numbers of its graduates to four different colleges will observe during the years that different types of pupils appear to succeed differentially in these colleges. Pupils with outstanding mathematical aptitude do particularly well in College A, but this aptitude does not seem to help them in College B. On the other hand, many students who are socially advanced and verbally fluent do well in College C, but students similar to these who enter College A frequently fail. The counselor uses this information in counseling pupils, and if the counselor's observations are accurate, this information is helpful. The counselor will find the information increasingly useful, however, if he finds a way for categorizing students according to his predictive observations and actually relates these categories to success in the four colleges. In this way, he would be able to say to himself and to his counselees that of every 100 students with ability such as theirs, a given proportion succeed in College A, a given proportion succeed in College B, and so on. Occasionally the counselor will find that his tabulations fail to bear out his intuitive impressions, and consequently he will be able to avoid predictions based on false premises. Equally important, however, are the opportunities of quantifying observations, easing communication, and attaching an estimate of error to the data.

USING DIFFERENT INFORMATION

The best way to learn how to use information in counseling is to use it, but practical learning experiences can be supplemented by reviewing the experiences of others. We will be helped by examining some of the experiences and problems of persons working with psychological tests of academic ability, educational achievement, special ability, vocational interest, and personality, and with other kinds of information about pupils.

THE CASE OF MARTIN

Martin Brown was a thin, rather shy boy completing his senior year in high school when he came to the university counselor. Speaking easily and smiling readily throughout the interview, he said that he wanted to attend the university, but did not know what to take. He thought some aptitude tests would help him.

Martin had a part-time job and decided to attend the university only after his employer had discussed several times with him the advantages of a college education and had convinced Martin of the desirability of going to college. In high school he had liked but not done well in mathematics, so in order to learn more, he had repeated his algebra course in an evening school. When he talked to the counselor, he was taking a correspondence course in engineering, since he thought he would like to be an engineer, though he realized this was a very difficult course and thought perhaps he first ought to take a general course in college. In high school he had done well in but not liked typing and bookkeeping. He had thought of going into business.

Martin's father was a mechanic and did not care what his son became, as long as he did not become a mechanic. The father thought his own occupation dirty and was especially concerned about the amount of time his wife spent keeping his clothes clean. Martin and his father spent much time keeping the boy's motorcycle and car in repair.

Martin said his health was good and his hobbies included hunting and fishing. While in high school he had worked part time in a supermarket, in a machine shop, and as a gardener. His high school counselor, on the basis of his high school tests, had suggested that he consider being an electrician or plumber.

The university counselor talked with the high school counselor and learned that Martin had obtained his highest grades in shop courses. His high school percentile rank was 62 because of his good grades in these courses, but throughout his school career his academic achievement had been low. In the sixth grade his grade level in reading was 4.7 on the Metropolitan Achievement Test, and on this test his average grade level was 4.9. In the eighth grade, the Stanford Achievement Test placed him at the sixth-grade level. On the Cooperative English Test taken in the eleventh grade, his score placed him in the lower 1 per cent of university freshmen. On the Kuhlmann-Anderson Test taken in the sixth grade, his IQ was 89. In the ninth grade his percentile scores on the Differential Aptitude Tests, using ninth-grade norms, were: verbal reasoning—6, number ability—28, abstract reasoning—40, spatial relations—40, mechanical reasoning—16, and clerical speed and accuracy—1. His score on the American Council on Education Psychological Examination in the eleventh grade placed him in the lower 2 per cent of high school juniors who had become university freshmen.

In spite of this consistent information, the university counselor had Martin take the Ohio Psychological Examination on which he obtained a score placing him in the lower 2 per cent of university freshmen. On the Cooperative Mathematics Test he fell in the lower 3 per cent of engineering students, and on a retest of the Differential Aptitude Tests his percentile scores were, using norms based on university students in a two-year general college course: verbal reasoning—10, number ability—69, abstract reasoning—35, spatial relations—43, mechanical reasoning—14, clerical speed and accuracy—9, and language usage–spelling—1. The counselor did not know that Martin had previously taken this battery of tests when he gave them, and later, when the original scores became available, the counselor had no way of taking into account the practice effect on the retests. The counselor assumed that the retest scores provided overestimates of Martin's true abilities, but he suspected there would be relatively little practice effect on the Differential Aptitude Tests after a three-year interval.

On the Kuder Preference Record, Martin obtained percentile scores of 95 on musical, 93 on clerical, 89 on artistic, and 53 on computational. All other percentile scores were below 50. On the Strong Vocational Interest Blank, he obtained A's on the scales for farmer, carpenter, policeman, and office man, and scores of B+ on scales for printer, mathematics and physical science teacher, industrial education teacher, vocational agriculture teacher, senior certified public accountant, and banker. On the Minnesota Multiphasic Personality Inventory, the scores were generally elevated, indicating personal conflict and psychological discomfort, but none of these scores were high enough to indicate an extreme problem.

All of the information collected influenced the course of counseling. The Kuhlmann-Anderson Test, the American Council on Education Psychological Examination, the Differential Aptitude Tests, and the Ohio test—all suggested that Martin did not have enough ability for a highly academic university course. His extra-high school experience in some mathematics and engineering courses tended to verify this judgment. The achievement tests and high school grades provided supporting evidence.

The interest tests and the information Martin revealed in the interviews about his family background, his hobbies, and his aspirations suggested that he might find ultimate satisfaction in jobs not requiring vocational preparation in a college. During two or three interviews, Martin realized that his own motivation to attend college was not high, but that he was being overly influenced by his employer. The university counselor agreed that it might be worthwhile for Martin to attempt a university course of a general and elementary nature for at least a few months if he wished. Although he did not actively encourage Martin, at the same time he attempted to help Martin realize that he might later discover that the plan was not the best one for him.

Martin returned to the counselor after one quarter at the university and said he was satisfied with his experience, but he wished to leave the university and hoped to work. The counselor and Martin discussed again the implications of the information, and Martin decided to accept a job offered by the owner of a neighboring nursery. This employer had been favorably impressed by Martin's friendliness, serious attitude, and common sense. The counselor assisted Martin in selecting adult education courses that would help to prepare him for advancement in this work, and later reports showed satisfactory progress both in his job and in his courses.

Almost all of the information collected was used during counseling. The counselor and Martin both considered test scores, work history, family background, high school experiences, reports from the high school counselor, and scores on achievement, special aptitude, and vocational interest tests. Without the other information, the scores on the academic aptitude tests could have been used only in a negative way. Martin could have been told or warned that his probability for success in the university was small. The other information, however, allowed the counselor to approach the problem more constructively and to help reduce future frustration and disappointment.

Other pupils similar to Martin may wish to embark on courses of action which, according to all the counselor's information, will lead to failure. The counselor's function is not necessarily to prevent the pupil from taking a particular road, but rather to help the pupil become aware of more promising alternatives in case the road selected does lead to failure. One of the most important jobs of the counselor is to help the pupil realize that being unable to meet certain requirements does not necessarily mean the pupil is a failure; rather, it may mean that the pupil has tried one alternative to learn if it is the correct one, and having discovered that it is not, he has succeeded in learning that some other alternative should be chosen.

THE CASE OF MARIETTA

Marietta was a junior when she saw her school counselor. The counselor knew that Marietta came from a large family living on a farm, that she was quiet, submissive, and shy, and that in school she had never shown any outstanding academic promise. She was not active in extra-curricular affairs and according to her classroom teachers, had not done well in classes. The counselor invited Marietta to her office to discuss her plans. Marietta said that she had not done well in school and that she did not have the ability to do better. She planned to work as a telephone operator for a while after graduation from high school and hoped then to be married.

Marietta had been tested in the statewide testing program, and the report to her high school indicated that she had a percentile rank of 70 on the American Council on Education Psychological Examination, using norms which compared her with entering college freshmen. Her scores on the Cooperative English Test, Form Z, lower level, were a percentile rank of 10 on Mechanics of Expression and 11 on Effectiveness of Expression, with a first percentile rank on total English score. The English norms also were based on entering college freshmen. The other test data available to the counselor described a girl of below-average ability who had never performed well on tests.

When the counselor reviewed Marietta's case, she wondered if an error could have been made by the statewide testing agency in reporting her college aptitude score to the school. She wisely wrote to the director of the agency, called Marietta's scores to his attention, and asked that they be checked. A check in the central files indicated that the ACE percentile rank should have been reported as 1, rather than 70; the Mechanics of Expression percentile rank on the English test should have been reported as 7, instead of 10; and the Effectiveness of Expression percentile rank should have been 1, instead of the 11 that was reported. The original percentile rank on the total English test was correct.

The counselor's treatment of Marietta's case illustrates well the care with which a counselor should review all available information, especially when one or two items of data are incongruent with other data.

Tests must be administered to students by counselors who are human and who are subject to human error in spite of all the effort made to reduce these errors to a minimum. Tests are processed and prepared for scoring by persons similarly prone to error. Many times tests are scored and reports are prepared by IBM machines and other electrical equipment. In spite of the efficiency of IBM machines and modern scoring devices, none are yet 100 per cent accurate, and no system has ever been devised which allows all errors to be detected and corrected before scores are reported to counselors. Consequently, the counselor must look at every test score, just as he looks at all other information, with a small question mark and realize that error possibly may explain some of the information at hand.

USING INFORMATION IN PLANNING

The following case of two brothers, who in many ways were different from each other, illustrates how information is used in counseling high school students. One of these brothers most likely will attend college after he graduates from high school; the other may attend college, but is equally likely to obtain post-high school training some place other than in college. The boys have different abilities and different expressed interests, and perhaps different measured interests, different aptitudes, and different backgrounds of information. To work effectively with these boys, their counselors and teachers must have information about them continually through high school.

The Nestor boys were students in a small city high school and were sons of an insurance salesman who himself had graduated from that school. Donald, seventeen years old, was in the twelfth grade and was planning to attend college, while Lloyd, fifteen years of age, was quite undecided about his plans, but expressed more interest in activities involving mechanical apparatus than in academic pursuits.

When Donald was in the eleventh grade, he had been inspired to become an engineer, influenced in part by advice given to him by a local industrialist during a "college and career day." His only work experience, which he had enjoyed, had been in selling, and he had no experience even indirectly related to engineering. His school grades had been evenly divided between A's and B's with the exception of four grades of B, D, D, and C in mathematics. The test scores for the two boys are presented in Figures 9.5 to 9.7.

Instead of discouraging Donald from seriously considering engineering, his school counselor called to his attention other occupations that would allow him to use his abilities to his best advantage. In the twelfth grade the counselor spoke with him several times, twice with Donald and his parents together. The outcome was that Donald decided engineering was inappropriate and that he should enter college and take a two-year general course. During that time he could decide if he should subsequently take a college or university course in business administration or if he should leave college at the end of two years and obtain his occupational training on the job, perhaps in something related to selling.

At this time Lloyd was too young to approach a definite decision, but in light of his expressed interest, the counselor helped Lloyd and his

FIGURE 9.5
DONALD'S TEST PROFILE
UNIVERSITY OF MINNESOTA
Office of the Dean of Students
Student Counseling Bureau
Summary Profile

Name: Nestor, Donald   Class: Senior   Sex: Male   Age: 17

Date	Name of test	Percentile	Norm group
3/49	American Council on Education Psychological Examination (high school edition)	89	High school: 9th grade
1/52	American Council on Education Psychological Examination (college edition)	83	Minnesota college freshmen
3/49	Differential Aptitude Test		High school:
	Verbal..........................	89	9th grade
	Numerical.......................	50	9th grade
	Abstract........................	45	9th grade
	Spatial.........................	38	9th grade
	Mechanical......................	38	9th grade
	Clerical........................	21	9th grade
	Spelling........................	75	9th grade
	Sentence........................	92	9th grade
3/49	Cooperative Mathematics..............	50	9th grade
3/49	Cooperative Social Studies.............	93	9th grade
3/49	Cooperative Natural Sciences...........	91	9th grade
3/49	Cooperative English		
	Mechanics.......................	90	9th grade
	Effectiveness.....................	94	9th grade
	Reading Comprehension.............	91	9th grade
1/52	Cooperative English—Total............	90	Minnesota college freshmen

parents plan how he could take advantage of every opportunity that might provide additional experience in mechanical and related work. The counselor also worked with Lloyd and his English teacher to improve his reading skills.

When pupils enter high school, they have to choose the general direction in which they will go. Will they take the academic road leading toward college, the road leading toward trade schools and apprenticeship training, the road leading directly toward employment, or the road lead-

FIGURE 9.6
DONALD'S INTEREST PROFILE
STRONG VOCATIONAL INTEREST BLANK—MEN

Name: Nestor, Donald   Age: 17   Date: January, 1952

Group	Occupation	Score
I	Artist....	C+
	Psychologist....	B−
	Architect....	C
	Physician....	C
	Osteopath....	C
	Dentist....	C
	Veterinarian....	C
II	Mathematician....	C
	Physicist....	C
	Engineer....	C
	Chemist....	C
III	Production Manager....	C+
IV	Farmer....	B−
	Aviator....	C+
	Carpenter....	B−
	Printer....	B
	Math Physical Science Teacher....	B−
	Industrial Arts Teacher....	B−
	Vocational Agriculture Teacher....	C+
	Policeman....	C+
	Forest Service Man....	C
V	Y.M.C.A. Physical Director....	A
	Personnel Director....	A
	Public Administrator....	A
	Y.M.C.A. Secretary....	B+
	Social Science High School Teacher....	B+
	City School Superintendent....	B+
	Minister....	B
VI	Musician....	C
VII	C.P.A....	A
VIII	Senior C.P.A....	B
	Accountant....	B−
	Office Man....	B
	Purchasing Agent....	B−
	Banker....	B
	Mortician....	C+
	Pharmacist....	B−
IX	Sales Manager....	A
	Real Estate Salesman....	A
	Life Insurance Salesman....	A
X	Advertising Man....	B−
	Lawyer....	B−
	Author-Journalist....	C+
XI	President—Manufacturing Concern....	B−

Interest Maturity, 50
Occupational Level, 43
Masculinity-Femininity, 52

ing to what, for lack of a better term, might be called a general education? Admittedly, none of these is an unalterable choice, and the choice made at the beginning of the high school period should be regarded as tentative and subject to later change. Nevertheless, the appropriateness of this choice determines in part the efficiency with which a pupil will be able to use his years in high school.

The age at which pupils are ready to make choices varies greatly, and a few pupils are in a position to make definite and permanent decisions

FIGURE 9.7
LLOYD'S TEST PROFILE
UNIVERSITY OF MINNESOTA
Office of the Dean of Students
Student Counseling Bureau
Summary Profile

Name: Nestor, Lloyd   Class: Sophomore   Sex: Male   Age: 15

Date	Name of test	Percentile	Norm group
3/51	American Council on Education Psychological Examination (high school edition)	55	High School: 9th grade
3/51	Differential Aptitude Test		
	Verbal..............................	55	9th grade
	Numerical............................	62	9th grade
	Abstract.............................	48	9th grade
	Spatial..............................	92	9th grade
	Mechanical...........................	95	9th grade
	Clerical.............................	12	9th grade
	Spelling.............................	14	9th grade
	Sentences	21	9th grade
3/51	Cooperative Mathematics.................	48	9th grade
3/51	Cooperative Social Studies...............	53	9th grade
3/51	Cooperative Natural Sciences.............	61	9th grade
3/51	Cooperative English		
	Mechanics............................	22	9th grade
	Effectiveness........................	41	9th grade
	Reading Comprehension................	18	9th grade

while relatively young. On the other hand, many are not ready for these decisions until after they complete high school. Arriving at educational and vocational decisions is a process extending through long periods of time (Super, 1957; Super et al., 1957), and there is no point in time at which it occurs. This means that the planning of pupils' programs must take into account the fact that decisions may change, that room must be left for new plans, and that life programs cannot be mapped rigidly even by the most skillful counselor.

By the time a pupil arrives at a choice point when action must be taken, he and his teachers should have a good idea of what his abilities and aptitudes are, what the general nature of his interests is, and what informational background he has.

CHOICE POINTS

The information we have been discussing is used repeatedly by counselors as they assist pupils in evaluating choice points. A few of these major points are of a kind that occur only once or only a few times. Other choice points occur repeatedly. For instance, specific courses must be considered and evaluated repeatedly in terms of pupil attitude and interest and chosen accordingly. Sometimes decisions must be made regarding the assignment of students to sections of courses, and when students are classified according to aptitude and achievement backgrounds, decisions again must be made.

Every week and perhaps every day the teacher will make and help the pupil make decisions that should depend on the information we are discussing. Class assignments and projects will be selected on the basis of the information about the pupil. Methods of motivating pupils will be selected more efficiently if the pupil's own interests and aptitudes are considered. Remedial measures can be provided for pupils who are retarded in specific areas or deficient in basic skills. The effectiveness of any attempt to individualize classroom instruction and high school planning depends on the use of objective and reliable information about individuals.

Choice points often appear outside the classroom. High school counselors and teachers help pupils select cocurricular activities appropriate in terms of interest, personality, and aptitudes. Some pupils who have meager musical backgrounds can be encouraged to participate in musical activities, not with the hope that they will become star performers, but rather in order to enrich their own backgrounds so that they can derive greater satisfaction from life. Other pupils with just as meager backgrounds but perhaps with inadequate musical aptitude will be encouraged to participate in other kinds of activities, because for these pupils music may be far too great a failure experience.

Some pupils begin to make their post-high school plans as early as the ninth grade and even before that, but most delay definite planning until the beginning of the twelfth grade. Some evidence suggests that for some students plans made early are more valid than plans made late (Dyer, 1939), but many high school pupils simply are not mature enough to make plans before the twelfth grade. Regardless of when these plans are made, however, the more information considered, the more realistic and appropriate they will be. The student projecting himself into the future and thinking of marriage, of occupations, or of community responsibilities should know his own strengths and limitations if such plans are not to eventuate in frustration.

One of the major purposes of collecting and providing the kind of information we have discussed is to help the student know himself.

QUESTIONS FOR STUDY

1. Speculate on the case of Martin if all the basic data were essentially the same as described, except his Kuhlmann-Anderson IQ was 114, his abstract reasoning percentile score 87, and a Wechsler IQ 121.
2. What special problems are related to the use of a personality inventory in a school testing program?
3. Discuss the advantages and disadvantages of using a vocational interest inventory in grade 9; in grade 12.
4. What errors are likely in making inferences about a pupil on the basis of knowledge about his family, his church, his neighborhood?
5. A pupil consistently achieves at a higher level than one would predict from scores on repeated ability tests. Does this mean the pupil is working too hard, standards are too low, the tests are invalid?

REFERENCES

Bingham, W. V., & Freyd, M. *Procedures in employment psychology.* New York: McGraw-Hill, 1926.

Darley, J. G. Tested maladjustment related to clinically diagnosed maladjustment. *J. appl. Psychol.,* 1937, **21,** 632–642.

Dyer, D. T. The relation between vocational interests of men in college and their subsequent occupational histories for ten years. *J. appl. Psychol.,* 1939, **23,** 283.

Johnston, J. B. *Who should go to college?* Minneapolis: University of Minnesota Press, 1930.

Lindquist, E. F. *Educational measurement.* Washington, D.C.: American Council on Education, 1951.

Meehl, P. E. *Clinical versus statistical prediction.* Minneapolis: University of Minnesota Press, 1954.

Meehl, P. E., & Rosen, A. Antecedent probability and the efficiency of psychometric signs, patterns or cutting scores. *Psychol. Bull.,* 1955, **52,** 194–216.

Remmers, H. H., & Gage, N. L. *Educational measurement and evaluation.* (Rev. ed.) New York: Harper & Row, 1955.

Ross, C. C. *Measurement in today's school.* (3rd ed., rev. by J. C. Stanley) Englewood Cliffs, N.J.: Prentice-Hall, 1954.

Sarbin, T. R. The logic of prediction in psychology. *Psychol. Rev.,* 1944, **51,** 210–228.

Super, D. E. Vocational development: the process of compromise or synthesis. *J. counsel. Psychol.,* 1956, **3,** 249–253.

Super, D. E. *The psychology of careers: an introduction to vocational development.* New York: Harper & Row, 1957.

Super, D. E., et al. *Vocational development: a framework for research.* New York: Teachers Coll., Columbia University, Bureau of Publications, 1957.

Swanson, E. O., Mervin, J. C., and Berdie, R. F. Expectancy tables for freshmen entering Minnesota colleges, *Res. Bull. Office of the Dean of Students,* 1961, **3** (2), 1–35.

Wesman, A. G. Expectancy tables—a way of interpreting test validity. *Test Serv. Bull.* New York: Psychological Corporation, 1949, **38,** 11–15.

CHAPTER 10

Learning about Occupational and Educational Opportunities

A knowledge of the educational and occupational opportunities available to the high school graduate is a prime requisite for the effective high school counselor. Young people, understandably, have but limited knowledge about the world of work and the requirements and characteristics of the vast number of jobs in which persons are gainfully employed. Moreover, youth is influenced by the traditions of our culture, such as the value of adhering to the white-collar job, the stereotype of occupations, the social-status hierarchy of jobs, and the belief that with hard work and persistence anyone can achieve his chosen goal. Lack of information about jobs, worker characteristics, and the fluid and dynamic nature of the marketplace, as well as about training and other educational opportunities, results all too frequently in occupational and educational maladjustment. The high school pupil, then, must be assisted, encouraged, and counseled to obtain better understanding, not only of himself, but also of the facets which make up the world of work.

Although some pupils may by accident or fortuitous circumstances choose and enter an appropriate and satisfying occupation, most pupils, in order to ensure a greater certainty of occupational success, require a more rational and realistic approach based on accurate information about occupations.

THE CASE OF JIM

Jim is a seventeen-year-old high school senior in a large metropolitan school system. He has taken courses in English, social studies, mathematics, science, and shop. His grades have been average except in shop courses, in which he has consistently earned A's and B's. The cumulative record in the counselor's office shows that Jim is considered by his teachers to be a quiet, conscientious pupil, well liked by his peers, and a good citizen. The shop instructor remarks in an anecdotal entry that Jim not only has developed an interest in radio and other similar technical fields, but also has demonstrated a facility and competence unusual for a person of his limited experience.

The results of the school's testing program, which have been posted in Jim's cumulative record, show that in comparison with his high school peers, he has an understanding of the subject matter areas better than one might expect from a C pupil. Scholastic ability test scores indicate that he is in the upper 15 per cent when compared to his classmates. A test of differential aptitudes bears out the shop teacher's impression that Jim has unusual ability, for the results reveal that he is in the upper 5 per cent in mechanical comprehension, spatial relations, and abstract reasoning.

The interest inventory shows that Jim's interests are similar to those of men successfully engaged in the physical sciences, such as engineering, physics, chemistry, and mathematics, and to those of men successfully engaged in technical work—carpenters, mathematics and physical science teachers, industrial arts teachers, and men in forest service. The cumulative record also shows that Jim's father graduated from the eighth grade and is employed as a semiskilled laborer. Jim's mother graduated from high school, and except for a few years of work as a clerk prior to her marriage and some occasional part-time work at department stores as extra help during sales, has been a full-time housewife and mother.

Granted that there is additional relevant information concerning Jim available to and known by the counselor; we have sketched only enough to be able to raise some pertinent questions. Where does Jim go after high school? Should he enter college or a technical school for further education? Should he enlist in the military services, applying for one of their specific training programs? Should he go directly into the job market, and if so, what kinds of jobs does he apply for, where are these available, and what kind of a future do they offer him? These questions must be considered and answered by each "Jim" as he decides what his future holds for him.

Every counselor, then, must have in addition to his understanding of human behavior, abilities, aptitudes, interests, and values, an understanding of the educational and occupational world. The Dictionary of Occupational Titles (U.S. Government Printing Office, 1949), published by the United States Employment Service, identifies more than 20,000 defined jobs and lists some 40,000 job titles.

OCCUPATIONAL INFORMATION

No counselor, regardless of how experienced he is, will possess accurate, current knowledge of the requirements, availability, status, remuneration, and other relevant characteristics of each one in the vast array of occupations. Counselors, however, can and must have knowledge about the organization and structure of the job world and about sources of occupational information. They also must have the ability to aid the pupil in translating occupational information into meaningful understandings for himself.

Where does the counselor look for occupational information? This question has no simple answer, for the sources are numerous and even bewildering in their array. Books, pamphlets, magazine articles, and films published by public, private, and professional agencies contribute to the large body of available occupational information material. These materials vary in their content, some describing the basic structure of jobs and job classification, others describing a particular occupation, and still others giving information about a constellation or group of related occupations. Some of these materials are available free on request; others need to be purchased. Some the counselor will find easily, whereas others he will have to discover through his own resourcefulness. The occupational materials differ in treatment, readability, currency, style, and format. Thus, as the counselor gains acquaintance with occupational information, he will be called upon to judge the quality of the material he wishes to use with his pupils. A useful guide to effective evaluation is contained in the report entitled "Standards for Use in Preparing and Evaluating Occupational Literature" (1950) prepared by the Publications Committee of the Occupational Research Division of the National Vocational Guidance Association.

If occupational information materials are to be useful to the pupil, they must be easily available to him. Whether these materials are kept in the school library, in a special reading room, or elsewhere, they must be organized and filed so that any student can find without difficulty the information he is seeking. Moreover, the organizational plan or file must have flexibility to permit the integration of new materials without disruption, and the arrangement itself should help make the materials inviting and appealing to pupils. Many schools arrange their libraries of pamphlets and leaflets in an alphabetical file, so that students can more easily locate the material. Other schools have adopted or adapted the filing system plans offered by commercial publishing companies. The authors of this text prefer a filing system based on the Dictionary of Occupational Titles, believing that the inconvenience of having to use an index to locate material is outweighed by the pupil's gain in knowledge of the broad classification of occupations.

WHAT HAPPENS TO HIGH SCHOOL PUPILS?

The counselor must know about educational and training facilities and job opportunities, but equally important is knowledge about what happens to his pupils when they leave school. The need for comprehensive and accurate information about pupils in school has been repeatedly stressed (Conant, 1959), but just as important for evaluating the objectives, policies, and counseling of a school is knowledge about the adult activities of the alumni.

As an example, a school in a suburban community had for several generations been sending a large proportion of its graduates to college. Only a few graduates went to work immediately after leaving school, and even fewer went to industrial and trade schools. As the community became older, it became more industrialized, and this resulted in a change in the student population and a shift in the post-high school careers of its graduates. Whereas 60 to 70 per cent of the graduates previously had gone to college, later only 30 to 40 per cent did. Almost a third of the graduates were planning to take further training in industrial schools, and another third were planning to seek jobs immediately after graduation. Information obtained from a series of follow-up studies of graduates revealed to the school the need for continuing study of its traditional college preparatory emphasis and suggested that the staff must revise old and develop new programs to meet the needs of new generations of students.

School counselors are the persons most immediately concerned with the educational and vocational plans of pupils, and frequently they are asked to provide to school administrators and teachers information about the school's graduates. The questions about the status of the alumni vary, but usually at least four categories of questions must be answered if a school is to know about the life for which it is preparing its pupils.

The first category pertains to the general status of the body of graduates. How many are employed and in what jobs, how many are obtaining advanced training and education and in what programs and schools, how many are married and what is their familial status, how have they met their military obligations, how have they contributed to the community at large, and what are their attitudes toward and comments about school? These general questions lead to broad descriptions of the graduates that have direct relevance for the kind of school the community needs.

In addition to knowing what happens to the total group of high school graduates, we are interested in information about specific subgroups. For example, what happens to the boys as compared to the girls, what happens to pupils coming from rural areas as compared to those coming from urban areas, what happens to pupils coming from different socio-economic levels, what happens to pupils at different ability levels?

We also are concerned with the question of predicting post-high school behavior, and this immediately raises the question as to how this behavior of graduates is related to other variables. For example, what are the relationships between scores earned on academic ability tests and college attendance, between scores on the Strong Vocational Interest Blank and occupational criteria, between vocational interests expressed in the ninth grade and later occupational criteria, between extracurricular activity participation in high school and activity records in college and in the community?

Once we have learned as much as we can about the behaviors most typical of pupils from certain groups and obtained information about relationships between this behavior and other variables, then we, as counselors, are in a position to make predictions as to probable outcomes for individual students and to assist pupils and their families if they wish to alter these probabilities.

The final question pertains to the relationship between the knowledge we have acquired about the behavior of our graduates and the broad needs of society. The social responsibilities of the school and the counselor, particularly as these pertain to society's manpower needs, require that society in general be kept informed as to how well the schools are meeting its needs. When the country, through its employers, its military organizations, and its other governmental units, expresses a need for thousands of engineers or nurses or teachers, and these needs are not being met, then the schools and other agencies together must see what can be done to meet these needs either by increasing the supply or altering the demand through better use of the available supply (Berdie, 1960).

PLANNING AND CONDUCTING FOLLOW-UP STUDIES

Some of the questions above can be answered in part by references to information collected by various social agencies. For example, census data every ten years provide information concerning the general educational level of the community, and analyses of these data are presented by sex, by states, and by other categories. State and professional licensing and certifying boards frequently can provide information concerning the numbers of persons entering various occupations and estimates concerning the future needs in these occupations. Much of this type of information is presented periodically in government publications, particularly those issued by the U.S. Bureau of the Census (*Statistical Abstract of the United States*), and in newspapers and news magazines.

Most schools, however, find that if they are to obtain all of the information they wish in the form in which it is helpful, they must plan and conduct their own investigations in order to learn what their graduates are doing. The collection of information about graduates usually is called a "follow-up" study. Procedures for planning and conducting such a study are worth careful review (California State Department of Education, 1950).

Some suggested steps in planning and conducting a follow-up study of high school students can be listed.

1. Discuss with the administrative staff of the school the needs for a follow-up study and the general types of information such a study can provide.

2. Discuss with counselors, teachers, and administrators the specific purposes of the study and the information that would help the school.

3. Select from the above group of persons a smaller working group to formulate specific objectives for the study and to prepare a working proposal.

4. Review these objectives and proposals with the entire school staff to obtain suggestions and support.

5. Prepare formats of the tables designed to present the information relevant to the questions underlying the purpose of the study.

Once the planning has advanced through step 5, use the services of a statistician and a research expert for steps 6, 7, and 8. Development of an accurate and efficient questionnaire or data sheet is a highly specialized business. Poor wording or poor arrangement of the questions may actually make the data collected unreliable and invalid. It is possible to build certain checks on reliability and validity right into the questionnaire itself. Even though a questionnaire is well constructed in terms of reliability and validity, it may be poorly organized, and much time and money may be spent needlessly in summarizing the data. Frequently much precoding of questions is possible. When it is desirable to analyze the data on automatic data-processing equipment, there are many ways of facilitating this process. The specialist can help decide if use of data-processing equipment is feasible and adapt the questionnaire to the appropriate format.

Since mailing, collecting, and analyzing the questionnaires are likely to be an expensive process, it may be highly desirable to obtain only a sample of the graduated seniors. In this case the services of a good statistician are indispensable. He can help decide how large a sample is needed and can specify the percentages of different groups that need to be in the sample. It is well known, for instance, that persons with more education are more responsive to questionnaires. For example, if 80 per cent of those who went to college and only 50 per cent of those who had no further education after high school return the questionnaire, conclusions drawn about the data will be spurious and any plans based on the findings might be misdirected.

6. In consideration of the above steps, design the instrument for obtaining information from students, parents, employers, and other sources.

UNIVERSITY OF MINNESOTA
OFFICE OF THE DEAN OF STUDENTS
STUDENT COUNSELING BUREAU

H.S._____1-3

Ident. No._____4-6

Four Years After High School
For High School Graduates of 1950

In order to provide information about the activities of high school students during the years following graduation, you are being asked to answer the questions below. Your answers will be handled in confidence.

Directions: Write in the answer or place a (√) after the appropriate word or phrase.

Name (print) _____
            Last   First   Middle

Present Address:_____
            Number   Street   Post Office (City and Zone)   State

Address at which you can always be reached:_____
                              Number   Street   Post Office (City and Zone)   State

7. Your marital status: Single____(0) Engaged to be married____(1) Married____(2) Divorced____(3) Widowed____(4).

8. Number of children: 0____, 1____, 2____, 3____, 4____

9-10. If you are married what is occupation of your husband or wife?_____

11-17. Schools attended since graduating from high school. Include all schools attended.

Check (√) the kind of school and amount of time attended and write in the name of the school.

Kind of School	Name of School	Less Than 1 yr.	1 yr. to 2 yrs.	2 yrs. to 3 yrs.	More Than 3 yrs.
None					
11. Trade School		(1)____	(2)____	(3)____	(4)____
12. Business School		(1)____	(2)____	(3)____	(4)____
13. Nursing		(1)____	(2)____	(3)____	(4)____
14. Teacher's College		(1)____	(2)____	(3)____	(4)____
15. Junior College		(1)____	(2)____	(3)____	(4)____
16. College or University		(1)____	(2)____	(3)____	(4)____
17. Other (specify)		(1)____	(2)____	(3)____	(4)____

18-19. Nature of training (mechanic, law, nursing, stenographic, etc.) _____

20-21. What is your present principal occupation (typist, college student, housewife, farmer, army, etc.)_____

22. Period of time so occupied: From_____ to_____
                                    year   year

If you are **not** a student or housewife, briefly describe your duties, telling exactly what you do:

_____

_____

_____

23. What is your present earned income? If you are paid by the hour, check your hourly wage; if you are paid by the month, check your average monthly wage or income.

Hourly Wage
(0)____less than $1 an hour
(1)____$1.00 to $1.49 an hour
(2)____$1.50 to $1.99 an hour
(3)____$2.00 to $2.49 an hour
(4)____$2.50 to $2.99 an hour
(5)____over $3.00 an hour

Monthly Wage
(0)____less than $170 a month
(1)____$170 to $259 a month
(2)____$260 to $345 a month
(3)____$346 to $432 a month
(4)____$433 to $519 a month
(5)____over $520 a month

24-32. Occupational Experience: Please list all principal full-time jobs you have held since high school graduation. List most recent first. If you have served a company in more than one capacity make separate entries.

From Mo. & Year	To Mo. & Year	Company	Job title and brief description of work performed	Reason why you took this job
____	____	_____	_____	_____
____	____	_____	_____	_____
____	____	_____	_____	_____
____	____	_____	_____	_____
____	____	_____	_____	_____

About one-third of high school graduates in Minnesota attend college.

33-47. If you did not go to college what were your main reasons for not going?

Check those which apply.

33. _____Preferred other type training to regular college.
34. _____Was not interested in school work; didn't like school.
35. _____Wanted to go to work right away.
36. _____Parents, relatives, or friends discouraged me from college.
37. _____I was needed to help at home.
38. _____My family couldn't give me any financial assistance.
39. _____Wanted to make money quickly.
40. _____Took job which went so well I didn't want to leave it.
41. _____Felt I could do all right financially without college education.
42. _____Had to enter military service.
43. _____Felt I didn't have ability for college work.
44. _____No college was near enough to make it worth while.
45. _____The work I wished to do did not require college preparation.
46. _____Planned early marriage.
47. _____Other (Specify)_____

48-59. If you did attend college, what were your main reasons for attending?

Check those which apply to you.

48. To prepare for a vocation _____ _____
49. To be with old school friends_____ _____
50. To get a liberal education _____ _____
51. To please parents or friends_____ _____
52. To be independent _____ _____
53. To make friends and helpful connections_____ _____
54. It was the "thing to do"_____ _____

55. Foregone conclusion, never questioned why___ _____
56. Would enable me to make more money_____ _____
57. "Everyone here" went_____ _____
58. Liked school _____ _____
59. Other (Specify) _____

_____
_____

60-69. **Whether or not** you went to college, check the persons below who encouraged you to go to college:

60. _____Parents
61. _____H.S. Teachers
62. _____Brothers and Sisters
63. _____Other Relatives
64. _____H.S. Principal

65. _____H.S. or College Counselor
66. _____Pastor, Priest, or Rabbi
67. _____Friends
68. _____Others (write in)_____

In order to indicate how satisfied you are in your **present** occupation, or with your status as student or housewife, please check the appropriate answer to each of the following four questions.

69. Choose the **one** of the following statements which best tells how well you like your present occupation or present status:

(1) _____I hate it.
(2) _____I dislike it.
(3) _____I don't like it.
(4) _____I am indifferent to it.

(5) _____I like it.
(6) _____I am enthusiastic about it.
(7) _____I like it better than I could possibly like anything else.

70. Check **one** of the following to show how you think you compare with other people:

(7) _____No one likes his occupation better than I like mine.
(6) _____I like my occupation much better than most people like theirs.
(5) _____I like my occupation better than most people like theirs.
(4) _____I like my occupation about as well as most people like theirs.
(3) _____I dislike my occupation more than most people dislike theirs.
(2) _____I dislike my occupation much more than most people dislike theirs.
(1) _____No one dislikes his occupation more than I dislike mine.

71. Check **one** of the following to show how much of the time you feel satisfied with your occupation or status:

(7) _____All of the time.
(6) _____Most of the time.
(5) _____A good deal of the time.
(4) _____About half of the time.

(3) _____Occasionally.
(2) _____Seldom.
(1) _____Never.

72. Check the **one** of the following which best tells how you feel about your occupation or status:

(1) _____I would change my occupation at once if I had anything else to which I could change.
(2) _____I would change to almost any other occupation which was practical.
(3) _____I would like to change my occupation.
(4) _____I would like to change my occupation for another somewhat similar to it.
(5) _____I am not eager to change my occupation but I would do so if it were more practical.
(6) _____I can not think of any occupation for which I would exchange mine.
(7) _____I would not exchange my occupation for any other.

80. (1)

7-24.   If other than a housewife, check the reasons for undertaking your present occupation or course of study. (Check as many as apply to you.)

7. To prepare for a vocation................................ _____
8. To be with old school friends....................... _____
9. To get a liberal education............................... _____
10. To start making money quickly..................... _____
11. To please parents or friends........................ _____
12. To be independent.. _____
13. To make friends and helpful connections..... _____
14. Advised by parents....................................... _____
15. Advised by counselors................................. _____
16. Advised by teachers..................................... _____

17. It was the "thing to do"............................. _____
18. Foregone conclusion, never questioned why _____
19. Would enable me to make more
money eventually _____
20. "Everyone here" did this .... _____
21. Tired of studying, had enough education ..... _____
22. Only thing I could afford to do .... _____
23. Like school .... _____
24. Other (write in)_____

25-26.   In what occupation do you think you will most probably be working ten years from now? Naturally you won't know for sure but make the best guess you can.

27.   If you are not now attending school, are you planning to attend school within the next three years? yes____, no____(o) If yes to question 27, what kind of school?

Trade School .. ___ ___ ____(1)   Nurses School .. _ _ _ ____(3)   Junior College   ____(5)
Business School ... _ ____(2)   Teacher's College _____(4)   Other (specify) _____
College or University ____(6)   if yes, what course will you take?_____

28-29.   If yes to question 27, what are your reasons for planning to attend school?

How will you finance this education?_____

If you already have attended college, how did you pay your expenses?

		Check proportion of total expenses				
		0-20%	21-40%	41-60%	61-80%	81-100%
30.	Parents or other members of family including wife or husband	____(0)	____(1)	____(2)	____(3)	____(4)
31.	Worked and earned money while attending college and during summers	____(0)	____(1)	____(2)	____(3)	____(4)
32.	My own funds saved prior to beginning college	____(0)	____(1)	____(2)	____(3)	____(4)
33.	Borrowed funds (loans)	____(0)	____(1)	____(2)	____(3)	____(4)
34.	Scholarships	____(0)	____(1)	____(2)	____(3)	____(4)
35.	Veterans benefit	____(0)	____(1)	____(2)	____(3)	____(4)
36.	Other _____ (specify)	____(0)	____(1)	____(2)	____(3)	____(4)

Military Service (to be answered by men only)

37.   What is your present status with respect to the armed service requirement?
(0)____Now in active service.
(1)____Have completed armed service requirements.

If you checked (1) above, are you maintaining active reserve status? yes____, no____

If you are not now or have not been in active military service, check one of the following.
(2)____Am attending school and am deferred by Selective Service Examination or grades.
(3)____Am attending school, am in Army or Air Force R.O.T.C.
(4)____Am attending school under Holloway Plan or Naval R.O.T.C.
(5)____Have been in active reserve training from age 18, am exempt from draft.
(6)____Am exempt from service requirements (dependents, essential occupation, C.O., etc.)
(7)____Not eligible for military service.

38.   Under which of the armed forces did you serve?

(0)____Army   (3)____Marines
(1)____Air Force   (4)____Coast Guard
(2)____Navy

39-40.   What special training did you receive besides basic training? (describe briefly)

41-42.   What type of work did you do in the service?_____

43.   Satisfaction with the active service. Satisfied____(0); neutral____(1); dissatisfied____(2).

44-57. What school, community, or other activities have you engaged in since leaving high school? (Check those which apply)
44. Veteran's organizations (e.g., American Legion, VFW)................................ _____
45. YMCA or YWCA... _____
46. Political organizations (DFL, GOP, etc.)... _____
47. Fraternal organizations (e.g., Masons, Elks, etc.)................................... _____
48. Neighborhood or other social groups, such as card playing groups .... _____
49. Church attendance .... _____
50. Church organizations .... _____
51. Study club .... _____
52. Sportsmen club or athletic organization.. _____
53. Fraternities or sororities .... _____
54. Charitable drives as a participant (e.g., Community Chest, Heart Fund, March of Dimes) .... _____
55. Volunteer service work (Big Brothers, 4-H Leader, Gray Ladies, etc.).......... _____
56. Trade or professional organizations (including labor union) .... _____
57. Other _____ _____
            (specify)
58. What offices or chairmanships have you held in any of these organizations?

Office	Organization
_____	_____
_____	_____
_____	_____

80. (2)   Identity No_____1-6

What magazines do you read regularly?
_____ 7. American
_____ 8. American Family
_____ 9. Argosy
_____ 10. Atlantic Monthly
_____ 11. Better Homes and Gardens
_____ 12. Capper's Farmer
_____ 13. Collier's
_____ 14. Coronet
_____ 15. Cosmopolitan
_____ 16. Country Gentlemen
_____ 17. Esquire
_____ 18. The Farmer
_____ 19. Farm Journal
_____ 20. Farmer's Union Herald
_____ 21. Fortune
_____ 22. Good Housekeeping
_____ 23. Harper's
_____ 24. Holiday
_____ 25. Hoard's Dairyman

_____ 26. Household
_____ 27. Life
_____ 28. Look
_____ 29. National Geographic
_____ 30. Nation's Agriculture
_____ 31. New Yorker
_____ 32. Newsweek
_____ 33. Pathfinder (Town Journal)
_____ 34. Popular Mechanics
_____ 35. Popular Science
_____ 36. Reader's Digest
_____ 37. Redbook
_____ 38. Saturday Evening Post
_____ 39. Successful Farming
_____ 40. Time
_____ 41. True
_____ 42. U. S. News
_____ 43. Wallace's Farmer
_____ 44. Other _____

45. Number of books (not school texts) read during the past six months?
0-3_____(0), 4-7_____(1), 8-11_____(2), 12-15_____(3), 16-19_____(4), 20 or more_____(5).
If you had the past four years of your life to live over again, what would you have done differently? Check those which apply.

46. _____gone into another kind of work.
47. _____gone to work for another employer.
48. _____gone into business for myself (or farm for myself).
49. _____gone to school other than college.
50. _____gone to college.
51. _____gone to a college other than the one to which I went.

52. _____taken another course of study in school.
53. _____lived in another section of the country.
54. _____moved out of the city.
55. _____moved to a city.
56. _____other (write in)_____

57-62. Apart from your major activity as an employed person, a student, or a housewife, what are your chief leisure time activities? Consider here the one or two things which you do in your spare time which take up the most time and effort. This could be political or religious work, leading a scout troop, a hobby such as metal craft or sewing, a sport such as hunting or golfing; it could be such things as simply movie going, reading, watching television, or listening to radio or records. List only those things which take up a considerable amount of your time. List your most important leisure time activity first:

1. _____
   (most important leisure time activity)

2. _____

3. _____

4. _____

80. (3)

This will involve the development of questionnaires and interview schedules and the preparation of such things as accompanying letters and news releases.

7. Select the sample from which the information is to be obtained. This sample may include all graduating pupils from specified years, pupils selected at random from these classes, or certain groups of pupils, including those who dropped out of school and those who remained.

8. Decide in advance the minimally acceptable return to be used in the study. Very few questionnaire or interview studies obtain 100 per cent response, but every attempt should be made to approach that number as closely as possible. If one obtains only a 30 per cent response after much effort, he is hardly justified in basing conclusions on that return because of possible biased response. Consequently, before the information is collected, the decision should be made that unless the response reaches a specified size, conclusions will not be drawn from the study.

9. Make sure the data returned are tabulated accurately and that all calculations and computations are carefully verified.

10. Review the preliminary results and conclusions with the advisory group and the members of the staff before preparing a final report, in order to incorporate their suggestions and comments into the report.

11. Develop with the advisory committee and members of the staff the most profitable ways for exploiting the information to achieve the most educational value and the best public relations value for the school and the counseling program.

As an example of the types of materials used in obtaining information, The figure on pp. 152–155 presents a questionnaire used in one study of high school graduates followed up four years after graduation.

Below, as another example, is a sample letter used to accompany follow-up questionnaires in another study.

Mr. John H. Jones
1000 Center Street
Oakland, California

Dear John:

Your high school is interested in knowing what you have been doing since you left school. We feel that through your experience we may be able to improve our programs so as to better meet the needs of the boys and girls still in school.

Will you please assist us by filling out and returning the enclosed questionnaire. The greater the number of responses, the greater will be the value of this survey. Your name will not be used in connection with your answers. The information furnished by you and your classmates will be used for statistical purposes only. However, if there are any questions which you do not care to answer, just omit them.

You can answer most of the questions very quickly, by means of a check mark or a few words. However, if you have any further comments or suggestions, we would be glad to have you write them in the spaces provided.

An immediate reply would be greatly appreciated.

> Thank you,
>
>> (Signed by school principal, or a counselor or teacher best known by the student.)

Name and address of a relative or friend through whom we can locate you in future years in case you are temporarily among the "missing."

(California State Department of Education, 1950)

INFORMATION FROM FOLLOW-UP STUDIES OF PUPILS

The first comprehensive attempts to obtain information about pupils who have left school were made during the depression of the 1930s, and since that time many follow-up studies have been completed on national, regional, state, and local groups.

The American Youth Commission of the American Council on Education was concerned with the problems of American youth during the depression of the thirties and set the stage for follow-up studies with the publication of its report *How Fare American Youth?* (Rainey, 1937). This report summarized population statistics and reviewed problems that youth face related to jobs, school, health, recreation, home, citizenship, and membership in subclasses such as Negro youth and rural youth.

In 1935 the Board of Regents of the State of New York initiated an inquiry into the character and costs of public education in that state, and this inquiry resulted in the publication of several studies. One comprehensive follow-up study entitled *When Youth Leave School* (Eckert & Marshall, 1938) was designed to obtain information related to the question of how well the secondary school was adjusting its program to the needs of boys and girls on the one hand and to the demands of society on the other. In June, 1936, a comprehensive testing program was administered to about 23,000 boys and girls in 62 high schools, and additional pupils in vocational schools were tested a year later. Information also was obtained from school officers about pupils, both those who remained in and those who had withdrawn from high school. Comparisons were made between students who withdrew prior to graduation and students who graduated.

Results indicated that more boys withdrew prior to graduation than girls, that about 20 per cent of the pupils who withdrew did so almost as soon as the law permitted, that a far smaller proportion of students who withdrew were in the college preparatory curriculum than in other curricula, and that the average student who withdrew had not completed the tenth grade. Students who withdrew prior to the end of their sophomore year in high school had for the most part taken few courses that emphasized useful skills and information, and they had only the most casual orientation to inevitable adult responsibilities. Students who withdrew were found to be less able academically as shown by tests, to come from socially and economically underprivileged homes, to be more often judged as incompetent in assuming duties of vocation or citizenship, and to have unresolved problems of planning later school and work.

This study provided for that era and that state a valuable picture of pupils who remained in and those who left school and suggested many explanations as to why pupils left school and to what extent this was the responsibility of the educational system.

A somewhat similar study (Bell, 1938) conducted for the American Youth Commission was based on information from 13,000 pupils in Maryland. This study showed that educational opportunities were not equally available on the basis of social class in Maryland. One conclusion was that "our present secondary school is still a highly selective institution adapted to the needs of a small minority of our population." The study also revealed a disturbing gap between school and employment; it was estimated that between 40 and 46 per cent of employable youth who had left school failed to obtain full-time employment within one year after leaving school. The study suggested a significant lack of appropriate and adequate vocational training and demonstrated a real need for guidance. The study concluded: "We need, therefore, a comprehensive program which must first of all develop a sociological approach to the problems and find ways of focusing all the efforts which society can make upon the individual youth and his needs. This is the starting point, and no amount of work is going to be of much value unless there is effective co-ordination at the point of operation, which is the individual youth."

Another follow-up study of a national statistical nature was published for the American Youth Commission in 1940, *Matching Youth and Jobs* (Bell, 1940). This study, along with the general report *Youth and the Future* (American Council on Education) published in 1942, provided a comprehensive picture of the status and problems of American youth during the time interval that started with the depression of the 1930s and ended with World War II. The effects of these studies upon American education are impossible to determine, but the information they contained was known by most American educators and undoubtedly influenced their thinking and planning.

One of the most influential follow-up studies relating the functions of the high school and the college was reported in 1938 by Learned and Wood and entitled *The Student and His Knowledge*. This was a report of the results of a comprehensive experimental examination program conducted in the state of Pennsylvania with the support of the Carnegie Foundation in 1928, 1930, and 1932. The authors based their investigation on this assumption:

Education is an exceedingly complex product. It includes every element that contributes to the effective insight and performance of a human being in what should be for him the largest possible field of influence. Certain of these elements may eventually yield to satisfactory measurement. Thus far, however, for only one element are trustworthy comparable measures available, namely, an individual's fabric of ideas—his knowledge, together with certain of his simpler skills.

Comprehensive, objective multiple-response achievement examinations were administered to high school seniors in 1928, to college seniors in the same year, to college sophomores in 1930, and to the latter group again when college seniors in 1932. The contents of the tests included natural science, mathematics, social sciences, languages and literature, both English and foreign, and contemporary Western and non-Western civilization. Pupils were followed during the years after testing, and relationships between test scores and educational progress and occupations were studied.

On the intelligence test, results indicated that of the high school students not going to college, 25 per cent made scores of 52 or higher (an arbitrarily selected score), whereas of the group going to college, more than one-half made scores lower than this. On the English test, 25 per cent of the high school graduates who were not going to college made scores better than the average score of the college-going group, and approximately the same was true on the algebra test. About 25 per cent of the pupils who went to college for at least two years after leaving high school had lower high school ability and achievement test scores than over one-half of those who left high school to go to work. The high school pupils who went to college had higher average scores, but many brilliant young minds were left behind because they could not pay for or were not motivated to attend college.

The study allowed comparisons to be made between high school pupils and college students preparing to become high school teachers. The median score of prospective teachers was 626 on the tests used, but 12 per cent of the high school seniors had scores higher than this. Seven per cent of the prospective teachers made lower scores than 36 per cent of the high school pupils. Thirteen per cent of the high school students scored higher than 44 per cent of the college group.

This study also revealed what were at that time amazing differences among colleges. Three colleges had students who obtained averages below the averages achieved by the high school students who were two years less advanced. Seven colleges had sophomores who obtained higher average scores than the college seniors in the state. Within institutions, variability also was great, and in each institution were found some sophomores who knew more than many seniors and some seniors who knew less than many sophomores.

The many kinds of information obtained in this study and later follow-ups of the same students reinforced the healthy skepticism of many about the validity of judging the extent of an individual's education on the basis of the amount of time spent in school. More forcefully, this study revealed the possibility of obtaining educationally relevant and useful information through broad-scale follow-up studies with particular emphasis on the use of objective and standardized tests.

The pre-World War II studies just described were designed to study weaknesses and strengths of selected aspects of the American educational system. The problems approached were defined in part by the economic conditions of the country during that time and in part by the increasing interest in questions related to educational philosophy. These studies were not designed to provide information particularly useful to the counselor, but even today the methods used and the data obtained have relevance for the counselor contemplating follow-up studies.

Systematic follow-up of school-leaving students has become a routine procedure in many high schools. A follow-up study in St. Cloud, Minnesota on Technical High School graduates class of 1941 is one brief example. The data were collected five years after graduation and were based on 110 questionnaires returned by a total group of 202 graduates. Since only 54 per cent of the graduating class responded, the generalizations which can be based on these data are strictly limited.

Of the 110 men and women respondents, 71 remained in their home community, 8 lived in other states, while the remainder lived in other towns and cities in Minnesota. Thirty-nine of the 54 women were married and had a total of 36 children, and 27 of the 56 men were married with a total of 18 children. Of the group of 75 who had attended school after completing high school, 24 went to a local state teachers college, 9 went to the state university, 10 attended schools of nursing, 8 attended other colleges and universities, 11 attended business colleges, and 13 attended trade schools and institutes. Job distributions of the kinds of jobs held by the entire group were obtained. Information also was obtained concerning the salaries of these former students, their military service, their job satisfaction, the definiteness of their occupational choice, and the date of their most recent occupational choice. Answers were obtained to questions concerning the individual who gave most help in choosing an occupation, the place where most important training was received, the subjects found most helpful in high school, the subjects considered least helpful in high school, and subjects the individual would have liked to but did not take. Several pages of comments made by former students also were included in the report.

This type of report provides to the high school information not only about what its graduates do, but about their attitudes and opinions concerning experiences in school.

THE UTILIZATION OF TALENT

More recent studies broader than those done on a local basis have for the most part been aimed at problems related to the utilization of human talent. The Educational Policies Commission begins its document *Man Power and Education* with this statement:

An inescapable responsibility of a democracy is the unceasing cultivation of individual talents and capabilities—all the abilities of all its people. To that ideal of promoting individual development is today added an unusually pressing need for the ability the nation can muster. The United States now finds itself in a situation in which the fullest possible development and use of all of its resources of trained man power is both more urgent and in some ways more difficult than it has ever been before in time of peace.

With this problem, American education is unavoidably involved and must be profoundly concerned. The fullest possible education of all Americans is the key to meeting man power needs.

With this emphasis, many speeches have been made and reports and articles published urging the community to discover new ways to encourage each youth to obtain the education and training most appropriate for him. Many national groups and organizations have been organized in order to search for solutions to manpower problems, and many educational associations have directed their attention to these problems. Three major follow-up studies will be described which have had as their purpose obtaining information that will enable schools and particularly counselors to help students maximize their education.

Each of these three studies was directed primarily toward the problem of the utilization of talent. Each, however, provided significant information concerning the problems of high school students and the needs which these problems expressed. The three studies were not only follow-up studies, they were also studies of plans and motivations of high school students.

The first study (Berdie, 1954) was started in 1950 to compare the characteristics of Minnesota high school students who did and did not attend college or university. Studies in Minnesota prior to 1940 as well as the everyday experience of teachers and counselors indicated that large proportions of talented students were not continuing their education after high school. This study was designed to obtain information about the motivations or lack of motivations of such students. In January, 1950, each high school in the state was asked to give to each of its graduating seniors a questionnaire which asked for information about their educational and occupational plans, family economic and social backgrounds, and other relevant aspects about the student's history and attitudes. The 25,000 students who completed these questionnaires included practically all of the public and private school graduates of that year. In addition to the data obtained from the questionnaire for each student, information was available about his rank in his high school graduating class, his score on the American Council on Education Psychological Examination, and his score on the Cooperative English Test. A small sample of students was selected, and the parents of these students were interviewed, as were a small sample of students themselves.

One year after high school graduation, a representative sample of these graduates was selected and each person in the sample was sent a questionnaire asking about his current status. In 1954, four years after the original study, a sample of students again was inventoried through the means of a questionnaire to determine the extent and kind of education and training obtained since high school (Corcoran & Keller, 1957).

The results showed that students who planned to attend college and university were more competent as shown by test scores and high school grades than students with other plans, but that a large proportion of similarly competent students had no plans for further education. Plans for further education were related to sex; more metropolitan boys than girls planned to attend college, and more farm girls than boys had such plans. Plans were related to urban-rural source; more city and small town children planned to attend college than did farm children. Plans also were related to social and economic level of the family. When socioeconomic level of the family was analyzed according to the economic resources available to the family as opposed to the social and cultural level of the family, these two conditions were found to have about equal weight in determining whether or not children attended college. In other words, although the financial resources of the family were important in determining the plans of the child, of equal importance was the educational and cultural background of the family.

The one-year follow-up study revealed that about the same proportion of young persons who expressed the intention of attending college actually did so, but that some of the graduates who originally had not planned to attend college did attend and about an equal proportion who originally had such plans did not carry them out. Again, the characteristics related to original plans for attending college tended to be the same characteristics related to the extent to which an individual fulfilled his original plans.

In the 1954 follow-up study, two samples were selected, the first being a stratified random sample of all the 1950 graduates. The 1,327 in this sample who responded included 69 per cent of the persons in the group to whom questionnaires were sent. The second sample included seniors with ACE scores of 120 or higher, placing them in the upper 10 per cent of high school seniors, in the upper 20 to 25 per cent of college freshmen. The 3,173 high-ability students who responded included 90 per cent of the group to whom questionnaires were sent.

In 1950, 50 per cent of the metropolitan men and 40 per cent of the metropolitan women planned to attend college, and one year later 54 per cent of the men and 39 per cent of the women reported they had attended college. In 1954, 62 per cent of the men and 48 per cent of the women reported they had attended college. Of the nonmetropolitan men, 33 per cent originally reported plans to attend college, as compared to 31 per cent of the nonmetropolitan women. In 1951, 34 per cent of the men and 39 per cent of the women reported they had attended college; and in 1954, 37 per cent of the men and 40 per cent of the women reported they had attended college. Thus, of metropolitan men in Minnesota during the first part of the 1950s, nearly two-thirds attended college within four years after high school graduation, and approximately one-half of the women attended college; whereas slightly over one-third of the nonmetropolitan men and 40 per cent of the women attended college. For purposes of comparison, an earlier study in 1938 revealed that 23 per cent of high school graduates attended college.

The results of this study, along with those of previous studies, indicated that the proportion of Minnesota youth attending college immediately after high school increased significantly between 1938 and 1950. The location of a Minnesota high school was found to be significantly related to a pupil's chances of attending college, as was his sex. The plans a pupil expressed during high school were related to college attendance, as was his ability to do college work shown by aptitude test scores and high school achievement. Motivation for attending college depended both on financial resources and family and pupil attitudes; a program to provide financial aid through scholarships and loans would not in and of itself solve the problem of utilizing human talent, unless it were accompanied by efforts to change attitudes toward education and increase motivation to obtain higher education. The results of this study suggested a great need for qualified counselors to work with pupils long before they reached their senior year in high school and for an even greater need for counselors to work with the parents of students as well as with the students themselves.

A comparable study was completed on high school graduates of 1957 from Wisconsin (Little, 1958). Information was obtained from 95 per cent of the graduates, and the analysis reported plans of pupils rather than actual behavior. Of the boys in the upper 20 per cent of their class as shown by academic aptitude tests, 72 per cent had plans to attend college immediately, and an additional 6 per cent had plans for further schooling. Thus, 78 per cent of the superior group as here defined planned to continue their education. Among the upper 10 per cent of the high school graduates, 82 per cent had immediate college plans. Among the girls, 40 per cent of the upper 20 per cent in ability had immediate college plans, but 23 per cent in addition planned some further schooling. Thus, of the superior girls, 63 per cent planned to continue their education.

Of all Wisconsin boys planning to attend college, 27 per cent were in the upper 10 per cent according to scores on the academic aptitude test, 41 per cent were in the upper 20 per cent, 77 per cent were in the upper 50 per cent, and only 5 per cent of those planning to attend college were in the lower 20 per cent. Of the girls, 24 per cent of those planning to attend college were in the upper 10 per cent, 39 per cent in the upper 20 per cent, and 77 per cent in the upper one-half. Again, only 5 per cent of the girls planning to attend college were in the lower 20 per cent of their class in ability.

As was found in other studies, college plans were related to parental occupations. Of the children of parents in professional or executive positions, 64 per cent planned to attend college. Of the children of skilled workers, 27 per cent planned to attend, and only 18 per cent of the children of farmers had plans for higher education.

The percentage of graduates planning to attend college increased with the size of the high school for both boys and girls. This perhaps was more a function of income and education of parental groups than of high school size directly. Again, a direct relationship was found between the pupil's report of his family's economic condition and his plans to attend college. Again, a follow-up study revealed that the proportion of pupils who attended college was the same as the proportion who originally had such plans. The number changing plans in one way balanced the number who changed plans in the other way.

This study also compared the status and progress of students with the college admission requirements in the state university, and the survey concluded:

At best, standards of admission based upon measures such as those tested here are imperfect if the purpose is to select students who will persist to graduation. They select many students who do not persist; they reject a substantial number who do persist. While the evidence is clear that high mental test score plus high achievement in high school studies are very strong predictors of college performance, individual differences among students of equal promise, in terms of these factors, are also strong. This says nothing of the differences in quality of performance. . . . There may be more pay dirt in refining the educational process for the very able students who are coming to college than in using finer screens on the group who are coming . . . at least until better types of screen are invented (verifax copy of the Wisconsin survey, p. 8).

The results of these two comprehensive studies done in adjacent states during different years but during the same decade were surprisingly similar. In spite of the similarity, however, caution must be taken in generalizing from Minnesota and Wisconsin to other states, and such generalizations to be sound must be based on studies of the students in the areas of concern. Some studies are available in Kentucky and Arkansas (Beezer & Hjelm, 1961; Kentucky, 1958; Smith, 1955; Stroup & Andrew, 1959; White, 1952).

The third study (Cole, 1955), a product of the College Entrance Examination Board and the National Science Foundation, was an analysis of information about 32,750 United States public high school seniors in 438 high schools in 1955. The analysis presented information about the plans for higher education of the average-ability group (middle 30 per cent), high-ability group (top 30 per cent), and low-ability group (bottom 40 per cent). Ability was defined by scores on a brief academic aptitude test specially developed for this project.

In the upper 30 per cent of seniors studied, 35 per cent came from the West, 34 per cent from the Northeast, 29 per cent from the southern part of the country, and 20 per cent from the South. As in the local studies, this national study revealed a relationship between occupation of father and plans of children. In the high-ability group, 83 per cent of the boys whose fathers were physicians and 65 per cent of the boys whose fathers were in scientific occupations planned to attend college, whereas only 38 per cent of the sons of farmers and 25 per cent of the sons of semiskilled workers had such plans. Even in this high-ability group, plans were related to scores on the test.

An interesting suggestion emerged from the results. Two-thirds of the high-ability boys who discussed college with their teachers or counselors were planning to attend college, whereas only 21 per cent of those with no such contacts intended to attend college. Although almost one-half of the high-ability students without college plans indicated that lack of money was a reason, about 25 per cent of the boys and 45 per cent of the girls reported they lacked a college goal. The authors of the study concluded: "This suggests that there is considerable validity in believing that, despite the importance of financial need, lack of motivation for college is a stronger deterrent to college-going among those of high ability who do not go to college" (*Higher Education,* Vol. 12, November, 1955, p. 37).

The follow-up study of these students obtained data from approximately 6,500 boys and girls. Of the boys in the upper 30 per cent in ability, 68 per cent planned to attend college, 79 per cent of those who planned actually attended college, and 19 per cent of those who did not plan to attend college actually attended college. In the middle 30 per cent, 43 per cent planned to attend college, 65 per cent of these actually attended college, and 13 per cent of those who did not plan to attend college actually did so. In the lower 40 per cent, 48 per cent planned to attend college, 45 per cent of these did attend college, and 5 per cent of those who originally had no such plans changed them. The following table taken from the summary report reveals these figures.

ABILITY RELATED TO COLLEGE ATTENDANCE

	Boys			Girls		
	High	Middle	Low	High	Middle	Low
Per cent planning to go.........	68	43	28	58	36	25
Per cent of those planning who actually went................	79	65	45	76	60	42
Per cent not planning to go.....	32	57	72	42	64	75
Per cent of those not planning who went..................	19	13	5	9	7	4

Source: From ETS Developments Report "Factors Affecting Attendance at College Are Same Factors Affecting College Plans," Vol. 5, March, 1957.

Many other types of follow-up studies have provided information of value to counselors. One study (Roessel, 1954) compared Minnesota Multiphasic Personality Inventory scores of ninth-grade Minneapolis public school students tested in 1948 who graduated and ninth-grade students of the same year who left school prior to graduation. Nine of the ten MMPI scales showed significant differences between the two groups, with the dropouts obtaining significantly higher mean scores than the graduates. Another study (Gough, 1956), based on approximately 7,500 boys and girls from 25 high schools in 21 states, used the California Psychological Inventory to develop a scale to predict which high-ability high school students would and would not attend college. Differences were found between the groups who attended and who did not attend college on existing scales and on enough items to constitute a separate scale.

Another kind of follow-up study was reported by Swanson (1955), who gathered information in 1951 about male graduates from twelve Minneapolis and St. Paul, Minnesota, public high schools of the years 1925 to 1929. Superior students were defined as those having an average college aptitude test percentile score and high school percentile rank of 80. Personal interviews with eighty-eight of these high-ability students showed that the high-ability students who had attended college had higher incomes in 1951 than did noncollege-trained contemporaries of equal ability. Comparisons also were made between the incomes of the high-ability noncollege-trained persons and the incomes of men in general of a similar age. When the two groups were compared on the basis of background factors, such as parental education, home ownership, and reported income of father at the time of the subject's high school career, significant differences were found.

A follow-up study more recent than any of these was published by Thorndike and Hagen. This was not a follow-up study of high school students, but rather a follow-up study of Air Force cadets tested during World War II. The purpose of the study was to relate test scores and information available during the war to the subsequent careers of these persons. In general, the groups of cadets who were in different occupations several years after the war were characterized by differences in test scores and background information, but within any one occupational group, test scores and other information were not related to the income of the individual, his reported satisfaction with his job, or his self-reported success in his occupation.

These and similar follow-up studies provide to counselors information about the subsequent careers of their counselees. They help counselors appreciate the relationships between family and other background factors and problems that face the counselee, his probable courses of action, and the probabilities of his success. Results such as these help counselors, as well as the teachers and principals, appreciate the nature of the population with which they work and are necessary not only for helping to counsel individual students, but also for planning and conducting a school program that best meets the needs of the largest proportion of pupils.

THE PROCESS OF OCCUPATIONAL CHOICE

The choice of an occupation is the end product of a process which extends over a long period of time. Even little children are curious about and interested in the manifold activities apparent in their environment. The policeman who helps them across the street each morning as they go to school, the postman who delivers the postcard Aunt Matilda has sent while on vacation, the road maintenance men with their fascinating rollers, sweepers, and dump trucks, the work of dentist or shoe repair-

man or the clerk at the nearest drugstore are all interesting objects of
concern.

At an early stage, the child begins to accumulate knowledge about
some of the activities that make up an occupation. In his elementary
school years, he inevitably learns more about the world of work. Through
reading, observing, and questioning, the young person slowly gains occupational information. This may be neither a self-initiated nor a conscious effort to learn. It arises from the individual's curiosity concerning
the world about him, from encouragement and guidance by adults in his
environment, and from a large number of other influences extant in his
circumstances. As the pupil progresses into high school, the approach to
choosing an occupation necessarily becomes less general. Pupils can now
appraise more realistically their abilities, aptitudes, interests, and values
and make judgments about the things or activities which bring them
satisfaction or dissatisfaction, as well as identify their strengths or weaknesses. Hobbies, part-time job experience, in- and out-of-school participation, class experience and grades earned are brought into focus in the
pupil's developing concept of himself. A pupil can begin to give serious
attention and study to the responsibilities of adult life, particularly his
occupation. A man's occupation includes more than being employed,
meeting the job requirements, and performing his daily functions. A
man's choice of an occupation, in a sense, determines the kinds and
sources of his satisfaction and the life style that he can expect in the
years ahead. These facets of adulthood must receive consideration by
the pupil as he makes his occupational choice.

TEACHING OCCUPATIONAL INFORMATION

There are two principal ways of presenting occupational information
to pupils: individual and group. Much of the dissemination of general
occupational information can be effectively planned for group consumption. Classroom units in social studies or English can be used to dis-
seminate occupational information to groups. Here the group can explore the relatedness of families of occupations, the needs and trends of
the community, the nation's utilization of manpower, and the relationship of personal characteristics and self-understanding to job satisfaction.
One or two occupations can be thoroughly explored to illustrate how to
use occupational information. Homeroom and extracurricular programs,
career conferences, college days, field trips, bulletin-board displays, and
movies are group activities that can also effectively assist the pupil in
gaining occupational information.

The other method of presenting occupational information is through
counseling interviews. Here the counselor and the pupil must start with
an understanding of the attributes, capabilities, needs, and aspirations of

the pupil. The counselor must make judgments about the timing, direction, and scope of the information to be examined, the way it is to be explored, and what relevant information is appropriate for that particular pupil. The counselor must aid the pupil in evaluating the occupational information he already has and assist him in locating supplementary or complimentary sources of further information or tryout. The counselor, too, needs at times to help a pupil understand and appreciate that a final occupational choice may come only after further extended tryout and evaluation, and that this process is quite normally an evolving, individual one. No pupil should be made to feel atypical or unusual if he comes to high school graduation without having a more definitive plan than "I'm going to college and then into an occupation where I will work with people." Certainly if he has both the ability and motivation requisite for college success and has a realistic picture of the probable satisfaction and competence that working with people connotes, then he need not know at this juncture of his development whether his eventual position will be in social work, recreation, teaching, or some other related occupation.

Concomitant with collecting, classifying and disseminating occupational information materials, the counselor also must maintain and impart information about post-high school training programs in collegiate institutions, technical and trade schools, the Armed Forces, and apprenticeships. The counselor must have available both for himself and for his students college catalogs, directories to colleges, and information about scholarship opportunities. He must have general information about higher education, such as is contained in the brochure *How About College? A Guide for Parents of College-bound Students* prepared by the American School Counselor Association (1960).

The majority of high school graduates do not continue their education by attending a collegiate institution. Most of them enter the employment market directly after graduation or seek noncollegiate training primarily vocational in nature. Susan may decide to enter a three-year hospital nurses training program; John may prepare himself as a welder by registering for an eighteen-month program in welding offered by an accredited trade school; Peter's post-high school plan is to become an apprentice bricklayer; Elsie is considering accepting a job as a telephone operator; and Charles's summer job as a gardener and nurseryman helper may have led to an offer to become a full-time helper at the local nursery. The counselor cannot assume that these are inappropriate choices for these pupils even if they possess the necessary academic ability to attend college. But the counselor should help to make these pupils aware of what their choices mean and see that they have the best information possible about the occupation they choose.

Obviously the pupil must have the necessary relevant information available as he explores alternative goals and means and determines rationally, on an informed basis, what he wishes his future to be. Specific information concerning various kinds of training programs, their availability, cost, requirements, and placement possibilities is needed in the counselor's repertoire of resource material. The counselor must have available catalogs of technical and vocational area schools, bulletins and directories of specialized schools and training programs, publications concerning apprenticeships, as well as guides for young workers entering the job market upon high school graduation.

Information concerning the male student's military obligation and the occupational training opportunities provided by the military services is another "must" in the counselor's compendium of knowledge. The Armed Forces provide brochures and pamphlets describing their various occupational training opportunities and these should be used by pupil and counselor alike.

Occupational and educational information, no matter how well selected and organized, how readily available, how inclusive and excellent in breadth and depth, cannot by itself become the basis for wise decision. Information is a necessary ingredient in the pupil's exploration and formulation of an educational and vocational choice; but the keystones of decision making are the student's assessment of his aptitudes, abilities, interests, values, strengths and weaknesses, and his appreciation of the demands and satisfactions contained in the vast array of occupational and educational opportunities available to him. The counselor's primary responsibility is to assist the pupil in his developing assessment of himself and in the translation and integration of information as his vocational choice evolves.

SPECIAL PROBLEMS OF GIRLS IN
POST-HIGH SCHOOL TRAINING AND VOCATIONS

Continuing trends in the rise of the employment of women and the changing character of women workers suggest that the counselor must include in his counseling, with girls especially, some particular attention to creating an awareness and an appreciation of the woman's role in our society.

In 1920, less than one out of every five workers was a woman. In 1960, nearly one-third of all workers were women. In 1920, 23 per cent of all women were in the labor force; in 1960, 35 per cent were employed. Early in the century, the working woman usually was single and in her late teens or early twenties, but the continuing trend toward a higher proportion of working women in our population (especially among married women) has produced a different picture.

Who are the employed women in today's labor market? Three of every ten married women are working. Two of every five women with children of school age are employed. Twenty per cent of the women in today's labor force are under the age of 25 and 50 per cent are over 40 years of age. Plotting these ages on a graph results in a U-shaped curve, with 46 per cent of the women between the ages of 18 and 24 working, a drop in percentage working for the age range of 25 to 44, and then a rise with 47 per cent of the women between the ages of 45 and 54 working. Many influences have contributed to this change: population growth, decline in the marriage age, increasing tendency of women to seek paid employment, growing variety of occupations available to women, and high levels of production and employment.

Life expectancy and work-life expectancy are important factors for women, as for men. In 1900, the average married woman had her last child at age 32, and she lived to age 64. In 1958, statistics showed that her last child was born, on the average, when she was 36 years old, and her life expectancy was 75 years. A single woman who now enters employment before 20 years of age will work, on the average, about 40 years, nearly reaching the men's average work-life expectancy of 43 years. Married women with no children (nearly 10 per cent of married women) now have a work-life expectancy of 31 years on the average. For married women with children, who reenter employment at about age 30 and have no more children after that time, the work-life expectancy is 23 years.

Automation and other developments in our society may modify trends relating to women workers. The best present prediction, however, is that today's high school girls should expect an average work-life ranging from 23 to 43 years. Education strongly affects what a woman's occupation will be. Education is an important determinant of the average income of the woman worker, and the chances that a woman will seek paid employment tend to increase with the amount of education she receives. College graduates are more likely to work than are nongraduates; about 40 per cent of women who are high school graduates are working, and the percentage rises to 55 per cent for those who are college graduates.

Our society today has a shortage of workers in a wide variety of jobs which require high-level training. In this framework, look at the following facts: two-thirds of the superior high school students not going to college in 1960 were women; one-fourth of the women capable of earning a college degree were not doing so; only one woman in three hundred who were capable of earning a Ph.D. degree proceeded that far. These are some of the reasons for the current statement that the manpower shortage is a shortage of woman power. Obviously, this educational pattern contributes to the low representation of women in the professions and in supervisory or managerial positions. We have long taken for granted that men, whether married or single, should plan for a full, productive, useful vocational life. Only recently have we become forcefully aware that women, too, whether married or single, have been responding to both a societal and a personal need for fuller realization of their potential vocational contribution. Without minimizing women's family contribution, we cannot ignore the present work-life expectancy figures. The former "either-or" (marriage *or* career) has now become "both over time" (marriage *and* career).

Young men and women both need to see the dualistic nature of many women's lives. Young women themselves need to look at the facts, accept them, and move toward intelligent, individual planning. The counselor's role here is obvious.

QUESTIONS FOR STUDY

1. Make a one-page outline of the information you would think most valuable to obtain in a follow-up study of recent graduates from your high school.
2. Are there several academically talented students in the senior class of your high school who have no plans for suitable further education? What specific information do you need to answer this question? If the answer is affirmative, what courses of action, if any, do you suggest?
3. Think of two instances from your own experience with students where occupational information was used, one involving what you would consider misuse of the information and one showing adequate professional use. Note the factors which differentiate the procedures in these two cases.
4. How should you weigh a student's tentative vocational plan in relation to other factors, in aiding him to choose the college he hopes to enter?
5. Suggest topics and references for two programs involving discussion by parents of the special problems of girls in post-high school education.

REFERENCES

American School Counselor Association. *How about college? A guide for parents of college-bound students.* Washington, D.C., 1960.

American Youth Commission. *Youth and the future.* Washington, D.C.: American Council on Education, 1942.

Baer, M. F., & Roeber, E. C. *Occupational information.* Chicago: Science Research, 1958.

Beezer, R. H., & Hjelm, H. F. *Factors related to college attendance.* Washington, D.C.: U.S. Department of Health, Education and Welfare, Cooperative Research Monograph, 1961, No. 8.

Bell, H. M. *Matching youth and jobs.* Washington, D.C.: American Council on Education, 1940.

Bell, H. M. *Youth tell their story*. Washington, D.C.: American Council on Education, 1938.

Berdie, R. F. *After high school—what?* Minneapolis: University of Minnesota Press, 1954.

Berdie, R. F. The counselor and his manpower responsibilities. *Personnel Guid. J.,* 1960, **38**, 458–463.

Bray, D. W. *Issues in the study of talent*. New York: King's Crown, 1954.

Burckel, C. E., & Hurt, H. W. (Eds.) *The college blue book*. Yonkers, N.Y.: Christian E. Burckel, 1956.

California State Department of Education. *Guide for making a follow-up study of school drop-outs and graduates*. Sacramento: Bureau of Occupational Information and Guidance, Jan., 1950, Bull. 13.

Cohen, N. M. *Vocational training directory of the United States*. Arlington, Va.: Potomac Press, 1958.

Cole, C. C., Jr. *Current loss of talent from high school to college: summary of report*. Washington, D.C.: U.S. Department of Health, Education and Welfare, Higher Education, Nov., 1955, Vol. XII, No. 3.

Conant, J. B. *The american high school today*. New York: McGraw-Hill, 1959.

Corcoran, Mary, & Keller, R. J. *College attendance of Minnesota high school seniors*. Minneapolis: University of Minnesota, Bureau of Institutional Research, Jan., 1957.

Eckert, Ruth E., & Marshall, T. O. *When youth leave school*. New York: McGraw-Hill, 1938.

Educational Policies Commission. *Manpower and education*. Washington, D.C.: National Education Association and American Association of School Administrators, 1956.

Educational Testing Service. Factors affecting attendance at college are same factors affecting college plans. *ETS Developments,* Mar., 1957, Vol. V, No. 3.

Eskow, S. *Guide to the two-year colleges*. Great Neck, N.Y.: Barron's Educational Series, 1960.

Forrester, Gertrude. *Occupational literature: an annotated bibliography*. New York: H. W. Wilson, 1958.

Gough, H. G. Some personality differences between high ability high school students who do, and do not, go to college. Paper delivered at Western Psychol. Ass., May, 1956.

Hoppock, R. *Occupational information*. New York: McGraw-Hill, 1957.

Irwin, Mary. (Ed.) *American universities and colleges*. Washington, D.C.: American Council on Education, 1960.

Karl, S. D. (Ed.) *The college handbook: 1961–1963*. Princeton, N.J.: College Entrance Examination Board, 1961.

Kentucky Cooperative Counseling and Testing Service. Rural drop-outs are studied. *Kentucky Cooperative Newsletter*. Lexington, 1958.

Kentucky Cooperative Counseling and Testing Service. State-wide testing tops 16,000 for new record. *Kentucky Cooperative Newsletter*. Lexington, 1958.

Learned, W. S., & Langmuir, C. R. *Misplacement in college*. 33rd Annual Report. New York: Carnegie Foundation for Advancement of Teaching, 1938. Pp. 34–62.

Learned, W. S., & Wood, B. D. *The student and his knowledge*. New York: Carnegie Foundation for Advancement of Teaching, Bull. No. 29, 1938.

Little, J. K. *State-wide inquiry into decisions of youth about education beyond high school*. Madison: University of Wisconsin, Sept., 1958.

Lovejoy, C. E. *College guide.* New York: Simon and Schuster, 1961.

Rainey, H. P. *How fare American youth?* New York: Appleton-Century, 1937.

Roessel, F. P. Minnesota multiphasic personality inventory results for high school drop-outs and graduates. Mimeographed report, Minneapolis Board of Education, Minneapolis, Minn., Apr. 20, 1954.

St. Cloud, Minnesota Office of Guidance Services. *Technical high school graduates class of 1951* and *class of 1955.* St. Cloud: Office of Guidance Services.

Shartle, C. *Occupational information: its development and application.* Englewood Cliff, N.J.: Prentice-Hall, 1952.

Smith, S. E. *Factors which prevent able young people from going to college.* Washington, D.C.: American Council on Education, Oct. 6–7, 1955.

Standards for use in preparing and evaluating occupational literature. *Occupations,* Feb., 1950.

Stroup, F., & Andrew, D. C. *Barriers to college attendance.* Washington, D.C.: U.S. Department of Health, Education and Welfare. Cooperative Research Project, May, 1959, No. 0008.

Swanson, E. O. Is college education worth while? *J. counsel. Psychol.,* 1955, **2**, No. 3.

Thorndike, R. L., & Hagen, E. *10,000 careers.* New York: Wiley, 1959.

U.S. Bureau of the Census. *Statistical abstract of the United States.* Washington, D.C.: U.S. Department of Commerce. Issued periodically.

U.S. Government Printing Office. *Dictionary of occupational titles.* Washington, D.C., 1949.

U.S. Government Printing Office. *Training opportunities for women and girls.* Women's Bureau Bulletin 274. Washington, D. C., 1960.

U.S. Government Printing Office. *Today's woman in tomorrow's world.* Women's Bureau Bulletin 276. Washington, D.C., 1960.

White, R. C. *These will go to college.* Cleveland: Press of Western Reserve University, 1952.

Wisconsin State Department of Public Instruction and School of Education. *My plans beyond high school.* Madison: University of Wisconsin, Apr., 1957.

Zapoleon, Marguerite W. *Occupational planning for women.* New York: Harper & Row, 1961.

CHAPTER 11

The Counseling Interview

The interview is the vehicle of counseling. It conveys between the two participants information about the questions, needs, and characteristics of the counselee and the attitude and competencies of the counselor. It allows the counselor to communicate to the pupil his reassurance, support, understanding, and knowledge of occupations and opportunities. We can conceive of counseling without tests, occupational information, or college bulletins; but we cannot conceive of it without the face-to-face meeting which allows the counselor and the counselee to discuss the matters at hand.

Several books and papers about counseling and interviewing present in great detail the relevant research and common folklore about the interview (Berdie, 1943; Bingham, Moore, & Gustad, 1959; Darley, 1950; Tyler, 1961). Here we will not attempt to treat comprehensively the counseling interview; we will attempt to discuss it with particular reference to educational and psychological testing.

THE PUPIL'S PURPOSES

Counseling, although a cooperative process involving both counselor and counselee, centers around the needs and purposes of the counselee. The counselor's and the school's purposes are important, but these are derived from and defined by the pupil's needs and purposes.

The purposes of counseling are determined jointly by the counselee, the institution or school in which counseling occurs, the counseling profession, and the individual counselor. Whenever the purposes of any one of these four are not compatible with the purposes of the others, conflict must result and confusion prevail in the ensuing counseling (Berdie, 1959).

Some of the counselee's purposes are revealed easily. He is aware of these and can discuss them freely. "I want to find out what college I should attend." Other purposes are less easily available to the counselor because the counselee is reluctant or unable to discuss them. Unwillingness may result from the pupil's embarrassment, guilt, or fear. His reasons for seeking counseling may result from inadequacies of which he is ashamed. They may result from actions or contemplations which he considers wrong. He may be seeking counseling for reasons usually incurring punishment. Inability to discuss his reasons may be a consequence of the pupil's lack of awareness of them or of his lack of skill in verbally describing attitudes and experiences of which he is aware.

Counselors quickly learn that most pupils have a "stated" reason for seeking counseling. This often is a "socially acceptable" reason and often is an accurate description of the student's need for counseling. Sometimes, however, the stated reason is given by the pupil because he is reluctant to present the "real" reason and sometimes he does not know the real reason. Sometimes the pupil is trying out the counselor to see if the counselor is interested and sensitive enough to help find the basic problem and thus to help the pupil.

The counselee's felt or stated need may be for information, support, love, friendship, or training in skills of learning, problem solving, or decision making. He may want definition and clarification of goals and values or an opportunity to think. Usually several needs are present in the counselee, and these change during counseling.

THE COUNSELOR'S PURPOSES

LEARNING ABOUT PUPILS

The counseling interview provides an opportunity for the counselor to understand the pupil. Let us here repeat our assumption that improvement in the counselee's self-understanding is related to the counselor's understanding of the pupil. Much information about persons can be obtained in an interview. Most information can be gained in a variety of ways, and the counselor has to select the most economical and accurate means for obtaining any information.

Obviously, a counselor can learn most easily about a counselee's appearance through direct observation in the interview. Whether he is large or small, light or dark, handsome or plain can be determined more easily in the interview than through means of physical measurement or reports from others. Nevertheless, interview observations are not completely accurate and are subject to the same errors of perception and judgment as are other personal observations (Hollingsworth, 1922). For example, a student's appearance on one day is only a sample of how he usually looks. He may look neat on Monday and sloppy on Tuesday. Other errors can affect judgments of appearance in interviews.

Observation in the interview also provides an opportunity for the counselor to learn about a person's speech. Again, the counselor must be aware of his own limitations and of the extent to which a person's speech changes from day to day or from situation to situation. Nevertheless, an observant counselor will be able to identify a student who shows a marked stutter, who lisps, who uses a limited speaking vocabulary, or who uses language usually considered socially unacceptable.

Counselors sometimes make inferences about students' abilities, educational achievements, and interests while observing their speech and behavior in interviews. The relationships between such judgments and indexes of these characteristics obtained through other means, usually psychological tests, are not high, and the wise counselor will place little faith in his own ability to make such judgments from interview observations alone.

Interview observations about the pupil's behavior in social situations are somewhat more useful, not necessarily because these observations can be made more reliably than observations of intellect or interest, but rather because other means for obtaining such information are so limited. A pupil in an interview is speaking with another person, and if he is easily embarrassed or confused when speaking with others, he perhaps is going to show signs of embarrassment when he is being interviewed. However, a generalization such as this must be made with extreme caution. One counselee with great poise and assurance told a counselor that she was embarrassed and had little to say when talking with others. When the counselor said that she seemed to be quite poised and comfortable in the interview, the counselee immediately commented that she had no difficulty when speaking with older persons.

The interview provides an opportunity for the counselor to synthesize information obtained about the counselee as well as to collect new information and confirm data already gathered. A counselor continually is perceiving from a variety of sources additional bits of data about the counselee. He can more easily assemble these bits of information into meaningful patterns when the counselee is participating in the interview. When data do not fit together to form a pattern, the counselor and the counselee together can explain discrepancies, find additional information that provides a more appropriate framework for the assembled facts, and discover the reasons for apparent contradictions.

Understanding pupils consists not only of collecting, verifying, and synthesizing information, but also of comprehending it. The counseling interview provides a situation where the counselor can discover the meaning of the information he has formed into coherent patterns. The counselor may be able to gain such comprehension when he reviews all of the available information in the absence of the counselee, but he can best approach the question, "What does this all mean?" with the counselee participating in the interview.

THE ACTS OF COUNSELING

The counselor uses the interview not only to increase his understanding of the pupil, but also to initiate and maintain the counseling process. Through the means of the interview, he establishes a relationship which allows the counselee to define his own and the counselor's roles, responsibilities, and functions. Only in the interview can the counselee begin to perceive his counselor as a person who is interested in him, who can help him, who provides no threat, who is a source of information, and who, as a teacher, can assist in developing his skill to solve personal problems. Only in the interview can the counselee begin to perceive counseling as a cooperative process which for success depends on the efforts of both the counselor and himself. Only in the interview can he begin to understand that he himself must arrive at many important decisions and that the counselor's role is not to make these decisions, but rather to aid him in making decisions that eventually will result in satisfaction and success.

In the interview the counselor can select tests and other means for obtaining information about the pupil and discuss this information with him. A pupil's history could be reviewed by the counselor, as mentioned earlier, without the counselee's presence, and tests then could be selected and given by the counselor. A report of the test scores could be prepared and given to the pupil outside of an interview, and the obtained information might help the pupil to arrive at satisfactory decisions. The interview, however, allows the counselor to prepare the pupil for tests, to motivate him to take tests, to provide a necessary background of information that will help him understand tests, and to provide information about the test results that will be incorporated into the pupil's perception of himself.

In addition to allowing the counselor to initiate and maintain the counseling process, the interview also aids the counselor to stimulate and guide the learning of the pupil first about himself, and then about his social environment. The counselor uses the interview to ask questions which direct the pupil's attention in one direction or another, to suggest that certain problems be explored, to provide information while the pupil progresses toward his goal, and to encourage the pupil in his search for knowledge about himself and about his relationships with others.

Thus, the interview has many purposes. Some of them can be attained without an interview, but others require an interview if they are to be achieved efficiently and completely.

LEARNING FROM INTERVIEWS

Our repeated assumption in this text has been that the counselor, in order to be of most use to his counselee, must understand the pupil, and that such understanding can result only from careful consideration of much information about him. Let us concern ourselves now with the counselor's use of the interview to learn about pupils.

Interview judgments, like test scores, must be evaluated on the basis of their reliability and validity. Errors of judgment derived through interviews have sources in the counselor, in the counselee, and in other aspects of the interview.

THE COUNSELOR AS A SOURCE OF ERROR

Many behavior cues may be present in the interview which the counselor fails to perceive. The counselor may not hear the counselee sigh, nor see a tear that appears in his eyes, nor observe the pupil's slight smile of satisfaction when he discusses his experiences in chemistry class. Obviously the counselor will be unable to incorporate this unperceived information into his evaluation of the pupil. The counselor must be a good observer and must be perceptive.

The counselor as he observes behaviors may distort their meaning by attempting to force them into preconceived categories. For example, a counselor who had much experience with alcoholic men listened to a pupil describe some of the conflicts he had with his father. Later the pupil casually mentioned that his father stopped in a bar before he came home. The counselor erroneously inferred that the source of the pupil's trouble was an alcoholic parent. The counselor with a strongly psychoanalytic orientation may overinterpret or misinterpret observations concerning the relationship between the pupil and his father or may force the pupil's report of fantasy into interesting, but not accurate Freudian interpretations (Rice, 1929).

In an interview the counselor may influence directly the very behavior he is observing, and thus another error of judgment looms. By phrasing questions in certain ways, the counselor predetermines the responses. If the counselor introduces his questions with "Don't you think," the pupil is more likely to say "yes" than if the counselor's statement were "You don't believe that" (Payne, 1951). If the counselor continually talks about financial problems and asks many questions about the pupil's economic status, the pupil's emphasis on money during that and future interviews mainly may reflect the counselor's concern rather than his own.

For example, one high school pupil came to his counselor to discuss the wisdom of taking a fourth year of mathematics. The counselor asked him many questions about his social life, how often he went to parties, whether he went on dates, and whether he had a girl. Later the counselor noted in his interview report that the pupil had come to talk about a course, but was really concerned about his heterosexual adjustment.

The type of person the counselor is partially determines the information provided by the pupil. Some boys and girls respond differently to

men and women counselors. Some elderly counselors arouse one response
in one student and another response in another student. These different
responses result from previous associations of the counselee. These associations may be so strong that they prevent a counselor from working
well with a student, and transfer to another counselor may be necessary.
The counselor may have noncounseling duties such as teaching or discipline in addition to counseling, and these can influence how pupils react
to him.

THE PUPIL AS A SOURCE OF ERROR

Some sources of error in interview judgments are found in the pupil.
As has been noted, pupils react differently in different situations with
different persons, and a counselor might erroneously decide that a boy
is shy and timid when actually he is that way only when with adults,
with women, or in a formal office situation. This essentially is a question
of the generality of behavior. Do persons tend to be shy and retiring in
all situations with all persons; do they tend to be hostile, aggressive,
cheerful, or bizarre in all situations with all persons; or do they tend to
act specifically and differently in various situations? Any judgments based
on pupils' behavior in interviews must take this into consideration.
Obviously, the more opportunities a counselor has to observe a pupil in
a variety of situations with many different persons, the more valid will
be his judgment about that pupil. Often the counselor will request information about a pupil's extra-interview behavior from persons best
able to observe it—classroom teachers, coaches, and parents—in order
to supplement his interview observations. These extra-interview reports
then will be integrated with other data to arrive at a valid description
of the pupil.

The counselor also must be aware that pupils are influenced by temporary and superficial experiences, and as a result behavior at any one
time may deviate from the pupil's usual behavior. A counselor might
observe that a boy is drowsy and sleepy during the interview and consequently report that he lacks interest in his work, is not interested in other
persons, and is not courteous. The fact may be that the pupil had only
three hours of sleep the preceding night after returning with his family
from a long automobile trip. An interview two or three days later might
show him to be lively, wide-awake, and most cooperative.

The pupil's behavior in an interview can be influenced by the weather,
his health, a pleasant or unpleasant experience just prior to the interview,
anticipation of a pleasant or unpleasant experience following the interview, eagerness or anxiety directly or indirectly connected with the
counseling interview, or other temporary situations.

Closely related to the extent to which generalizations can be made is
the question of the validity of judgments about interview behavior as

they are used to predict future behavior. Will a boy who is friendly, socially aggressive, and poised in a counseling interview behave the same way two or ten years later when he is attempting to sell an insurance policy? Will a girl who in an interview reacts warmly, sympathetically, and with much understanding react the same way after she completes college and becomes a fourth-grade teacher? These questions are similar to those one must ask when making predictions from rating scales, psychological tests, and other means of observing behavior (Kelly & Fiske, 1951).

SOURCES OF ERROR IN THE SITUATION

Some sources of error in interview judgments are found neither in the counselor nor the pupil, but rather in other aspects of the counseling situation. Many interruptions and distractions during an interview can influence both the counselor and the counselee so that erroneous judgments will be made. When either the counselor or the counselee is uncomfortable because a chair is not suitable, the temperature or the lighting in the room is annoying, or other irritants are present, judgments may be in error. The reputation of the counseling program or of the counselor may arouse certain reactions on the part of the pupil which in turn influence the counselor, and this aspect of the relationship may result in accurate or inaccurate judgments.

If the information learned about the counselee is to be accurate and relevant, the counselor must be aware of the following questions:

1. What are the characteristics he is trying to assess?

2. Have the counselor's experience and training provided him with a basis for identifying and evaluating these characteristics? (Does he have a norm?)

3. Can the counselor *objectively* observe expressions of these characteristics to determine their importance and meaning?

4. Is the counselor aware of the many possible conditions that determine the meaning of these expressions?

5. Is the interview situation itself conducive to the elicitation of these expressions?

TEST SELECTION IN COUNSELING INTERVIEWS

Many counselors use the first interview for test selection and the second interview for test interpretation. In the first interview, the counselor collects information about the pupil, comments on the information that is not available, decides which tests can provide the needed information, and arranges for the pupil to take the tests. In the second interview he describes the test results to the pupil and attempts to incorporate this information into that previously discussed.

Although this process has never been proved ineffective, many counselors find it distasteful. The first interview should not be a diagnostic interview and the second a treatment, but rather the entire counseling process should help the counselee understand himself and help him use this new self-understanding. Information obtained during the first interview may help in the selection of tests, but more importantly it helps the counselor and the counselee start to design a general pattern in which all of the information about the pupil can be assembled so the pupil can obtain a clear picture of himself.

A pupil may come to a counselor to discuss a choice between an engineering college or a vocational school. The counselor may review with the pupil all of the available information about his general academic ability, mathematics achievement and aptitude, hobbies, work experience, and family background. The counselor or the counselor and the student together then may decide that the pupil should take mathematics, mechanical comprehension, and vocational interest tests and return later to discuss the test scores. The second interview may then consist of a review of the test scores and of other information.

Using an alternative approach, when the pupil first comes to discuss his choice with a counselor, the counselor may discuss the pupil's academic achievement, mathematics background, hobbies, and work experience as these all relate to the experiences of engineers, the expectations of schools and employers, and the basic personality needs of the student. They will consider the meaning of this information as it affects the student's choice. During the interview the counselor may mention, if the pupil does not, that some information is lacking and tests might fill some of these gaps.

Instead of using an interview as a means for interpreting tests, the sophisticated counselor will refer to tests as they raise questions in the interview, will use test scores to support or question information as it is considered, and will use test scores as cues to introduce topics, ask questions, and suggest that the pupil evaluate or reevaluate his own abilities or interests.

Bordin and Bixler (1946) have suggested that the more responsibility the counselee assumes in selecting tests, the more effectively can tests be used. They suggest that the counselor provide enough information about testing, about types of tests, and about specific tests to enable the pupil to make sensible judgments concerning appropriate tests. Too much discussion of testing in an interview, however, influences the pupil and the counselor to place too much reliance on test scores. The question is not only whether the counselee can select tests as appropriately as the counselor, but also whether the time and effort required to teach the pupil how to select tests is justified by the assumed increase in the pupil's acceptance and understanding of the process. A counselor's casual statement suggesting that the pupil take a test and a simple and brief explanation of the purposes of the test may avoid undue emphasis and provide the counselor and the counselee time to devote to problems and attitudes not related to testing.

A comparison made by Gustad and Tuma (1957) of the effects on client behavior of different methods of test introduction and interpretation in the counseling interview demonstrated that the different methods had little effect on the subsequent behavior of clients. At present the choice of the best method of test selection and interpretation in the interview must be considered a matter of counselor preference rather than demonstrated effectiveness.

THE USE OF THE INTERVIEW TO INFLUENCE LEARNING AND ATTITUDES

The counselor's main use of the interview is not to learn about the pupil, but rather to use information to help the pupil learn about himself. Here are some general principles to be considered in this use of the interview:

1. The interview is a cooperative venture in which the counselee has certain responsibilities, the counselor other responsibilities, and the two participants share further responsibilities. The counselor acknowledges the counselee's responsibility for selecting the initial topic of conversation, usually by asking the pupil what he would like to discuss, how he happened to come to the counselor, or "What's on your mind today, Bob?" The counselor has responsibility for establishing limits in counseling, particularly those pertinent to time, but also in some cases those pertinent to topics discussed and intensity with which they are discussed. The counselor and the counselee both have responsibility for deciding how much time during the interview is to be devoted to various topics and when new topics or problems should be introduced. The interview time does not belong to the counselee any more than it belongs to the counselor. Rather, this is a situation where two people are working cooperatively for the purpose of aiding and improving the ultimate condition of the counselee.

2. The relationship between the counselor and the counselee begins as soon as they see one another. Many pupils are ready to discuss their important problems when they begin to talk with a counselor, others are more comfortable if they spend a short time becoming acquainted with the counselor. The initial and introductory conversation need not extend throughout a large part of the interview. Pupils feel most satisfied when they and the counselor can begin to talk about the topics at hand soon after the beginning of the interview. Comments about the weather, the books the counselee is carrying, or the counselor's regret that the pupil

had to wait a few minutes usually are enough to make the two persons feel comfortable with one another.

3. The counseling interview must have a purpose, and the goals for the interview must be limited. The purpose of the school counselor is not to reconstruct the personality of the pupil; even the most experienced and ambitious psychoanalyst approaches this goal with caution (Colby, 1951). The counselor's goals are restricted, and he hopes that whatever the pupil learns in the counseling interview will perhaps influence certain other aspects of his life (Tyler, 1958). The counselor should define his purposes during counseling in terms of vocational choice, educational progress, family adjustments, relationships with friends, and other definable objectives. During counseling the counselor and the counselee cannot move continually from working toward one objective to working toward another.

4. The counselee infers the attitude of the counselor from his speech and behavior. If the counselee is to see the counselor as friendly and sincere, the counselor's behavior must produce this impression. He cannot act this way unless he truly is friendly and sincere. The counselor's main and primary motivation in counseling must be to help the student, and consequently he must act so that the student perceives this.

5. Counseling is a process that occurs during time, and the pacing, or timing, of counseling is important. An hour devoted to careful discussion of one, two, or three topics may result in the pupil's understanding and learning. An hour crowded with discussion about six or ten important topics may result only in confusion and anxiety. Ideas presented too quickly, questions asked without adequate time to consider previous answers, and a machine-gun style of speaking may produce an interview which the counselee leaves breathlessly wondering what has been happening. A leisurely pace during the interview with enough time for the counselor and the counselee to contemplate without wasting time in prolonged discussion of irrelevant topics is not only efficient, but also effective counseling.

6. Closely related to pacing is the use of pauses during an interview. Many beginning counselors feel compelled to speak or have the counselee speak throughout the entire period. A few seconds of silence to a beginning counselor appears much longer than it really is. Counselors who make recordings of their interviews frequently notice that what they remembered as a long pause, when listened to, was a short and natural silence. A period of silence extending through one or even more minutes during an interview provides to both participants an opportunity to consider what they have been discussing, to think of new topics, and to try to organize their information and ideas. The most active counseling may occur in the mind of the counselee during these periods of silence.

7. The counseling interview is a communications device, and if it is to be effective, the counselor must use symbols that are understood by the counselee and that have relatively the same meaning for both persons. The vocabulary and the concepts used by the counselor must be within the span of comprehension of the counselee. The counselor must adapt his vocabulary and concepts to the capacity of the counselee, and he must remember that the pupil may attach to words meanings other than those assumed by himself. A counseling interview with a student with an IQ of 90 in the eighth grade should be different from a counseling interview with a college sophomore who has an IQ of 140. Counselors must be particularly careful to avoid using technical terms and professional jargon. For example, few pupils would understand a counselor if he said, "Your occupational profile resembles that of engineers" or "You don't have any reject patterns on the Strong."

8. The mechanics of communication sometimes interfere with counseling. The counselee must hear what the counselor says if he is to understand it. The counselor must speak loudly enough for the counselee to hear him; he must enunciate clearly; he must direct his speech toward the counselee; and he must not allow a pipe in or a hand before his mouth to interfere with communication.

9. Questions are useful in the counseling interview for more than eliciting information. They can be used effectively to direct the pupil's attention toward topics, to encourage him to explore further certain problems, to focus the course of the interview in one or another direction. Questions also can be leading questions which encourage the student to view a statement in a special way or to arrive at a foregone conclusion. Leading questions can be used effectively or deceptively, and the counselor must judge when this method can be used most appropriately in the interview.

10. The counseling interview is a learning and teaching situation. Much of the learning consists of reformulation and restructuring of information and attitudes already present within the pupil, but much new information also is presented in counseling. Information taught in counseling must be presented clearly. It should be offered so that it appears relevant to the pupil. Use should be made of examples and illustrations. Frequently information should be given repeatedly and in a variety of ways. The student should participate actively in the learning process by providing his own illustrations and by asking and answering questions.

11. Counselors frequently have to decide when to advise and when to refrain from advising pupils, particularly when counselees ask such questions as, "What would you do if you were me?" Whether or not to advise depends on the persons involved and the type of advice requested.

When a pupil is independent and mature and in the past has demonstrated his ability to solve his own problems and receive advice as advice (not prescription), the counselor might express an opinion, whereas he might be quite reluctant to do so with a pupil who was overly dependent or who had habitually sought to have others make his decisions. The counselor's experience and knowledge should be made available to the pupil, but only insofar as the pupil is able to incorporate this into his own decision making.

12. The setting in which the counseling interview occurs is important. There must be privacy, physical comfort, and freedom from distractions. The counselor and the counselee must have comfortable chairs; the lighting and the temperature must be appropriate; the telephone must not interrupt; the noise of typewriters in an adjacent office must not make hearing difficult; and the band rehearsal in the next room must not distract both participants.

SUMMARY

The counseling interview has been discussed as it relates to the counselor's use of tests in order to help pupils increase their self-understanding. Many aspects of the counseling interview have not been considered here, such as the counselor's responses to emotional reactions of his counselees (Rogers, 1951) or the incorporation of the counselor's values into the counseling process (Williamson, 1958, 1959). In the counseling interview, many things occur: psychotherapy, teaching occupational and educational information, developing study and reading skills, and developing interpersonal relations. The emphasis here has been on the use of the interview to expand the student's knowledge of himself.

The objectives of both the counselor and the counselee and the responsibilities of both of these persons for determining the purposes of counseling have been considered. The counseling interview has been viewed as a learning situation in which the counselor is the teacher, the counselee is the student, and the content of the course is the counselee himself. Most of the principles that apply to learning in the classroom can be reinterpreted to apply equally as well to learning in the counseling interview.

Attention also has been given to the process of test selection and interpretation in the counseling interview. The choice and interpretation of tests are part of the counseling process and are not something apart. Tests are selected and explained as the need arises; information from tests may be used explicitly by the counselor as he discusses test results with students, or test scores may provide cues to the counselor which help him make choices even though they may not be discussed directly with the pupil.

QUESTIONS FOR STUDY

1. In what ways does a counseling interview differ from a social conversation?
2. In what ways, if any, would counseling interviews differ if conducted by:
   a. A communist?
   b. A Catholic priest?
   c. A "Babbitt"?
   d. An aesthetic?
   e. An operationalist?
3. What should determine the duration of a counseling interview?
4. Prepare a list of personality and behavior characteristics that can be observed accurately in an interview and another list of characteristics more difficult to observe accurately.
5. Discuss the use of pauses in counseling interviews.
6. Why would some people object to the idea of "using techniques" in an interview?

REFERENCES

Berdie, R. F. Counseling principles and presumptions. *J. counsel. Psychol.*, 1959, 6, 175–182.

Berdie, R. F. Psychological processes in the interview. *J. soc. Psychol.*, 1943, 18, 3–31.

Bingham, W. V., Moore, B. V., & Gustad, J. W. *How to interview.* New York: Harper & Row, 1959.

Bordin, E. S., & Bixler, R. H. Test selection: a process of counseling. *Educ. psychol. Measmt.*, 1946, 6, 361–374. Reprinted in A. H. Brayfield (Ed.), *Readings in modern methods of counseling.* New York: Appleton-Century-Crofts, 1950. Pp. 173–183.

Colby, K. M. *A primer for psychotherapists.* New York: Ronald, 1951.

Darley, J. G. Conduct of the interview. In A. H. Brayfield (Ed.), *Readings in modern methods of counseling.* New York: Appleton-Century-Crofts, 1950. Pp. 265–271.

Gustad, J. W., & Tuma, A. H. The effects of different methods of test introduction and interpretation on client learning in counseling. *J. counsel. Psychol.*, 1957, 4, 313–317.

Hollingsworth, H. L. *Judging human character.* New York, London: Appleton, 1922.

Kelly, E. L., & Fiske, D. W. *The prediction of performance in clinical psychology.* Ann Arbor: University of Michigan Press, 1951.

Payne, S. L. *The art of asking questions.* Princeton, N.J.: Princeton University Press, 1951.

Rice, S. Contagious bias in the interview: a methodological note. *Amer. J. Sociol.*, 1929, 35, 420–423.

Rogers, C. *Client centered therapy.* New York: Houghton Mifflin, 1951.

Tyler, Leona. *The work of the counselor.* New York: Appleton-Century-Crofts, 1961.

Tyler, Leona. Theoretical principles underlying the counseling process. *J. counsel. Psychol.*, 1958, 5, 3–10.

Williamson, E. G. Value orientation in counseling. *Personnel Guid. J.*, 1958, 36, 520–528.

Williamson, E. G. The meaning of communication in counseling. *Personnel Guid. J.*, 1959, 38, 6–14.

CHAPTER 12

Counseling Relationships

We already have defined counseling as listening and talking with an individual about the needs, characteristics, and behaviors which make him similar to or different from other persons, with emphasis in the discussion on the rational meaning and the emotional implication of these characteristics. This process depends on the relationship between the counselor and the counselee, and this relationship in turn is a function of how the counselee perceives his counselor. The pupil perceives the counselor in defined ways, and these perceptions are determined not only by what the counselor does and says in the interviews, but also by the pupil's expectations perhaps formed long before he ever met the counselor. As the pupil perceives the counselor, he develops certain attitudes, feelings, and expectations toward the counselor and behaves accordingly. On the other hand, the counselor behaves similarly toward the pupil. His perception of the pupil is determined by what the pupil says and does in the interview, as well as by information and impressions of the pupil obtained before the interview. On the bases of his perceptions, the counselor responds to the pupil with understanding, with sympathy, with hostility, with anxiety, with affection, or with other appropriate or inappropriate feelings.

When we consider the attitudes and feelings that these two persons have toward one another and the behavior that results directly from these, we are considering the counseling relationship. The relationship between the counselor and his pupil, or the counselor and the parent, or the counselor and the teacher, determines the effectiveness of much of what the counselor does, and these counseling relationships can in a sense be considered the vectors of counseling.

Relationships between counselors and others are determined by the same experiences and conditions that influence all interpersonal relationships. Freud suggested that the relationship between an individual and his intimates essentially recapitulated the relationship between the individual and his parents or persons who played the part of parents during childhood. Thus, the attitudes of a patient toward his psychoanalyst develop as did similar attitudes when the patient was a child. The patient relives earlier emotional experiences. The development of this relationship Freud labeled "transference." He stressed that transference was not a relationship that developed between two persons in casual contact with one another, but rather that an intense and enduring relationship between patient and psychiatrist was necessary if transference were to evolve.

Although the relationships between counselors and others, including pupils, their parents, and their teachers, cannot be described as transference, other experiences pupils have had with individuals seen as similar to the counselor influence the reaction of the pupil to his counselor. Thus, if a counselor looks or talks like or in another way reminds a pupil of a favorite uncle, of a disliked grade school teacher, or of a domineering mother, then the pupil's immediate reactions will be influenced by these earlier experiences. As these early experiences are out of the control of the counselor, and in fact he may be unaware of them, he hardly can assume responsibility for many of the ways in which the pupil reacts toward him.

Another determinant of the relationship between the counselor and others consists of the social expectation, that is, how society expects a pupil, a parent, or a teacher to react to a counselor. Parents are expected to act toward teachers with a certain amount of respect, with extreme courtesy, and at times with perhaps some hidden derision. Counselors have not been with us long enough to establish clearly defined social expectations, but these expectations are developing, and the reactions to counselors now are being influenced by them.

RELATIONSHIPS BETWEEN COUNSELORS AND PUPILS

Perhaps because of the poverty of research on counseling relationships, many dogmatic assertions have been presented, usually with little evidence to support them (Berdie, 1959). One of these dogmas contends that the pupil must come voluntarily and of his own desire to the counselor if the counselor is to help him. Another is that the counselor cannot be seen by the pupil as a disciplinarian if counseling is to be effective. Yet another is that the counselor must be seen by the pupil as being "on his side." Particularly the counselor must not be perceived by the pupil as a representative of society at large, of the teacher, of the family, or of any group that maintains an authoritative relationship with the pupil.

Experience suggests that when the above conditions are maintained, counseling is easier than when they are not. Sometimes under these conditions counseling is possible, whereas if conditions were different, it might not be. On the other hand, experience also suggests that in some instances counseling can be effective even when the counselor plays a disciplinarian's role, when he is seen by the pupil as representing society, or when the pupil is counseled in spite of his reluctance or perhaps even aversion.

Counselors should attempt to do their counseling whenever possible in situations where pupils actively seek such help; they should be seen by pupils as being other than disciplinarians; they should attempt not to represent indiscriminately and unreasoningly to the pupil the mores and morals of society. When the counselor is unable to control conditions to this extent, however, he should not decide that counseling is impossible, but rather should expect that the probability of success will be somewhat different than it would be if he had such control.

The relationship between the pupil and the counselor is determined in large part by the way in which the pupil perceives the counselor's attitude toward him (Berdie, 1951). No one has adequately demonstrated the relationship between the counselor's attitude and the attitude as perceived by the counselee, but most pupils are sensitive and able to obtain a moderately accurate perception of the counselor's attitude. Thus, a counselor who really is not friendly or accepting or supporting, but by his actions or words tries to convey that he is, most likely is seen as he really is by the counselee. Fortunately, not very many hostile or non-accepting persons become counselors, and counselors are not often tempted to appear other than as they are.

THE INSULATION OF THE COUNSELING INTERVIEW

To some pupils the counseling situation provides a psychologically insulated opportunity whereby they can talk with a person with whom they have minimum ego involvement and yet talk as they usually do only with persons with whom they are emotionally involved. This kind of insulation may minimize the effects of the counselor's attitude, and in a sense the counselee is reacting not to the counselor as a person who has attitudes and feelings, but rather to his own stereotype or idea of what a counselor should resemble.

Pupils are accustomed to discussing their personal affairs with persons with whom they have enduring and close relationships. They discuss their affections, their anxieties, and their hopes with parents, relatives, or close friends. When they engage in these discussions, almost always they are aware of how the listener is reacting. In these conversations, both persons continually evaluate how the conversation will affect their own future mutual relationship. During counseling, however, the discussion can be seen by the pupil as having no bearing on the future personal relationship between the counselor and the counselee, because no such relationship is anticipated. Consequently some pupils truthfully may react to the counselor in the sense of, "I don't care what he thinks of me." Sometimes, however, the counselor, as seen by the pupil, assumes the role of "all others" or "people in general," and the pupil's reaction to the counselor depends on his sensitivity to what others think of him.

Thus, we cannot assume that for every pupil the counselor's attitudes toward him are equally important. Many pupils, even in a psychologically insulated situation, nevertheless have strong needs for regard; and consequently they may personalize the relationship with the counselor and even become dependent on him.

The relationship between the counselor and the pupil is affected not only by experiences during counseling, but also by experiences outside the interviewing room. The manner in which these relationships are affected varies from pupil to pupil. Some pupils will respond more positively to a counselor after they have played a game of softball with him at a school picnic. Other pupils after this noncounseling experience will react by being unable to move into a counseling relationship with the counselor as easily as they could have previously. The counselor who isolates himself from pupils and limits his contacts with them only to formal counseling interviews may facilitate a counseling relationship with some pupils, but make it more difficult for others.

Some people have suggested that how a counselor feels about a student may be more important than what a counselor does. Most persons, however, regardless of the type of counseling they prefer, agree with the statement made by Rogers (1949).

It has been our experience that the counselor who tries to use a "method" is doomed to be unsuccessful unless this method is genuinely in line with his own attitudes. On the other hand, the counselor whose attitudes are of the type which facilitate therapy may be only partially successful, because his attitudes are inadequately implemented by appropriate methods and techniques.

Thus, the relationship between the counselor and the counselee is not something apart from either one of the two individuals, nor is it something apart from what the counselor does or says, but rather it is a product of the feelings of the counselor and the counselee and the behavior shown by these two persons during counseling.

RELATIONSHIPS WITH PARENTS

Counselors no later than 1955 were minimizing the role of parents in counseling. Earlier texts on counseling (Hahn & MacLean, 1950; Shostrom & Brammer, 1952; Tyler, 1953; Williamson, 1950) either failed to mention altogether the work the counselor must do with the parent or gave it only a few paragraphs of discussion (Berdie, 1955).

The cumulative experience of counselors, however, supported by the research which indicates the importance of family experiences in determining occupational and educational plans, has emphasized the importance of the mother and father in counseling. The decisions made by children to attend college or to enter certain occupations, and more important the attitudes related to these decisions, are formed in the home often long before the counselor or the high school has known the pupil. Serious emotional problems for the most part start to develop in early childhood, and symptoms predictive of many mental diseases can be traced back before the child even entered school. For example, a study by Warnken (1957) demonstrated that adults who were hospitalized because of schizophrenia were observed to be different from other children by their teachers as early as the primary grades. No other single influence is as effective in determining the direction of the child's life as his relationships with his parents. Any attempt to counsel him without providing adequate attention to these relationships is folly, and frequently the relationship between the counselor and the parent is an effective vehicle for influencing the parent-child relationship.

The counselor can serve serveral functions in his relationships with parents. He can:

Teach the parents about adolescent behavior

Inform parents about the purposes, organization, and activities of the school

Inform parents about the purposes and procedures of the counseling program in the school

Inform parents about the needs, characteristics, abilities, interests, and personalities of their own children

Aid parents develop understandings, techniques, and attitudes that will improve their relationships with their children

Provide support to parents as they seek to resolve their own problems and meet their own needs

Aid parents and children together to find solutions to specific problems.

TEACHING PARENTS ABOUT ADOLESCENTS

Let us consider these functions in greater detail. The counselor, because of his training and experience, presumably has a larger fund of information about what adolescents do and why they do it than most parents have. The experience with adolescents of most parents is limited to observations they have made of themselves as children, of their friends at that time, of their own children, usually relatively few in number, and to the indirect experiences and reports of friends and family. Thus, many parents have inadequate frames of reference within which to evaluate or judge the behavior of their own children. A parent, for example, who was intellectually gifted as a child and who associated with similar children may have had little experience with children of average intelligence. When by some genetic event he himself has a child of average intelligence, he may find the behavior and reactions of this child somewhat confusing. Similarly, a father who as an adolescent was primarily interested in athletics and sports and whose friends were similarly inclined may be puzzled and bewildered by an adolescent son whose interests, rather than being in athletics, are in science, or music, or art, or writing. A mother who is and always has been socially skillful and interested in relationships with other persons may be unable to determine whether her daughter who is more introspective is merely a normally shy and somewhat quiet girl or if she is a neurotic or perhaps even psychotic child. A father who considers himself a self-made man and who reports to his family that he has been self-supporting since the age of twelve may not understand whether his own son is unusually lazy and unreliable or whether he is fairly typical of other boys reared in a culture similar to the one provided by the father.

A few sources of information are available to parents concerning adolescent behavior, and perhaps one of the best publications which can be placed in their hands by a counselor is issued by the Children's Bureau of the Social Security Administration, U.S. Department of Health, Education, and Welfare, *The Adolescent in Your Family* (1954). This 110-page volume discusses the phenomenon of adolescence, the influence of early life experiences, the implications of physical change, the development of independence and breaking away from childhood, the development of responsible behavior, the roles of friends and companions, the adjustment to the opposite sex, the development of emotions in adolescence, the health needs of adolescents, and role of the parent in helping adolescents plan their educational and vocational futures.

The counselor often can serve a useful purpose by discussing with parents the questions they have about adolescent behavior and providing to parents standards of reference that will allow them to evaluate the behavior of their own children. Essentially, parents are concerned with the question, "When should we worry and do something about a situation, and when should we accept it as normal?" In providing information he has obtained from his own experiences and from his studies of abnormal psychology, child development, and the psychology of individual differences, the counselor can aid the parent to view his own child more objectively and plan more sensibly.

TEACHING PARENTS ABOUT THE SCHOOL

The counselor also serves a useful purpose in interpreting the school to parents. Modern educational policy and practice have been subjected to so much discussion, criticism, countercriticism, and evaluation that parents, as much as professional educators, are confused by the discrepant statements made about education. To what extent does a child's school provide for his own individual needs? To what extent does it emphasize traditional or classical learnings? To what extent does it provide an opportunity for the child to develop initiative, imagination, and creativity? To what extent does it help the child learn about the limits that society imposes on his behavior? Does the school approach these problems in an authoritative or a democratic way? How is the child's time scheduled in school? Who helps make decisions regarding the child? What are the school's and the teachers' attitudes toward homework and independent study? What does the school's reporting system actually mean? Do teachers welcome visits from parents? How much assistance with schoolwork does the school expect the parent to provide the child? What activities does the school sanction and which ones does it discourage? Parents face all these questions at one time or another, and they can be better informed and more comfortable as a result of discussion of these questions with counselors, teachers, and administrators.

The modern school is a complex and confusing institution. Parents are the strongest supporters of education, and when the counselor helps parents better understand the strengths and weaknesses of the school, he not only provides the parents a service, but perhaps even more, he provides a service to the community. The counselor of course shares this responsibility with every other member of the staff, and by no means is he the school's sole public relations representative.

The reaction of a child to counseling frequently depends on the reaction of the parent to counseling, and most parents know relatively little about counseling and even less about the role of the school counselor. Before World War II, the number of school counselors was small, and of today's parents, perhaps fewer than 10 per cent, when they were in high school, had experience with school counselors. Most parents know at least something about teachers and principals, as pupils they had experience with these persons, but most of them know little about counselors; one of the counselor's incessant tasks is to interpret his own role to parents.

Frequently this can be done effectively in group sessions, at PTA meetings, before community clubs and organizations, and in conferences with groups of parents. Always, however, it must be done again each time the counselor meets with a parent. Thus, when a counselor invites a parent to see him about his child, the counselor must carefully define his own role to the parent, making sure that the parent realizes the counselor's responsibilities, authority, limitations, concern and interest with the child and his parents, and his appreciation of the child's needs. As counselors work effectively with parents, parental and subsequently community support of counseling will enable counselors to extend their services to an increasing number of pupils.

TEACHING PARENTS ABOUT THEIR CHILDREN

Many parents have resorted to counselors for information about their own children. Although they may need information, at least as seen by the counselor, about the general subject of adolescence, about the school, and about counseling, usually they are interested primarily in their own children. The counselor should appreciate that most parents know far more about their children than do counselors, and the counselor best serves in this function by providing information the parent does not have and in helping the parent reformulate, when appropriate, his total view of the child.

Most parents of high school pupils know the general intellectual level of their child. They know whether the child is superior, inferior, or average intellectually. Some parents, however, have misjudged the intellectual ability of their children and assumed they had inferior ability when the fact was they had superior aptitude, or on the other hand, they have perceived their child as being an intellectually gifted child when he was only an average child. The parents' emphatic request for test scores, particularly IQs, should be interpreted by the counselor as a seeking of information and reassurance concerning the intellectual status of their child. For several decades, psychologists, psychometricians, and educators have assumed they should not reveal test scores to parents, particularly scores on tests of intellectual ability. Instead they have interpreted scores using descriptive phrases. In spite of questions concerning the wisdom of this policy, the many hazards of providing specific test scores to parents support this approach, and only in unusual cases, and seldom in response to parental pressure, should specific test scores be provided to parents. The following interview excerpt shows how one counselor dealt with this problem:

COUNSELOR: I can understand your concern about Joseph, Mrs. Hatch. In elementary school he obtained very good grades. I junior high school his grades were still good, although not as good as they had been before. But during the past year and a half in high school his grades have really dropped.
PARENT: I feel sure that he has enough ability to do well in high school, and I just can't understand why he doesn't.
COUNSELOR: You don't think that his trouble in school this year is a result of lack of ability?
PARENT: No, I am sure he has enough ability. He has a room of his own to study in and a nice desk. We don't let him look at television when he is supposed to study, and he has to do his studying before he does anything else.

COUNSELOR: In spite of the fact that study conditions seem to be very good, he still doesn't do well.

PARENT: That's right. Now, what I would really like to find out is whether he has as good ability as his father, and I think he has. I know he has taken some intelligence tests, and I would like to find out what his IQ is.

COUNSELOR: Yes, he has taken some intelligence tests. I believe he started to take these when he was in the third grade, and we have several test scores for him.

PARENT: What is his IQ?

COUNSELOR: All of these tests, going way back to the third grade, indicate that Joseph is a moderately bright boy. More recent tests show he is well above average for high school students, and certainly he has enough ability to do well in high school. He should be able to find a college in which he will be a good student.

PARENT: But what is his IQ?

COUNSELOR: I am reluctant to give specific test scores to either pupils or parents. In fact, I never do that, but I am sure that the kind of information we can discuss will be just as useful, perhaps more useful to you than the test scores. We know, for instance, that Joseph has very good verbal ability. He can handle words very well. His ability to deal with numbers is about average, a little below that of his verbal ability, but nevertheless, these two together indicate that he has enough ability to do well in high school. These test scores consistently place him in the upper one-third of high school students. He is not in the upper 5 or 10 per cent, but he is well above average, and enough above average so I am sure that you and I can conclude that his trouble in school during the past year or so is not due to lack of ability. We must look for other reasons.

The research described in Chapter 10 emphasized the importance of parental attitudes and home atmosphere as a determinant of pupils' plans and behavior. If pupils are to make educational and vocational plans appropriate for their abilities and needs, parents, as soon as possible, must have a realistic perception of these abilities and needs. If a father and mother are to encourage a child to consider appropriate types of schools, they must have enough information about the child to help decide what is appropriate. If high-ability children are to be encouraged to attend college by their parents, their parents must know that these children have the potential for college long before such a decision has to be made, and family discussion and conversation must be based on this assumption. The parent of each child, year by year, should learn more about the ability and the potential of his child and should have the opportunity to discuss with counselors and teachers the implications of this information. Even understanding their own children will not result in all parents encouraging their children to use their abilities, and counselors often must talk with parents and attempt to motivate them to encourage their children.

Parents need information not only about the abilities of their children, but also about their other characteristics. A parent who has had an opportunity each year to review with a counselor or a teacher the scores his child has made currently and in previous years on the Iowa Tests of Basic Skills or Iowa Tests of Educational Development can obtain accurate information about how his child is progressing in school, how his child compares this year to last year, and how his child compares to other children who have succeeded or failed in a variety of curricula.

A parent who knows that on the Strong Vocational Interest Blank his child's interests are comparable or similar to the interests of men successful in engineering, chemistry, and physics, but dissimilar to the interests of men in accounting, banking, and other business occupations will be less prone to urge his reluctant son to enter the family business than if he did not have this information. A parent who knows how counselors, teachers, and other pupils react to his child is in a better position to study his own reactions to his child than if he did not have this information. The information that the counselor provides to a parent about his own child frequently is the very information the parent requires in order to understand his child's needs.

HELPING PARENTS LEARN WHAT TO DO WITH THEIR CHILDREN

Parents not only require information about their children, but they frequently can benefit from information and advice concerning ways of living with their children. Some parents wish to discuss with counselors the extent to which their children require stricter discipline or more leniency at home, or greater or less independence. Some parents can benefit from discussing the place of punishment and reward in raising the adolescent. Some parents can learn with a counselor how the adolescent can best be aided to handle money, or to establish and maintain appropriate relationships with the opposite sex, or to explore educational and vocational opportunities. The counselor is not expected to teach the parent how to be a parent, but often the counselor can aid the parent in developing certain skills, attitudes, and approaches that help solve problems.

Counselors sometimes aid parents by helping with relatively specific problems. Often, children who have developed adequate emotional control over their social behavior and who have learned how to use efficiently their abilities and potentials encounter problems and conflicts that perplex parents. A pupil may decide to leave school before the parents consider he is ready, or another may decide to marry when the parents consider him too young, or a boy may decide to be an engineer when the parents think he lacks mathematical ability. Counselors can provide opportunities for parents to review the nature of the problem, to study the source of the problem, to understand the pupil's perception of the situation, and to explore possible ways in which the parents can approach the problem.

THE COUNSELOR PROVIDES SUPPORT TO PARENTS

Finally, the counselor sometimes serves an important role by providing psychological support to parents. Parents, both as fathers and mothers and as adults, have problems and emotional needs of their own. Problems that parents have with children may be expressions of other and perhaps more basic problems of the parents themselves. Fathers can feel inadequate and anxious because of the economic competition in which they find themselves; mothers may feel unwanted and superfluous because of the increasing independence of other members of the family. The behavior of children may be a recapitulation of similar behavior of the parents, and parents may remember with anxiety and guilt their own past behaviors and thus project these anxieties onto their children. The counselor usually is not in a position to provide psychotherapy to parents, and seldom does the counselor have an opportunity to provide intensive or effective counseling in order to help parents solve their own problems, but the counselor can provide emotional support and understanding and sometimes effectively refer the parent to other sources of help. This is indicated in the following excerpt from an interview.

COUNSELOR: You're afraid that if Dick doesn't go to college next fall, he never will?
FATHER: I meant to go to state college after I worked a year, but never did.
COUNSELOR: So if Dick enlists after he graduates, you feel he may do what you did?
FATHER: Yes. After a few months my mother became ill, and the family needed whatever money I could earn. Then after a couple of years, I was married and college was out. Now, I've really paid for it.
COUNSELOR: And yet, you're successful in your job, have an awfully nice family, and seem to have a good life.
FATHER: But I always feel I should have gone to college. I'm sure I would have been able to get further.
COUNSELOR: You mean on your job?
FATHER: No, I guess not that. I've done very well there. I'd just feel better about it.
COUNSELOR: You don't want Dick to feel this same way?
FATHER: Yes, but no. I guess I'm getting what's good for me and what's good for him mixed up.

HOW PARENTS AND COUNSELORS PERCEIVE ONE ANOTHER

Counselors sometimes imply that the problems of pupils originate in unwise, selfish, or emotionally unstable parents, and they may conclude that if children could be raised by perfect parents or without parents, pupils would be able to avoid many of their perplexing problems. Loevinger (1953) has indentified what she has called the "mother-blaming complex among psychologists," and she describes this as "the tendency of an adult to identify himself with the child and the child's insatiable demands upon the mother." This mother blaming has become a rather prominent part of our culture, as was demonstrated by the popularity of books by Strecker (1946) and Wylie (1942) during the 1940s. These books and corresponding discussions in professional counseling journals most often refer to the harmful effects of the mother on the child, although counselors often include the father among those most responsible for the child's problems.

This attitude toward pupils' parents suggests that many counselors have failed to solve their own conflicts involving authority, insofar as these conflicts usually have their source in the relationships between parent and child. As a result of this lack of understanding, counselors sometimes mistakenly describe as one of their main functions the helping of the pupil to achieve independence, when more properly he needs not to achieve independence, but rather needs to develop a mature and appropriate set of dependency relationships with others. The way to help a person live happily with his family is not to move him out of the family so that he can be independent and at the same time lose those satisfactions inherent in the family situation, but rather to help him develop comfortable and appropriate dependency relationships so that the family fills for him certain emotional needs and at the same time allows him adequate opportunity to develop both emotionally and socially.

In working with parents, counselors frequently have opportunity to observe a variety of types of conflict between pupils and parents. Some of these conflicts result from the two parties possessing discrepant interests, values, and attitudes. Some conflicts are due to immature emotional dependencies between the students and the parents, and not always are these immaturities on the side of the pupil. Other conflicts are due to inadequate communication between parents and pupils. Still others are due to inadequate, but habitualized skills of dealing with other persons.

The counselor usually is concerned with making the pupil feel more comfortable in his relationship with his parents. Sometimes this can be done only by removing the adolescent from the immediate environment of the family, but too often the counselor thinks this is the only alternative. Realistically, seldom can this be done. Sometimes the pupil can be made more comfortable by being assisted in changing his perception of his parents and in developing a new acceptance of them through obtaining an understanding of his parents' needs and problems. Sometimes pupils can be helped by providing them with a new repertoire of behaviors involving their relationships with parents.

THE PARENT AS A COUNSELING RESOURCE

Counselors must remember that the parent is an important counseling resource. The parent knows the pupil through living in close emotional and physical proximity and frequently can actively cooperate with the counselor in helping the pupil.

Our assumption in this text has been that the more information the counselor has about the pupil, the better his understanding of the pupil's needs will be, and the better they can work together. Much of the information obtained about pupils is derived from interviews, school records, and psychological tests. Sometimes reports can be obtained from teachers and other pupils. A new perspective of the pupil, however, is offered by the parent, who can illuminate not only the counselee's present behavior, but also provide information about his development. Concerning a pupil who was quiet and subdued at school, the counselor would know one thing if his parents reported that he was hostile and aggressive at home and another thing if his parents reported that he was comfortable at home.

More directly, the parent frequently has control over the pupil's physical and social environment. Whether the pupil has adequate study space, whether he is provided with adequate opportunity for social activity and recreation, and whether he has opportunity to consider occupational and educational alternatives depend on the parents. Whether the pupil has many visitors in his home or spends much time visiting others can be influenced through parent and counselor cooperation.

Parents provide a natural source of emotional support for pupils, and counselors can help parents realize the importance of having their children learn that they are accepted and loved in their family. Essentially, this means bringing to an overt behavior level that which is already at a conscious level in order to help parents satisfy some of the important needs of their children.

In summary, many parents need support from counselors. When a parent is concerned about his child, when he feels he has done his best as a parent and realizes his own limitations, there may be little more he can do. As the pupil makes his trial-and-error attempts to mature, however, parents may need reassurance and support from counselors.

Finally, parents may benefit from the same counseling obtained by their children. The parent who seriously told the counselor that he was perplexed because his adolescent son was in difficulty revealed a real need when he stated, "I can't understand it, since I have only two rules he has to follow: first, he has to pick up after himself and not leave things lying around; and second, he has to do what he is told to do when he is told to do it."

As the parent gains new understanding of his own needs, as he learns more about his own psychological defenses, as he practices new skills in maintaining satisfactory relations with others, the behavior of the pupil should reflect these changes.

RELATIONSHIPS WITH TEACHERS

The only concept of counseling relevant for educational objectives is one which defines the counselor as a member of the educational team carrying shared and mutual responsibility for conducting the school's broad program. For counselors to be accepted by the school and the community, they must work continually and closely with others employed in the school. When the counselor is perceived as a clinical or service adjunct in the school, then his role becomes minor and unimportant.

Because of this we must consider, in addition to the relationships between the counselor and the pupil and the counselor and the parent, the equally important relationship between the counselor and the classroom teacher. What the counselor and the teacher know about one another and their respective jobs, how they feel about one another, and how they behave toward and with one another, influence the extent to which both can help pupils.

Most teachers believe they know and many teachers actually do know more about classroom teaching and related problems than do most counselors. Nevertheless, counselors are far from naïve about teaching, for in all states that provide certificates to counselors, teaching experience is one of the requirements for certification. On the other hand, most counselors believe they know, and many actually do know, more about counseling than do teachers. Both the counselor and the teacher have a sincere and intense interest and concern with their own activities, and this sometimes, unfortunately, may result in reduced esteem for the function of the other person. Both must recognize that the purposes of the modern school can be attained only if each is allowed and encouraged to do the best he can in his own special job and that the success of each in working with children depends on the effectiveness of the work done by the other.

The important relationship between the counselor and the teacher revolves around five functions:

1. Classroom guidance programs
2. Consultation of the teacher with the counselor regarding individual pupils in the classroom
3. Consultation by the counselor with the teacher regarding counselees
4. Consultation with the counselor by the teacher regarding teaching and professional problems

5. Joint activity of the counselor and the teacher regarding school, curricular, extracurricular, personnel, and administrative problems and programs

CLASSROOM GUIDANCE PROGRAMS

The nature of this interaction depends on the organization of the school's counseling and guidance program. One of the most common methods of organization provides for the social studies teacher in the eighth, ninth, or tenth grade to teach a unit on occupations. Sometimes the counselor is invited to teach this unit; more often the counselor consults with the teacher, assists in outlining the content of the unit, provides material to be included, and arranges for special resources such as films, tests, books and monographs, and visitors to the class (Willey & Strong, 1957).

Counselors frequently have some responsibility for the instructional and classroom testing program when standardized tests are used. In some schools the counselor carries primary responsibility for these programs; in other schools the counselor serves as a consultant who provides information and advice upon request. The counselor is expected to have current and reliable information concerning available tests and to provide sound judgments and relevant information when these are called for.

Schools with homeroom organizations or "block classes" assign to classroom teachers responsibilities for a variety of counseling and guidance functions, and the professional counselors in the school carry varying degrees of responsibility for these programs. They may supervise and actually administer broader aspects of homeroom programs, or they may only participate in general discussions of these programs in teacher meetings and during other occasions.

In each of these respects, the counselor is expected to be well informed about available methods and materials, to have information about experimental evaluation and other related research concerning group and classroom methods, and to have an attitude that allows and encourages teachers to seek help and consultation and that provides for continuing development of teachers to better use these programs.

CONSULTATION BY TEACHERS WITH COUNSELORS REGARDING INDIVIDUAL
    STUDENT PROBLEMS

Each teacher inevitably will have pupils who present special problems in the classroom. Sometimes these pupils are particularly gifted and require intellectual stimulation and advanced work and assignments. Sometimes pupils are retarded, either because of limited aptitudes and abilities or because of educational deficiencies that might be remediable. Sometimes pupils are excessively shy and withdrawn; sometimes they are disorderly and insolent; sometimes they are disturbed and emotionally upset. In each instance, the teacher is called on to draw from all of his or her information and experience in order to best understand and to determine the best way of treating the pupil. The counselor serves a useful function here by first providing the teacher with additional information about the pupil from cumulative records, test scores, counseling records, and other sources; and secondly, by discussing with the teacher the meaning and implication of all available information about the pupil. In this way, the teacher and the counselor together can identify hypotheses which might help explain the pupil's behavior, evaluate the evidence which supports or fails to support these hypotheses, and draw conclusions or diagnoses concerning the pupil's behavior and his problems which lead to the exploration of alternative courses of action.

Counselors also, using cumulative records, test scores, and reports from others, can identify pupils needing special attention of whom the teacher is unaware. The counselor thus identifies and calls to the teacher's notice pupils who have reading disabilities, emotional or health problems, exceptional talents, or unusual interests.

CONSULTATION BY THE COUNSELOR WITH THE TEACHER REGARDING COUNSELEES

The counselor's perception of counselees usually is determined in large part by the impression the pupil makes in an interviewing room. Additional information, of course, is obtained from the student's cumulative folder, but frequently the best and most helpful kind of information is obtained from the teacher who is in a position to observe the pupil as he approaches his schoolwork, as he lives with his schoolmates, and as he participates in out-of-classroom activities. Teachers can tell counselors how students behave, and these observations and reports sometimes do and sometimes do not agree with the reports obtained directly from the pupil or from the observations made by the counselor. In these instances the counselor needs the teacher in order to adequately understand the pupil, just as much as in the previous instance the teacher needed the counselor.

PROBLEMS OF TEACHER PRACTICE AND PERSONALITY

The counselor is not trained and generally not expected to provide counseling services to teachers regarding their own problems; but as a counselor establishes his or her reputation in a school as being a real aid to pupils, teachers sometimes make tentative requests for such assistance regarding their own problems. In general, counselors can provide sympathetic understanding, but usually should quickly help the teacher find other sources of help. Counselors cannot effectively counsel members of their own family or close friends, and neither can they effectively counsel colleagues or others whom they know well or with whom they have frequent contact outside the counseling relationship.

Counselors sometimes can aid teachers in improving their own teaching and classroom behavior. Often counselors are tempted to move quite directly when they sense problems. For example, one counselor heard several reports that a teacher applied varying types of punishment in the classroom designed more, it seemed, to make pupils lose status with themselves and others and to provide personal satisfaction to the teacher than to improve the pupil's behavior. Was this only a "technique" the teacher used or was it an expression of a basic personality need? Would advice from the counselor help or hinder? Another counselor heard of a teacher who was using financial rewards and punishments in the classroom, punishing some students by fining them, rewarding others by payment from the fund. Knowing this was counter to school policy, and perhaps illegal, the counselor was tempted to move directly and halt these practices. In cases similar to these, counselors should not assume administrative responsibilities. They can, however, call to the attention of principals or other administrators broad and general types of practices that may require attention in the school without revealing the names of those teachers practicing them or without being identified themselves as supervisors. Thus, if a counselor finds that much cheating is allowed in one teacher's classes, he might discuss with the principal and with all teachers the need to carefully study the problem of cheating throughout the school. In this general area of relationships between counselors and teachers, no general recipes are adequate, and in each case the counselor must carefully evaluate and consider the entire situation and make use of his best judgment.

COOPERATION BY THE COUNSELOR AND TEACHER ON SCHOOL PROGRAMS AND PROBLEMS

One of the counselor's most important relationships with the teacher occurs in situations from which evolve school policies and programs. Counselors are members of the school faculty. In some instances counselors are asked to serve on or as chairmen of committees, often committees on testing or group-guidance programs. Sometimes these committees are primarily concerned with aspects of the school which are noncounseling, but which depend largely on information and opinions that the counselor can provide. The school curriculum is determined by many things, and among these is the nature of the student body. The counselor usually can know more about the general characteristics of the student body than can most other persons in the school.

Many problems require decisions in the school, problems which have no absolutely right or wrong solution. Often the counselor can participate in this decision making as a well-informed and objective person, who nevertheless is no specialist with these particular problems. The counselor will be able to maintain the respect of others in the school most easily if he or she carefully refrains from speaking about these problems with great authority. For example, questions such as these may arise: How should we handle students who are married in high school? Should they be allowed to remain in school? Should they be allowed to participate in activities? Should they be encouraged to associate with other children? What kind of clothing is appropriate for pupils to wear in school? What types of report cards and forms should be used in the school? Should the senior class be allowed to have its prom in a downtown hotel which has a bar? Should students who have formed religious clubs or associations be allowed to use the cafeteria and classrooms during activity hours and lunch periods? With these types of questions, the counselor can assist, just as others in the school can, but always the counselor must refrain from wearing his cloak as a counselor when moving into problems for which his professional training has offered no special preparation. He has many responsibilities directly related to his role as a professional counselor and others related to his less specialized role as a member of the school staff.

In summary, the relationships between the counselor and the teacher are expressed primarily through the day-to-day and face-to-face contacts between the two, the participation of both in the in-service training of each other, the consultation with one another concerning both general problems and problems about individual students, the referral of pupils from one to the other for specialized kinds of assistance, and cooperative activity in dealing with broad and general school problems and policies.

COUNSELORS' RELATIONSHIPS WITH SCHOOL ADMINISTRATORS

What the counselor actually does, the assignment given to him by his administrator, and the functions he is allowed to serve best define the quality of the relationship between the counselor and his administrator. The very existence of the counselor in the school indicates that the administration of the school is somewhat favorably disposed toward counseling. Having a counselor in the school, however, is not sufficient to indicate a favorable relationship; the counselor may be there because the administration considers it the thing to do. The counselor may be on the staff because of pressure the administration was unable to resist.

An administrator, either a principal or a superintendent, who under-

stands the proper role of counseling in a school, who is sympathetic with
the purposes and methods of counseling, and who has confidence in the
professional competence and personal qualities of his counselors will
provide an opportunity for the counselor to devote his energy and time
to proper counseling activities. The administrator who lacks these characteristics, on the other hand, may restrict the counseling activities of
the counselor by assigning him administrative, clerical, and teaching assignments that more rightfully belong to others employed in the school.
Some surveys of how counselors distribute their time on the job suggest
that this occurs in some schools.

In 1949, Arnold (1949) sent questionnaires to high school counselors
in Ohio and found that the 126 who responded said the function which
demanded most of their time was related to attendance and tardiness
problems. The next most time-demanding activities were counseling on
personal, social, or school problems and discipline. Vocational and educational counseling ranked fifth, only slightly ahead of clerical work
related to guidance.

Martyn (1957) reported that 35 school counselors near San Francisco
judged they devoted between 43 and 80 per cent of their time to clerical
work.

At the other end of the country, Purcell (1957) reported that, of 154
counselors around Long Island, 15 per cent said they prepared the
school's master schedule, 64 per cent worked with attendance problems,
75 per cent administered tests, 39 per cent scored tests, 35 per cent recorded tests results, and 70 per cent judged that they spent one-half hour
per day or more on clerical work.

Tennyson (1958), in a questionnaire study of 152 Missouri counselors,
reported that 47 per cent of their time was spent in counseling, and a
total of 60 per cent of their time was devoted to a category called "assistance to students," a category which included counseling. They reported devoting 21 per cent of their time to activities included in a category called "assistance to administration." Generalizations cannot be
made from these few studies to counselors throughout the entire country,
and conditions in counseling change greatly from year to year, so that
surveys made a few years ago may not accurately reflect conditions today. In many schools, however, the clerical and administrative assignments of the counselor are quite obvious, and each hour the counselor
devotes to duties other than counseling, duties that perhaps could be
done more efficiently and more economically by other persons, results in
an hour's less counseling service being provided to the pupils in that
school.

Counselors often are concerned with the same problems which concern
school administrators, and the counselor who proves himself to be ef-

ficient in carrying out his duties and who shows good judgment and ability to relate well to other persons impresses the school administrator as a person capable of doing some or many of the things usually done by the administrator. Inevitably the administrator will be tempted to seek the help of the counselor in noncounseling duties, and sometimes the counselor is faced with the rather difficult task of demonstrating to the principal or superintendent the adverse effect on the counseling program and on individual students of devoting counselor's time to these other assignments.

In recognition of the many demands made by schools on the time of the counselor, a conference called by the American Personnel and Guidance Association and supported by the American Association for the Advancement of Science in Ann Arbor, Michigan, during 1958, prepared a report (AAAS, 1958) which contained a brief description of the legitimate functions of the counselor in the school.

Seven areas of counselor responsibility described as the counselor's major functions were as follows:

(1) *Utilization of effective techniques and tools in counseling to assist students:* (a) in attaining realistic self-understanding; (b) in evaluating alternatives; (c) in formulating appropriate goals; (d) in making independent decisions about educational and vocational plans and personal adjustment.

(2) *Consultation with parents, school staff, and specialized personnel staff about student problems and plans.* The staff includes teachers, health personnel, social workers, school psychological workers, attendance personnel, and others. The counselor seeks to interpret and to achieve better understanding of student differences and problems, to encourage and maintain optimal conditions for pupil growth and development, and to derive help from these sources in his close work with the students. The team approach that characterizes case-study conferences to aid individual students carries over into staff interrelationships about such aspects of the school program as curriculum, teaching methods, formation of class groups, scheduling, and administrative procedures.

(3) *Maintenance of liaison relationships with community agencies and referral services.* The counselor must have supplementary and supportive welfare, therapeutic, and informational services to meet individual student needs.

(4) *Identification of individual talents and aptitudes.* The counselor conducts the school program of testing and of identifying and appraising talent and organizes the comprehensive cumulative pupil record plan that is essential to such a program. He also is obligated to develop channels and means for full utilization and interpretation of the data, for the purpose of understanding students more fully and helping them gain better self-understanding.

(5) *Provision of informational service to include the full range of educational and occupational information.* The counselor establishes means for utilizing information material and occupational files, school libraries, and counseling offices; for individual student counseling; for occupational units taught by classroom teachers; and for group approaches designed to acquaint students with appropriate environmental information.

(6) *Research and service studies.* The counselor has responsibility for contributing

data that will provide a clearer description of the school population being served, normative data for use in interpreting objective testing, follow-up studies of former students, and evaluation of counseling services and techniques.

(7) *Job placement of students and counsel on post-high school education.* The counselor has key responsibility for assisting students to take intelligent steps after graduation from high school. In large schools, the actual placement work may be performed by others in the guidance program, but the counselor still holds key responsibility.

The extent to which a school counselor is provided with opportunities to serve these functions, as opposed to demands that he devote his time to administrative, clerical, and classroom teaching responsibilities, provides an index of the counselor's relationship with his administration. The counselor must have the trust and faith of his principal and superintendent; it is not enough that he be competent, but also he must impress others with his competency. A reputation for competency can exist for a short time even when basic skill and integrity are absent. This reputation, however, can endure only if it is merited.

RELATIONSHIPS WITH OTHERS

The counselor must have primary concern with the relationships he maintains with pupils, their parents, teachers, and his supervisors, but also he must depend on other groups in the community for support if he is to effectively perform his mission. Particularly important here are the counselor's relationships with employers of school graduates and college and university staff members, usually those concerned with college admissions. Counselors must be informed about local employment opportunities, and such information is derived from a variety of sources including local, public, and private employment agencies, personnel offices of businesses, and individual employers. The counselor also must have established a reputation, so that employers have confidence in the recommendations he makes and in the referrals he sends. In some schools this relationship is encouraged by the membership of the counselor and other representatives from the school in community organizations, service clubs, churches, and other groups to which local employers belong. In some instances these relationships are maintained by systematic and regular visits of counselors with these persons.

Relationships with representatives of colleges and universities are initiated and stimulated through mutual membership in educational and professional organizations, invitations from the high school to college staff members to visit the local schools, visits made by high school counselors and teachers to colleges and universities attended by graduates, and attendance of high school and college staff members at conferences specifically designed to advance such relationships (Berdie & Snoke, 1959).

The relationships maintained by the counselor with the community at large, as shown by the general reputation of the counselor and the school counseling program in the community, affect the success of the entire counseling program. After years of successful counseling, a counselor hopes that he and his program have established a reputation which justifies the school's providing his service. The counselor who gives effective service, but does no more than that, sometimes fails to establish this reputation. In a sense the counselor has to be a public relations agent quick to take carefully reasoned advantage of opportunities to present to groups in the community descriptions of his objectives, his programs, and his problems. The world will not beat a path to the man who makes a better mousetrap unless it knows that his is a better product. Similarly, the community will not accept the counselor who is doing a good job unless it knows he is effective. Public relations, although not one of the major functions of the school counselor, certainly is a function that cannot be overlooked.

In summary, the relationships maintained by counselors with a variety of persons determine in large part the effectiveness of their work. Much of the counselor's work depends directly on the relationship between him and the persons with whom he works, particularly pupils, parents, and teachers. Counseling is much easier to do with persons who are well motivated for counseling, who are seeking counseling, and who are accepting of the services offered by the counselor. The community will provide the counselor with the opportunity to make his services available only as long as the counselor is able to convince the community that he has something to offer. Counseling relationships not only provide one of the most important avenues for counseling, but provide the very basis for developing counseling programs.

QUESTIONS FOR STUDY

1. To what extent are the terms "counseling" and "discipline" contradictory? To what extent are they compatible?
2. What are the problems and advantages of the part-time counselor who is also the baseball coach and has pupils both as counselees and athletes?
3. Discuss the dual role of the part-time counselor who both teaches a course and counsels.
4. List the questions you anticipate parents ask or would like to ask counselors.
5. What is the counselor's role in relation with parents concerning the school's grading system?
6. What resources are available in your home community that provide assistance to parents with severe emotional conflicts?

7. What should counselors know about the work of the classroom teacher to make them more understanding of the teacher's problems?
8. How can the counselor aid the teacher with "discipline" problems?
9. What are some administrative functions a counselor might perform legitimately?
10. Discuss the "public relations" responsibility of the counselor.

REFERENCES

American Association for the Advancement of Science. Identification and guidance of able students. Report on Conference on Testing and Counseling, University of Michigan, May 28–31, 1958.

Arnold, D. L. Time spent by counselors and deans on various activities. *Occupations*, 1949, **27**, 391–393.

Berdie, R. F. Counselor attitudes. *Educ. psychol. Measmt.*, 1951, **11**, 349–354.

Berdie, R. F. The counselor and the parent. *J. counsel. Psychol.*, 1955, **2**, 185–188.

Berdie, R. F. Counseling principles and presumptions. *J. counsel. Psychol.*, 1959, **6**, 175–182.

Berdie, R. F., & Snoke, M. S. A continuing experiment in high school-college relations. *J. higher Educ.*, 1959, **30**, 46–49.

Hahn, M., & MacLean, M. S. *General clinical counseling.* New York: McGraw-Hill, 1950.

Loevinger, Jane. The mother-blaming complex among psychologists. *Amer. Psychologist*, 1953, **8**, 748–750.

Martyn, K. A. We are wasting the counselor's time. *Calif. J. sec. Educ.*, 1957, **32**, 439–441.

Purcell, F. E. Counselor duties—a survey. *Sch. Counselor*, 1957, **4**, 35–38.

Rogers, C. R. The attitudes and orientation of the counselor in client-centered therapy. *J. consult. Psychol.*, 1949, **13**, 82–94.

Shostrom, E. L., & Brammer, L. M. *The dynamics of the counseling process.* New York: McGraw-Hill, 1952.

Strecker, E. A. *Their mothers' sons.* Philadelphia: Lippincott, 1946.

Tennyson, W. W. Time: the counselor's dilemma. *Personnel Guid. J.*, 1958, **37**, 129–135.

Tyler, Leona E. *The work of the counselor.* New York: Appleton-Century-Crofts, 1953.

U.S. Department of Health, Education, and Welfare. *The adolescent in your family.* Social Security Administration, Children's Bureau Publication 347, Washington, D.C., 1954.

Warnken, R. G. The educational background of male schizophrenic patients. Unpublished doctoral dissertation, University of Minnesota, 1957.

Willey, R. D., & Strong, W. M. *Group procedures in guidance.* New York: Harper & Row, 1957.

Williamson, E. G. *Counseling adolescents.* New York: McGraw-Hill, 1950.

Wylie, P. *Generation of vipers.* New York: Holt, 1942.

CHAPTER 13

Professional Responsibilities of the Counselor

Effective counseling influences the welfare of individuals and the structure and function of society. In the lives of most counselees, the role of the counselor is small, but not necessarily unimportant. Even without counseling most people achieve important understandings and make significant decisions rather similar to those that would have followed counseling. For many persons, however, counseling is one of the significant determinants of their decisions, and for some persons counseling may be the important determinant.

The outcomes of counseling depend first on what the counselor does, and second on the kind of person he is. This distinction between the deed and the doer is valid only to a limited extent, but the counselor's skills are different from his attitudes, and we must consider both his methods and his values (Berdie, 1951). In this chapter we are concerned primarily with the attitudes and ideas that reflect the counselor's values and ethics.

Counseling as a "helping" profession has as its primary purpose improving the welfare of others. This objective has been defined at various times in terms of adjustment, happiness, homeostasis, productivity, satisfaction, progress, or success. Immediately we can see how the definition of this objective depends on the values of the counselor. Puritanical values would direct such a definition toward work stability, psychoanalytic values toward freedom from repression, hedonistic values toward satisfying sensory stimulation, and deistic values toward a feeling of communion. Simply to say that all counselors are trying to make persons happy does not adequately solve the dilemma of counseling objectives, for counselors define "happiness" in terms of their own values and philosophy. Neither is it sufficient to say that problems of ethics for counselors are really not important insofar as all counselors are working toward the welfare of persons. A counselor in a fascist society might have quite different values and proceed differently from a counselor in another kind of social organization.

211

212 *Testing in Guidance and Counseling*

Consequently, if we are to discuss professional and ethical responsibilities of the counselor, we must limit ourselves to the counselor in the society in which we live; and also we must attempt to specify some of the ground rules that we hope will have acceptance from at least a large portion of the persons in that society. Some of these ground rules, as they affect counseling in our society, can be phrased in this way:

1. Each person should be given the opportunity to assume as quickly as he can as much individual responsibility as possible for his own decisions and actions.

2. The individual's freedom of action should be as great as possible within limits imposed by the need to protect the welfare and safety of others.

3. The individual's opportunity to develop into the person he desires to be should not be limited by his race, color, religion, national origin, or socioeconomic status.

4. A society characterized by diversity, rather than by conformity, is a more interesting one in which to live, and one which, in the long run, can best meet the needs of its members. Such diversity is to be encouraged.

5. Each individual in society shares responsibility for the welfare of every other member of society and in turn is dependent on others.

6. Each member of society plays a variety of roles and belongs to a number of subgroups, and the larger group must tolerate and encourage the loyalties of the individual toward these subcultures with which he is affiliated.

Immediately we must recognize that our discussion of professional responsibilities and ethics in counseling is "culture bound," and we consistently must refrain from being provincial and dogmatic in our approach to these problems. As we explore perplexing situations, perhaps the one thing that will become apparent is that in most instances, decisions have to be made in light of the specific situation and that the goodness or badness of the decisions usually depends on the soundness of the counselor's judgment, on the extent to which he perceives the implications of the facts involved, and on his willingness, once his principles become defined, to behave in accordance with these principles.

Counselors are responsible to their counselees and their counselees' families, to their school and their fellow staff members, and to their community at large. Almost always in counseling the interests of these diverse parties coincide, but occasionally the counselor faces a problem of divided loyalties. What might best benefit the counselee might be detrimental to others. Here the counselor must make a difficult decision.

The judgment of the counselor is the final determinant of the answer to these dilemmas. Rules, regulations, and school policies may facilitate the making of these decisions, but their ultimate effectiveness rests on the counselor himself; for this reason, counselors must regard themselves as members of a profession rather than as tradesmen (Darley, 1949; Wrenn, 1949). Their character, their sense of responsibility, their regard for the rights of others, their selflessness, although all integral parts of their personal values, also are components of their working selves (Berdie, 1960).

The "ethical" dilemmas faced by different workers vary from profession to profession. Physicians, lawyers, and ministers are all faced by questions whose answers depend on the worker's ethics. Closest to the questions faced by counselors are those which face psychologists, and counselors should be acquainted with the code of ethics adopted by the American Psychological Association (APA, 1958).

CONFIDENTIALITY

Throughout counseling the counselor must make decisions about what he does and the probable effects of these actions on his counselees. Decisions about communicating information should be made, among other decisions. The counselor is not completely deliberate in his proceedings. He does not always carefully weigh everything he says and does and select on the basis of a carefully reasoned process from all possible actions those which he desires, but he does make many decisions on the basis of the predicted outcomes of his actions. When he gives information to a pupil, he does this after deciding that the pupil will benefit from this learning. When he provides reassurance to a pupil, he does this after deciding that the pupil's anxiety needs alleviation. He gathers information about a pupil through the use of tests or questioning after careful deliberation.

In the same way, when a counselor reports information to others, the decision concerning this action should be made, as are other decisions in counseling, after considering all implications of the alternatives. Reporting information about a counselee to others who are in a position to affect the life of that person is a counseling process, just as is providing information directly to the pupil or providing him with reassurance. When to communicate information, to whom it should be communicated, and the manner of communication should be decided on the basis of predicted outcomes just as are questions concerning the use of other counseling techniques.

Many counselors have subscribed to a dogma of confidentiality, perhaps because this dogma relieves the individual counselor of making many difficult decisions (Gilbert, 1951). Some counselors will report no information about the counselee to anyone. Some will report information about counselees to others only when they have the explicit approval and permission of the counselee. Some counselors will report information about counselees only to a carefully designated list of persons. Some counselors will report only certain information to certain persons, all carefully prescribed in advance.

A point of view adopted by the present authors is that the reporting or communicating of counseling information essentially is similar to other techniques and procedures used in counseling and that the use of the communicating or reporting technique should be decided, not on the basis of dogma, but rather on the basis of the answers to the questions: (1) What are the probable effects of the use of this technique on the counselee? (2) What are its probable effects on other persons?

If the counselor concludes that the pupil will benefit through the reporting of information and that other persons will not be injured, then he should report the information. If reporting will injure either the client or other persons, the counselor will decide that the information should not be reported. This is similar to the process used in selecting other counseling techniques.

THE CASE OF JANE

Jane Bush was an attractive but shy high school sophomore who had no close relationship with anyone in the school other than her English teacher. The English teacher realized that Jane was increasingly unhappy and after several weeks of this observation discussed Jane with the school counselor. The counselor made a point of becoming acquainted with Jane and spoke with her several times, both informally in the halls and on the school grounds, and also in the counselor's office. Jane liked the counselor and over a period of several weeks told the counselor much about her own life and that of her family.

Jane's mother and father were well educated and intelligent persons, both active in their own professional activities. From Jane's description the counselor inferred that her mother was a warm, sympathetic, and understanding woman who had much interest in music and literature and very little interest in housekeeping. Jane described her house as a messy and poorly kept place and said that she refused to have friends visit her home because of its disorder. She quickly said that she would not discuss this with her parents because she realized how silly it really was, and she would not want to hurt her parents' feelings.

The counselor discussed the situation with the English teacher, who had met the parents several times, and after careful consideration decided that the mother's reaction to the girl's feelings would be quite positive. Consequently when the counselor talked with Jane's mother about her eleventh-grade program, she introduced the subject and described to the mother Jane's reactions and her feelings. As the counselor antici-pated, the mother listened with great understanding and made some minor modifications in the family living patterns that resulted in Jane's willingness to bring her friends to her home. Here the counselor made a decision to report information to another party intimately involved with the pupil with the expectation that this would be for the benefit of the pupil and to the injury of no one else. Further counseling was directed toward facilitating communication between Jane and her parents.

Often the parent takes the initiative in seeking information about his child, and the counselor must decide how this information can be com-municated so that it is most helpful to the pupil and his parents. The counselor must carefully delineate between observation and inference, hearsay and fact. He must be able to foresee the effects of such com-munication on both parent and child. He must recognize the parents' great concern with and responsibility for the child and at the same time be willing to communicate selectively. Only in a court can a counselor be *required or forced* to reveal information he possesses, but other social pressures sometimes are almost as effective as court action, and the counselor must be able to maintain his judgment even under these pres-sures.

Obviously, counseling information is never a topic of social conversa-tion, is never discussed with colleagues outside of a professional and private setting, and is never used to enhance the counselor's status or prestige.

THE CASE OF DENNIS

Another case is quite different. Dennis Gray was a high school senior who had taken the Differential Aptitude Tests in the ninth grade. His percentile ranks varied around 50, with a particularly low score on the mechanical comprehension test. His academic work had been better than one would have predicted from these tests, and he was graduating from a large high school in the upper 10 per cent of his class. He had taken mathematics for four years in high school, and his grades had been ex-cellent. His two years of shop work and mechanical drawing had re-sulted in only mediocre grades.

Dennis applied for admission to an engineering school in a mid-western university, and on the college aptitude test and mathematics test required of students entering that school, his scores were in the upper one-half of college freshmen. The admissions office of the school re-quested the high school counselor to send a report of all test scores available for Dennis which would help in deciding on his admission. After carefully reviewing all of the information, the counselor decided that the scores on the Differential Aptitude Tests did not provide an adequate description of the pupil's abilities and consequently did not report those scores. The report that was sent to the admissions office was based primarily on Dennis' academic record and the college aptitude tests he had taken in grades 11 and 12.

THE CASE OF ELLEN

Ellen Brown was graduating from high school after taking three years of typing, shorthand, and bookkeeping. Her grades in these courses were excellent, and her typewriting and shorthand skills were commendable. However, Ellen had never obtained good scores on tests of verbal or numerical ability. Ellen applied for a job which did not require much verbal or numerical ability and her prospective employer asked the high school counselor for a report of Ellen's test scores. The counselor, after discussing this with Ellen, wrote to the employer saying that the scores were quite irrelevant and that she would be unable to report them. She did include the report made by the commercial teacher that Ellen was one of the very superior students in her business classes and that both in her courses and on her job in the school, she had proved to be a thoroughly reliable and dependable person. Ellen was given the job on the basis of her proven skills and qualifications. The counselor's primary responsibility here was to Ellen, not to her prospective employer, but these interests do not conflict. Both the pupil and the employer benefit from appropriate placement; neither is aided when the counselor's sole purpose is to place the pupil in a job.

Making judgments about communicating counseling information frequently is difficult. The counselor usually will wish to consult with his colleagues when faced by these decisions in order to make sure that he has not overlooked any important possibilities and in order that his judgment may be reviewed and the validity of his conclusions examined.

THE CASE OF BILL

Bill Harris was a high school junior when his family moved to another city and enrolled Bill in a high school there. The new high school requested the counselor in the old school to forward Bill's personal record. The counselor in the former school who reviewed his record discovered that Bill had been involved in many personal difficulties in grades 8 and 9, but in grade 10 Bill had made a very good adjustment in the school and had had no difficulty whatsoever. After carefully reviewing all of the evidence, he decided that he would not report Bill's past difficulties to the new school, because Bill's family had solved most of the problems which had resulted in Bill's misbehavior. Before definitely making this decision, however, he discussed it with the assistant principal who asked a few questions about facts that the counselor had not considered.

Nevertheless, after this careful review, the decision remained that this particular information would not be reported to the new school, and the counselor felt much more secure in his judgment.

RECORDS

Confidentiality of information also depends on policies and procedures for maintaining counseling records. The counselor's records are not "public records" maintained for official or public purposes. The purpose of counseling records is to make available to counselors information about pupils that will help in counseling these pupils. Counseling records should be available only to counselors; when information in these records is to be communicated to others, it should be interpreted by counselors.

Test scores sometimes will be included in counseling records, sometimes in other personal records, and sometimes in both places. When scores are to be used by teachers and others in the school, they should be easily available to these persons in places other than the counseling record. When reports are to be sent to persons outside of the school, such as college admissions officers or prospective employers, great discretion is required. Again, no rules or directions can be formulated to provide for all instances other than the generalization that such reporting should never be done in a routine or casual fashion.

In summary, decisions about communicating information regarding students cannot be made on the basis of simple rules or dogmatic regulations. Rather, these decisions must result from careful reasoning, just as must other decisions about the counseling process. Decisions must be based on information about the content of the communication, the persons receiving the communication, and the probable effect of the communication on the student.

OTHER PROFESSIONAL RESPONSIBILITIES OF THE COUNSELOR

The major professional responsibility of the counselor is to provide his students with the best available counseling. Perhaps the only unethical act for the counselor is to provide poor counseling when it is within his power to provide good counseling. This means that the counselor continually must strive to be trained at the highest possible level.

As new methods, procedures, techniques, and principles are discovered in counseling, counselors must learn about them and learn to apply them. The training of a counselor is never completed; his professional responsibilities require that he read incessantly, attend professional meetings to learn of new developments, and continually associate with others in his profession to learn of new opinions and techniques.

This responsibility also extends to the finding of new professional frontiers. Professional associations publish journals and conduct meetings which have as their purposes the dissemination of new information. These professional organizations sponsor committees which deal with scientific and professional problems in counseling, and in these efforts organizations require the support of counselors. No counselor can belong to all of the organizations directly and indirectly related to his profession, but each counselor should lend his support to at least some of the groups which function primarily for the welfare of his counselees and his associates.

The counselor is responsible for knowing about available community resources and for making adequate use of them. Many pupils need to be referred to ministers, community agencies and clinics, physicians and psychiatrists, and youth and community organizations. The counselor must know his own limitations and how others in the community provide means for him to extend his services.

The extent to which the counselor can successfully fulfill his professional responsibilities depends largely on what we might call his personal integrity. His decisions must be based on his desire to help rather than on ease or expediency. He must be willing to sacrifice his time, his comfort, and sometimes his own welfare for the benefit of others. He must know about his own needs to be accepted and liked by others, to have status and security, and to progress in his profession, and he must be able to direct the behavior influenced by his needs. He must know and control his own prejudices and biases and must be tolerant of those who differ from him. We describe here a virtuous paragon with full realization of the humanity of counselors—they want money and fame and sex and fun, as do others—but the counselor cannot be a good counselor unless he also is a good man.

In summary, the professional responsibility of the counselor is to provide his own counselees and others the opportunity for obtaining the most effective and best counseling possible. This responsibility is not limited to counselees the counselor will see today, or this year, but includes counselees of future years. Actions of the counselor should not be decided on the basis of answers to the question "Is it right or wrong?" for this is all too easy, and such answers frequently are based on dogma or tradition; rather his decisions should be based on questions pertaining to predicted outcomes. "If I as a counselor take such an action, how will this affect others?"

QUESTIONS FOR STUDY

1. How can parents be given greater understanding of their children's potentials without reporting actual test scores to them?

2. What should a counselor's reply be when a principal asks him if a student, while being counseled, revealed he had cheated in an examination?
3. A teacher asks a counselor for permission to read the counselor's notes about a student in the teacher's class. What determines the actions of the counselor?
4. How can a school counselor keep aware of the research on counseling constantly being done?
5. What problems face a counselor who becomes increasingly aware of the extent to which his own marital conflicts are distracting him from his counseling? Who counsels the counselor?

REFERENCES

American Psychological Association. Standards of ethical behavior for psychologists. *Amer. Psychologist*, 1958, 13, 266–271.

Berdie, R. F. Counselor attitudes. *Educ. psychol. Measmt.*, 1951, 11, 349–354.

Berdie, R. F. Policies regarding the release of information about students. *J. counsel. Psychol.*, 1960, 7, 149–150.

Darley, J. G. An appraisal of the professional status of personnel work, Part II. In E. G. Williamson (Ed.), *Trends in student personnel work*. Minneapolis: University of Minnesota Press, 1949. Pp. 280–287.

Gilbert, W. M. Relationships between counseling organizations and other divisions. In R. F. Berdie (Ed.), *Concepts and programs of counseling*. Minneapolis: University of Minnesota Press, 1951. Pp. 42–55.

Wrenn, C. G. An appraisal of the professional status of personnel work, Part I. In E. G. Williamson (Ed.), *Trends in student personnel work*. Minneapolis: University of Minnesota Press, 1949. Pp. 264–279.

CHAPTER 14

Counseling Research

What kinds of jobs do our graduates hold as adults? Does the home-room teacher have a counseling function? Can group counseling supplement individual counseling in our schools? How effective are our procedures for reporting pupils' achievement to themselves and their parents? What are the post-high school plans of our twelfth graders, our ninth graders? What are the occupations of the parents of our pupils, and how much education have they had? How many of our high school pupils live on farms?

These are typical of the questions frequently asked school counselors. Research can reveal the answers to these questions. Research can supply answers to practical as well as theoretical questions, and the effective practicing counselor is aware of the importance of research as it helps him do his day-to-day work and contributes to scientific knowledge.

RESEARCH AND PROFESSIONAL DEVELOPMENT

The counselor who wishes to grow approaches his job with an evaluative point of view. He constantly questions the adequacy of his counseling program and its techniques. He tries out new programs and new approaches and evaluates them incessantly. Thus, the practicing counselor habitually inquires and develops a critical attitude toward what he does. Continuing inquisitiveness and searching for better answers result in expanding knowledge. The counselor who develops the habit of inquiry will grow in his position rather than become stale. However, he will not question his role to the extent that he becomes so anxious and insecure that his insecurity interferes with his effectiveness. The counselor assumes he is doing a good job, but at the same time realizes that a better job can be done.

Evaluation research which provides for regular follow-up of cases and results in feedback of information to the counselor about what has happened to his clients can be quite comforting and reassuring to him. For example, a high school counselor is reassured when he learns that Johnny Jones, coming from a very poor family with many siblings and a widowed mother, was able to win a scholarship from Harvard with the counselor's help. Equally rewarding is learning that Mary Smith graduated from the business college decided upon during consultation with the counselor and that she became a private secretary to an executive in a growing company. Probably neither of these people would have attained their goals without the help of the counselor.

Experience may help a counselor develop professionally, but further graduate training in counseling techniques and research is also essential to development. Graduate training in the summer and reading about research during the entire year can provide stimulation leading to professional growth. The counselor with the desire to increase his professional stature will read journals such as the *Personnel and Guidance Journal* and the *Journal of Counseling Psychology*. In addition, the counselor should learn about and read other educational and scientific journals.

The counselor, if he is trained and experienced, can serve as a research consultant for the school administrators and teaching faculty. This research will help the school administrators find definitive answers to school problems. The counselor, by adopting a research point of view, can promote genuine progress in the school program as he, by his example, influences the school administration to take a research approach and to base decisions on research results rather than on opinions or attitudes. Conscientious counselors contribute a certain percentage of their time to self-development and to research and the development of their profession. Depending on their work setting, for some counselors this percentage may be only 5, but for others it might approach 25 or even 50 per cent. Sometime in the future large school systems may be able to employ counselors to work full time on counseling research.

An important reason for practicing counselors to do research is that very often research hypotheses coming from the hunches of the practitioner tend to produce advances in the field. Because he is constantly being confronted with new problems, every practitioner can contribute something to the research knowledge in his field. Thus, from his store of experience with certain types of clients, the counselor can hypothesize about certain relationships, and his hypotheses when tested may confirm or suggest an extension to an existing theory which in turn advances the profession and suggests to others effective ways of counseling.

Research is necessary to enable the counseling profession to meet new demands being made on it every day. Research helps a profession and a practitioner grow. If practitioners contributed no research knowledge, the profession would not grow and before long would degenerate into a set of routine practices which would not continue to be particularly effective. Thus, research is important in aiding one's own professional growth, in improving one's techniques, in aiding the growth of the profession so that it does not become fixed and rigid, and in contributing to the objectives of the educational enterprise.

KINDS OF RESEARCH

The report of the conference on testing and counseling sponsored by the American Association for the Advancement of Science emphasized research and stated that the counselor has the responsibility to contribute data providing a clear description of the school population being served, normative data for tests, follow-up studies of former pupils, and evaluations of counseling services and techniques (AAAS, 1958).

Some examples of research that can be done by a counselor in a local school system are: the development of local norms for tests, descriptive research characterizing the student body, a follow-up of recent graduates, a follow-up of adults who have graduated some years past to determine what they are doing and to learn their reaction to the school curriculum, a study of the predictive power of tests, and the evaluation of counseling procedures.

DESCRIPTIVE STUDIES

Easiest perhaps is the research we call descriptive research, that is, research descriptive of the student body. This research describes important characteristics of the pupils in the school system. These research data may be important to the counselor, but are also an integral aspect of school administration. The simplest level of gathering research data is to count the number of pupils in the various grades and record their ages. The distribution of parental education, parental occupation, and the number of siblings may also be important for the counselor, teacher, and administrator to know. Whether the parents are married, divorced, widowed, or deceased are important data to learn. In some larger school systems, departments of pupil accounting have certain data punched on IBM cards from which distributions of pertinent characteristics can be obtained easily. One such approach is that of the Office of Child Accounting, Board of Education, Baltimore County, Towson, Maryland, which has been described by William J. Kinling (1960). According to Kinling, the Office of Child Accounting distributes to teachers, principals, and counselors rosters prepared by data-processing equipment. The rosters contain pupil information such as sex, curriculum, previous schools, bus transportation, grade repetition, and whether or not a clinical report is on file. Rosters have been prepared by homeroom assignment, by specific class assignment, such as third-period business arithmetic class, and even by IQ decile. A questionnaire completed by the school staff members demonstrated the worthwhileness of this approach.

Does providing information to teachers accomplish anything? Baker and Doyle (1959) have reported that making available to teachers objective data about pupils' ability resulted in teachers marking pupils to a greater extent on an individualized basis. In the school system they studied, the philosophy of marking required that marks be assigned according to the extent to which each pupil's progress was commensurate with his potential. Baker and Doyle interpreted a decreased relationship between marks and intelligence test scores, a decrease in the number of poor marks for pupils of relatively low intelligence, and an increase in the number of poor marks for more capable pupils as evidence that teachers were assigning marks differentially to a greater extent than they were before test data were made available.

Hoyt (1955) attempted to evaluate whether or not giving teachers information about the individual differences of their pupils resulted in a change in pupil achievement or in pupil attitudes toward the teachers. The study was stimulated by the exhortations of educators that teachers should know their pupils' characteristics. Hoyt established random sample experimental groups within eighth-grade classes in two Minnesota public junior high schools. Pupils were first classified by sex and three levels of scholastic aptitude. At each school from the subgroups formed each pupil was assigned at random to one of three experimental groups. The teachers of the experimental groups were then exposed to different amounts of information about their pupils. The amount of information made available to teachers varied from giving only pupils' names in one section to giving very complete test, cumulative record, and biographical data in another section. Pupils' achievement was measured by administration of objective tests in September at the beginning of the experiment and again in April at the end of the experiment. Pre- and post-experimental pupil attitudes toward particular teachers were measured by an inventory constructed by the experimenter from items taken from the Student Reaction Inventory (Grim & Hoyt, 1952). Each teacher answered questions requiring him to recall specific characteristics of pupils randomly selected from his experimental section.

Hoyt concluded that teacher knowledge of pupil characteristics was increased as a result of receiving pupil information, but pupil achievement did not increase differentially in relationship to amount of information given to the teacher. There was a definite tendency for pupil attitudes toward the teacher to improve in direct relationship to the teacher knowledge of pupil characteristics. Hoyt's study illustrates well the type of experimentation that can be done to obtain reliable answers to educational questions.

FOLLOW-UP STUDIES

Follow-up studies of high school graduates and nongraduates can be informative and important to the development of an effective counseling program. Follow-up studies should be done of recent graduates and those who graduated several years past. Relevant general questions are: What are these people doing now? How many of them obtained further education, and what kind of education was this? How many entered the labor market directly from high school, and what types of jobs have they held since entering the labor market? How adequately did the school curriculum prepare them for what they are now doing? What aspect of their school experience do they feel helped them most and what helped them least? What advice do they have for students currently enrolled in their high school?

PREDICTION STUDIES

Other research is concerned with prediction of school grades. How well does the Clerical Speed and Accuracy Test of the Differential Aptitude Tests correlate with course grades in bookkeeping? Does the high school edition of the American Council on Education Psychological Examination given in the ninth grade predict grades earned over the total high school period? How predictive are tenth-grade scores on a scholastic aptitude test of scores on the National Merit Scholarship screening test? Can the Differential Aptitude Tests help in assigning ninth-grade students to the curricula offered by the high school? The answers to these questions can be ascertained through what are generally called prediction studies. In prediction studies one is investigating the predictive validity of his measuring instruments (see Chapter 5). Some validity or prediction studies were discussed in Chapter 9 and demonstrations were presented of methods of using the results of such studies in counseling.

The following study by Doppelt, Seashore, and Odgers (1959) in evaluating the validity of the Differential Aptitude Test (DAT) for auto mechanics and machine shop students is a good example of a high school validation study. Pupils in machine shop and auto mechanics courses in seven Ohio vocational high schools were tested in the fall, 1954, at the beginning of grade 11. At the end of the fall term instructors rated their pupils on four traits: understanding trade information, job know-how, quality of work, and quantity of work. At the end of grade 12, the same pupils were again rated on the four characteristics and the relationships between the tests and both sets of ratings were evaluated.

The DAT Language Usage Test: Spelling was most highly correlated with grades 11 and 12 ratings of understanding trade information. The grade 12 ratings of this characteristic were also predicted significantly by scores on the DAT Number Ability, Abstract Reasoning, and Language Usage Test: Sentences. The prediction of over-all accomplishment of auto mechanics pupils was not satisfactory.

For machine shop pupils, the sum of scores on the DAT Mechanical Reasoning, Space Relations, and Abstract Reasoning tests provided useful predictions of both grade 11 and grade 12 ratings. The authors prepared expectancy tables (see Chapter 9) based on these findings to facilitate the use of the DAT by school personnel.

EVALUATING THE IMPACT OF SCHOOL EXPERIENCES

The effect of school experience as reflected by achievement tests is well established. However, for pupils there are other outcomes from school experience which might be reflected on instruments measuring aptitudes, opinions, personality, and social relationships.

A pioneer study evaluating outcomes of instruction other than specific achievement was conducted by the evaluation staff of the Eight-Year Study of the Progressive Education Association (Smith, Tyler, et al., 1942). The following titles of tests developed by the evaluation staff are indicative of the processes they tried to measure: Interpretation of Data, Nature of Proof, Analysis of Controversial Writing, and Beliefs on Social Issues.

A recent example of this type of research is a study by Mendicino (1958). He administered the Mechanical Reasoning and Space Relations tests of the Differential Aptitude Tests to an experimental group of 150 tenth-grade boys having taken courses in vocational machine shop and mechanical drawing and compared their test scores with those of a control group not in these courses. The two groups were comparable in age, race, and physical condition. They were tested during the first two weeks of the school year and again at the end. The mean scores for the two groups on initial and final tests were almost identical. The author concluded that one year's experience in vocational courses does not increase scores on mechanical reasoning or space relations tests.

RESEARCH ON COMMUNICATION

Another area of important research is concerned with the adequacy of communication between the school, the parent, and the pupil about the pupil's achievement. Research can be done on various types of report cards through soliciting parental reaction; by quizzing parents one can determine what kind of information was gained from report cards. Many schools attempt to report achievement test results to parents and to pupils. Here again the type of reporting procedure can be varied and the types evaluated systematically. Through systematic evaluation one can determine whether or not his reporting procedures are accomplishing their objectives. Many counselors attempt to communicate test and other counseling data to parents. This is an area needing a research approach. Finally, research on the type of teacher consultation employed by the school is needed.

The research approach of Funk and Becker (1952) in an industrial setting could easily be adapted to the school situation. These investigators developed an objective test covering content which management was attempting to communicate to employees. After communication was attempted, the objective test was administered to determine the extent to which communication had been successful. Many parents would cooperate in an analogous experiment to test the effectiveness of the communication media of the school. Randomly selected samples of parents could be exposed to different communication approaches, tested on the content communicated, and comparisons made among the groups. For example, if a school had administered the Iowa Tests of Educational Development and wished to educate parents as to the meaning of Iowa test scores, three groups of parents might be selected for experimentation. One group could be lectured about the Iowa tests. Another group might be subdivided into small groups for discussion, and the third group could receive only descriptive literature about the Iowa test scores and what they mean. Rather short tests of information transmitted would probably have sufficient reliability to detect group differences approaching practical as well as statistical significance.

RESEARCH ON THE COUNSELING PROCESS

Many counselors will be interested in doing research on the counseling process per se. Much research has been done on counselor techniques in the interview, but none of it is definitive, and considerably more research needs to be done. The *Journal of Counseling Psychology* and the *Personnel and Guidance Journal* contain articles on recent research on counseling techniques. Comprehensive research of this nature has been reported by Robinson (1950) and by Rogers and Dymond (1954). However, the high school counselor need not engage in so elaborate a research program. The interview research done by Weeks (1957) is an example of research that can be done at the high school level. Weeks analyzed 37 interviews with 20 high school boys by listening to recordings and at the same time reading typed transcriptions of these recordings. He rated the counselee's expressed affect (feeling or emotion) and compared judges' reliability of ratings and then determined the relationship of amount of affect expressed to the amount of talking done by the counselee.

Many schools use teachers as teacher-counselors, whereas others use teachers as advisors to individual students. Some schools use only full-time counselors to work in individual advising and counseling. One type of study is that which attempts to compare the relative effectiveness of teacher-counselors, teachers, and counselors as advisors.

Caravello (1958) studied the comparative effectiveness of counseling by teacher-counselors and guidance specialists. Post-high school records were compared of pupils, some of whom had been counseled only by teacher-counselors and some of whom had been counseled by a specialist. A control group of noncounseled pupils was also identified. There were no differences among the groups in employment status, but a significantly larger number of the counseled pupils continued their education. Approximately one-third of the pupils counseled by the specialist felt that counseling was helpful to them as compared to less than 10 per cent of those counseled by teacher-counselors. The pupils reported a strong preference for guidance from specialists.

Another program variation which can be evaluated is the method of assigning counselors to pupils in specified grades. For example, a counselor may be assigned to work year after year with ninth graders or with twelfth graders. In other systems the counselor is assigned to a group of pupils when they enter the ninth grade, and he works with these pupils throughout their high school experience; that is, he moves with the group as they progress from grade to grade. Both of these approaches have certain advantages and disadvantages. Which approach would work best in a given school would depend on many factors, a number of them specific to a given school.

Some counselors may wish to evaluate their total counseling program in a general way, whereas others will want to evaluate a specific technique within their program, and others will want to do both.

Caplan (1957) studied the effect of counseling on problem boys in a junior high school. The experimental group of the counseled students improved in self and ideal concepts significantly more than the non-counseled controls. Differential changes in achievement were less clear. However, prior to counseling, the experimental group obtained an average of 2.4 poor grades, whereas after counseling they obtained .9 such grades. The control group averages were 1.6 and 1.7 respectively.

Spivak (1957) has reported a brief study of the effect of reporting to seventh-grade teachers the kinds of problems checked by their pupils on the SRA Youth Inventory (Remmers & Shimberg, 1949). On retesting, the experimental group whose teachers had been informed of their problems showed a significant reduction in the number of problems checked, but a control group showed no significant reduction of problems on re-testing.

RESEARCH AND THEORY

Much research in schools and school systems will be stimulated by events or incidents occurring in the day-to-day counseling program. Such program-related research aids in evaluating the present program and helps in the improvement of the program. Research on theoretical questions may be of personal interest to the counselor, and it may or may not be directly beneficial to school or counseling programs. Some counselors do research of a more highly theoretical nature. This research most often contributes to the entire profession of counseling and many times will contribute to a parent science such as psychology or sociology.

An example of theoretical research accomplished at the high school level is a study by Reeves and Goldman (1957). They reported a test of the hypothesis that school maladjustment is related to discrepancies between externally measured social-class level and the pupil's own perception of his social-class level. They related the discrepancy between measures of these types of social-class levels to scores on the SRA Youth Inventory (Remmers & Shimberg, 1949) and the Ohio Social Acceptance Scale (OSAS) (Raths, 1943). For grades 9 to 11, there was no relationship of discrepancy scores and scores on the SRA Youth Inventory, but a significant relationship was found between the discrepancy scores and the OSAS. This study suggests that pupils whose self-perception of their social-class level was congruent with an external measure of social-class level were more accepted on a sociometric instrument by their peers. The maladjustment hypothesis needs further exploration. Another study of theoretical interest is one by Rose and Wall (1957) who extended the customary prestige study of occupations among white respondents to another race by conducting focused interviews with 68 Negro high school pupils who had been asked to rank 15 occupations.

As this research and the studies cited earlier indicate, it is possible for school counselors to engage in research of importance to the development of psychology and sociology.

SUMMARY

The concept of research and the maintenance of a research point of view is important to the school counselor because it promotes his own professional growth and contributes to the profession. In addition, the counselor may be able to contribute significantly to the entire educational program of his system through emphasis on research. Research may consist of descriptions of the student body, follow-up of former students, reporting techniques, grade prediction studies, research on counseling, and research of a theoretical scientific nature. All such research will contribute to specific school counseling programs as well as to the profession as a whole.

QUESTIONS FOR STUDY

1. Select a research article of interest to you from a recent issue of the *Personnel and Guidance Journal*. Outline the implications of this article for your counseling practices.
2. What descriptive information about the student body of a school is most relevant to the guidance program? What characteristics of parents are most relevant?
3. Can the research topics discussed in this chapter be ranked in their importance to a counseling and guidance program? If so, rank them.
4. Outline briefly a study to evaluate the predictive validity of a test or tests with which you are familiar. List the subjects to be tested, how and when they are to be tested, follow-up data, etc.
5. Design a procedure for the routine follow-up of counseling cases. Assume high school seniors are to be counseled and then followed up sometime after high school graduation. For what purposes should the seniors be followed up?
6. Within a single school system, how might one compare the relative effectiveness of teacher-counselors, teachers, and counselors as advisors? What indexes of effectiveness might be used?
7. In question 6, what factors specific to the given school system might influence the results of the study so that they would be different from those obtained in another school system?

REFERENCES

American Association for the Advancement of Science. *Identification and guidance of able students.* Report of Conference on Testing and Counseling, University of Michigan, May 28–31, 1958.

Baker, R. L., & Doyle, R. P. Teacher knowledge of pupil data and marking practices at the elementary school level. *Personnel Guid. J.,* 1959, 37, 644–647.

Berdie, R. F. Counseling. *Ann. Rev. Psychol.* Palo Alto, Calif.: Annual Reviews, 1959, 10, 345–370.

Caplan, S. W. The effect of group counseling on junior high school boys' concept of themselves in school. *J. counsel. Psychol.,* 1957, 4, 124–128.

Caravello, S. J. Effectiveness of high school guidance services. *Personnel Guid. J.,* 1958, 36, 323–325.

Doppelt, J. E., Seashore, H. G., & Odgers, J. H. Validation of the Differential Aptitude Tests for auto mechanics and machine shop students. *Personnel Guid. J.,* 1959, 37, 648–655.

Dugan, W. E. A study of the influence of teacher knowledge of individual pupil characteristics upon achievement and other developmental outcomes. Unpublished doctoral dissertation, University of Minnesota, 1942.

Funk, H., & Becker, R. C. Measuring the effectiveness of industrial communications. *Personnel,* 1952, 29, 237–240.

Grim, P. R., & Hoyt, C. J. Appraisal of teaching competency. *Educ. res. Bull.,* 1952, 31, 85–91.

Hoyt, K. B. A study of the effects of teacher knowledge of pupil characteristics on pupil achievement and attitudes towards classwork. *J. educ. Psychol.,* 1955, **46,** 302–310.

Kinling, W. J. The dissemination of guidance information using data processing equipment. *Personnel Guid. J.,* 1960, **39,** 220–221.

Mendicino, L. Mechanical reasoning and space perception: native capacity or experience. *Personnel Guid. J.,* 1958, **36,** 335–338.

Raths, L. E. Identifying social acceptance of children. *Educ. res. Bull.,* 1943, **32,** 72–74.

Reeves, J. M., & Goldman, L. Social class perceptions and school maladjustment. *Personnel Guid. J.,* 1957, **35,** 414–419.

Remmers, H. H., & Radler, D. H. *The American teenager.* Indianapolis: Bobbs-Merrill, 1957.

Remmers, H. H., & Shimberg. B. *SRA youth inventory manual.* Chicago: Science Research, 1949.

Robinson, F. P. *Principles and procedures in student counseling.* New York: Harper & Row, 1950.

Rogers, C. R., & Dymond, R. F. (Eds.) *Psychotherapy and personality change.* Chicago: University of Chicago Press, 1954.

Rose, A. W., & Wall, M. C. Social factors in the prestige ranking of occupations. *Personnel Guid. J.,* 1957, **35,** 270–275.

Smith, E. R., & Tyler, R. W., et al. Appraising and recording student progress. *Adventure in American Education.* New York: Harper & Row, 1942. Vol. 3.

Spivak, M. L. It pays to tell the teacher. *Personnel. Guid. J.,* 1957, **35,** 452–453.

Weeks, J. S. Level of affect in the counseling responses of high school senior boys. *J. counsel. Psychol.,* 1957, **4,** 297–303.

CHAPTER 15

Tests Used in Counseling

INTRODUCTION

Although the discussion in this text has been concerned with the use in counseling of tests in general, specific tests have been cited frequently and the reader by now should know much about some of the tests counselors use. Detailed information about counseling tests cannot be presented here because of space limitations. Such information can be obtained from other sources, the most useful being *The Mental Measurements Yearbooks* (Buros, 1938, 1940, 1949, 1953, 1959). Every time a counselor contemplates using a test he has not used before, he should first consult these yearbooks to learn what authorities think about the test, to acquire information about the test, and to learn of other sources of information.

In this chapter the authors present some information about a few carefully selected tests of ability, achievement, interest, and personality. They have chosen from among the tests of each kind those they consider most useful to counselors with the expectation that counselors considering using these tests will give to them further study and carefully read *The Mental Measurements Yearbook* reviews, the test manuals, analyses such as those in Super and Crites, *Appraising Vocational Fitness* (1962), and reviews in professional journals.

Many tests not described here can contribute to the work of counselors. Some of these are new and little is known of them. Some are seldom used and little experience has been accumulated. Some are not practical, economical, or efficient. Many tests have not been included here because of defects related to validity, reliability, format, interpretive information, norms, content, and other conditions which determine how useful tests are to counselors.

No single author, and no group of authors, can claim to be a final court which renders a judgment about the ultimate usefulness of tests, and the present authors make no such claim. These are tests which we have used and which we have seen others use, and our opinion is that we and others have found them useful.

GENERAL ABILITY TESTS

Title: Lorge-Thorndike Intelligence Tests
Authors: Irving Lorge and Robert L. Thorndike
Publisher: Houghton Mifflin Company
Date of Publication: 1954. Manual and technical manual, 1957

These are group tests of nonverbal and verbal intelligence and perhaps are the best of their kind. The authors state that these tests measure abstract intelligence, the ability to work with ideas and relationships among ideas. Suitable tests are available for testing in grades kindergarten through 12. The Primary Battery (Levels 1 and 2) consists of three nonreading tests for kindergarten and grades 1, 2, and 3. It includes subtests of oral vocabulary, pictorial classification and pictorial pairing.

The Verbal and Nonverbal Batteries (Levels 3, 4, and 5) are used in grades 4 to 12 and provide scores which can be used independently or in combination. The Verbal Battery includes the following subtests: Vocabulary, Verbal Classification, Sentence Completion, Arithmetic Reasoning, and Verbal Analogy (Levels 4 and 5 only). The Nonverbal Battery includes the following subtests: Pictorial Classification, Pictorial Analogies and Numerical Relationships.

Two forms, A and B, are available at each level. At Levels 3, 4, and 5 are a consumable edition (pupils mark in the test booklet) and a reusable edition (pupils mark on separate answer sheets which may be hand- or machine-scored). The Primary Battery is given without time limits, usually in three testing sessions. The actual working time on the Verbal Battery is 34 minutes, on the Nonverbal Battery, 27 minutes.

Alternate forms reliability coefficients range from .76 to .90 for the various levels within a single grade. Odd-even reliabilities also are high, ranging from .88 to .94 with the exception of one, .59, which resulted from an unmeaningful division of items. The data presented in the manual, including standard errors of measurement, show that the tests are of adequate reliability to use with individuals.

Evidence for the validity of these tests is still meager. The manual reports correlations of .87 and .76 respectively between the Lorge-Thorndike and reading and arithmetic grade equivalents derived from the Stanford Achievement Test. Another study, based on 214 cases, yielded a correlation of .67 between the Lorge-Thorndike (Level 4) given at the beginning of grade 9 and average achievement at the end of the ninth grade. This evidence of validity is encouraging, and further validation studies should be done.

Norms are based on the standardization sample of over 136,000 children in 44 communities in 22 states. This was a sample consisting of pupils from volunteering schools, so some bias may be present in the norms. However, the final norms were built so that each type of community in the stratified sample was represented in the norm group in the same proportion as it was found in the country as a whole. Four types of norms are given for the tests: IQs, grade percentiles, grade equivalents, and age equivalents. The grade percentiles will be most useful.

These tests are perhaps the best available group tests for measuring intelligence in grades kindergarten through 12.

Title: American Council on Education Psychological Examination (ACE)
Authors: High school forms prior to 1948 by L. L. and Thelma Gwinn Thurstone; forms of 1948 and 1953 by Educational Testing Service from materials developed by these authors; college form of 1947 by Thurstone; all other forms by Educational Testing Service from materials developed by these authors
Date of Publication: High school forms, 1944–1948; 1953
College forms, 1947–1949; 1952; 1954

These scholastic aptitude tests have been used widely in grades 9 to 12 (high school form) and with college freshmen (college form). Linguistic and quantitative part scores can be obtained, and the total score consists of the sum of these scores. The linguistic section of the high school edition consists of two parts, same-opposite (antonym-synonym multiple-choice items) and completions (items consisting of a word definition followed by five letters, one of which is the initial letter of the defined word). The college edition includes a verbal-analogies section in addition to these two sections. The high school edition includes two tests in the quantitative section: Arithmetic (thought problems in multiple-choice form) and Number Series (different sequences of seven numbers, each followed by alternative numbers, one of which continues the pattern of the stimulus series). The college edition includes, in addition, a Figure Analogies part in the quantitative section.

High school forms 1947, 1948, and 1953, college forms 1949, 1952, and 1954 will be kept available by the publisher as long as a substantial number of schools order them. The use of the ACE is declining, since newer tests are replacing it. In the 1940s and early 1950s, this test was the most widely used college aptitude test, and much research was done on it.

Working time for the high school edition is 55 minutes, whereas 60 minutes of working time is allowed for the college edition. Each of the several subparts is separately timed. The short time limits on the parts require care by the test administrator to ensure accurate testing. Both forms utilize the "rights only" scoring formula and can be hand- or machine-scored.

The reliabilities reported for total scores for both forms are quite high (about .90) and the reliabilities of the Q and L scores are almost as high. However, speed of response enters strongly into determination of scores and, hence, may cause the reliabilities to be overestimated.

Information about validity is not available from the test manuals. However, many validation studies at the college level have been reported in educational and psychological journals. The validities reported for the ACE tend to be lower than those reported for the Ohio State Psychological Examination and more recently constructed tests (Berdie, Dressel, & Kelso, 1951; Layton, 1954).

Norms for the high school editions are based on a sample of 19,500 pupils distributed among the grades 9 through 12. Separate norms for each grade are provided.

The norms for the college forms are based on scores reported by institutions using the test and hence have an unknown amount of bias included. Total score percentile rank tables are available for entering college freshmen by type of institution (four-year, teachers, and junior colleges) for all forms. Separate tables for men, women, and combined groups are available. Similar tables for Q and L scores are provided for all except the 1947 edition.

REFERENCES

Berdie, R., Dressel, P., & Kelso, P. Relative validity of the Q and L scores of the ACE psychological examination. *Educ. psychol. Measmt.*, 1951, 11, 803–812.

Layton, W. L. The relation of ninth grade test scores to twelfth grade test scores and high school rank. *J. appl. Psychol.*, 1954, 38, 10–11.

Title: California Test of Mental Maturity; California Short-Form Test of
      Mental Maturity
Authors: Elizabeth T. Sullivan, Willis W. Clark, and Ernest W. Tiegs
Publisher: California Test Bureau
Date of Publication: 1957

This is a paper and pencil intelligence test. The short form utilizes seven of the twelve subtests included in the long form. The subtests included in the long form were determined from an analysis by Sullivan in 1926 of the 1916 edition of the Stanford-Binet. The twelve subtests are combined to yield five part scores: memory, spatial relationships, logical reasoning, numerical reasoning, and verbal concepts. The subtests comprising memory are omitted in the short form. The scores from these part scores are not of sufficient reliability to use diagnostically with individuals. However, the twelve subtests in the long form and the seven subtests in the short form also yield language and nonlanguage scores which are sufficiently reliable for individual use at most grade levels.

Both forms are available in six levels: preprimary, for kindergarten and entering grade 1; primary, for grades 1 to 3; elementary, for grades 4 to 8; junior high, for grades 7 to 9; secondary, for grades 9 to 13; advanced, for grades 10 to college and adults.

The scoring formula used is "rights only." Language and nonlanguage and total scores are obtained in addition to the subtest scores. Because of the low reliabilities of the subtests, the diagnostic profile provided should not be used except for plotting language, nonlanguage, and total scores. Tests can be hand- or machine-scored.

The subtests have relatively short time limits, but the test manual states without evidence that these are essentially power tests. Approximate total test administration times (in minutes) are as follows:

Level	Short form	Long form
Preprimary..........	40	70
Primary.............	55	90
Elementary.........	60	110
Junior high.........	65	115
Secondary..........	65	115
Advanced..........	65	115

Reliability coefficients reported in the manual are of the internal consistency type which are influenced considerably by speed. Since these tests are timed, the reliability coefficients may be spuriously high. The coefficients reported for total scores on the long form for grades 1, 2, 5, 8, 12, and college freshmen are all above .90. The reliabilities of the language and nonlanguage scores are almost as high. Comparable reliabilities for the short form are not quite as high as those for the long form.

Much evidence demonstrating high relationships between these tests and other tests such as the Stanford-Binet and the Kuhlmann-Anderson is presented in the manual. To this extent the authors have demonstrated the validity of the tests. However, no evidence is presented of the ability of the tests to predict school achievement. Since these tests are used primarily in the educational setting to predict grades, such evidence is highly desirable.

Norms are based on an undescribed norm group of 25,000 cases for which control data from other standardized tests were available. Mental ages, IQs, and percentile ranks are provided.

REFERENCE

California Test Bureau, Summary of Investigations Number Three. *California Test of Mental Maturity.* Los Angeles, 1956.

Title: College Entrance Examination Board Scholastic Aptitude Test (CEEB-SAT)
Author and Publisher: Educational Testing Service for the College Entrance Examination Board
Date of Publication: New forms each year, 1926 to date

This test is a key part of the CEEB testing program and is one of the best known tests in this country among laymen and professional testers. It is a scholastic aptitude test administered six times a year (January, February, March, May, August, and December) at specified test centers established by Educational Testing Service. The test results are used by admissions officers of many colleges to select students. The test yields verbal and mathematical ability scores from five subtests each with a 30-minute time limit. The test requires 3 hours of working time and is given in a half-day testing session. A correction for guessing is made when the test is scored.

The reported reliabilities for the two subscores are approximately .90 and indicate sufficient reliability for the separate use of the subscores. Many validity studies have been reported for this test with results similar to those usually found with good scholastic aptitude tests. It is a quite effective predictor of achievement in many colleges.

Scores for the test are reported on a standard score system with a mean of 500 and a standard deviation of 100. A large number of norms are available for various college entrance candidates. For example, norms are available for public schools, independent schools, and all schools; for preliminary and final candidates; for boys and girls; for transfer students; for college sophomores and college students in various curricula.

Title: College Qualification Tests (CQT)
Authors: G. K. Bennett, M. G. Bennett, W. L. Wallace, and A. G. Wesman
Publisher: The Psychological Corporation
Date of Publication: 1955, and periodically

These are three ability tests suitable for use in counseling high school seniors, admitting students to college, and awarding scholarships. CQT-Verbal is a 15-minute synonym-antonym test. CQT-Numerical is a 35-minute test of basic mathematics skills, including arithmetic, algebra, and geometry. CQT-Information is a 30-minute test of social science and natural-physical science concepts with separate subscores and a total score. A total score combining scores on all three tests also is obtained. The tests may be machine- or hand-scored.

Each test is available in three forms, A, B, and C. Form A is available to high schools, Forms B and C are sold only to colleges and universities. The three tests can be purchased in a combination (single booklet) edition or as separate booklets.

Internal consistency reliability coefficients are good: mid-.90s for the total score and from the high .70s to the low .90s for the subtests. Validities reported for predicting college grades are quite good and average about .55.

Percentile norms are based on approximately 20,000 freshmen in 37 colleges and universities in 22 states; 8,000 freshmen in 20 junior colleges in 14 states; and 14,000 pupils in grades 11 and 12 in 38 high schools in 25 states.

Title: Cooperative School and College Ability Tests (SCAT)
Author: Cooperative Test Division
Publisher: Educational Testing Service
Date of Publication: 1955–1957

These are scholastic aptitude tests intended to aid in determining the capacity of pupils in grades 4 to 14 to succeed in school. These tests were designed to replace the American Council on Education Psychological Examination, although the tests probably do not measure the same factors. The SCAT were designed to measure school-learned abilities rather than abstract psychological traits. Four skills are measured: Part 1, getting the meaning of isolated sentences (15 minutes); Part 2, performing numerical computations rapidly (20 minutes); Part 3, associating meanings of isolated words (10 minutes); Part 4, solving arithmetic problems (25 minutes). Parts 1 and 3 are combined to yield a verbal score, Parts 2 and 4 to obtain a quantitative score, and all four parts to obtain a total aptitude score. At Level 1 (college freshmen and sophomores and superior grade 12) forms 1A, 1B, 1C, and 1D are available. For Level 2 (grades 10 to 12 and superior grade 9), Level 3 (grades 8 to 10), Level 4 (grades 6 to 8), Level 5 (grades 4 to 6) forms A and B are provided. Seventy minutes of actual working time are required. The tests may be administered in two sessions of about 45 minutes each or in one 80-minute session.

Scoring (rights only) can be done by hand or machine. Raw scores are changed to converted scores which render all verbal scores, all quantitative, and all total scores comparable regardless of the form or level used. *However,* the converted scores for the verbal tests cannot be directly compared with the converted scores for the quantitative tests and total tests. Comparison of a pupil's converted scores is possible only by converting them into percentile ranks of an appropriate norm group. Percentile bands are used instead of the more familiar percentile ranks. Thus, a pupil's score is plotted on the SCAT Student Profile as a band rather than a point. The use of bands rather than point scores emphasizes the lack of precision of a test score.

Internal consistency reliability coefficients for SCAT are quite high, at least .95 for all grades. However, these coefficients are spuriously high because of the speed factor. At some grade levels in the standardization group only about half the pupils completed subparts of the tests. Alternate forms and test-retest reliabilities have not yet been published. If the true reliabilities are substantially lower than those reported, then the percentile bands used in reporting scores are narrower than they should be and hence give promise of greater precision than warranted.

The validity of SCAT appears to be approximately that of the ACE and is typical of most scholastic aptitude tests.

Norms are based on a carefully designed sampling of American schools and colleges in the fall of 1956 and can be considered quite good. Of course, these norms, as do most norms, include the bias introduced by the fact that only those schools were included which were willing to participate in the testing program. Norms are presented in percentile bands for verbal, quantitative, and total test scores for each grade. These bands may be spuriously narrow as discussed in the paragraph on reliability above.

Title: The Henmon-Nelson Tests of Mental Ability, Revised Edition; and Revised Henmon-Nelson Tests of Mental Ability, College Level
Authors: Tom A. Lamke and M. J. Nelson; Paul C. Kelso (College Level)
Publisher: Houghton Mifflin Company
Date of Publication: 1957, 1958, 1960, 1961

These are group intelligence tests primarily designed to measure scholastic aptitude. The tests are available in four levels of difficulty: for grades 3 to 6, 6 to 9, 9 to 12, and for college students (freshmen to first-year graduate students). Forms A and B, similar in construction and difficulty, are available at each grade level. The ninety items (100 in the college form) in each test form are arranged in order of increasing difficulty and represent a variety of item forms to test different aspects of mental ability.

Mental age, percentile rank, and IQ can be obtained to express an individual's total score on the three lower forms of the tests. Percentile norms for college freshmen are available for the college form for quantitative and verbal parts and total scores. Scoring is accomplished through counting the number of right responses which are obvious to the scorer through the test's self-marking answer sheet. These tests are also available in the machine-scorable form.

The tests can be given easily in the usual class period, since the pupil is given 30 minutes to work on the test proper for the lower level forms and 40 minutes for the college level form.

Consumable or reusable test booklets are available for the lower three levels, and reusable booklets are available for the college edition. Self-marking or IBM answer sheets are available at all four levels.

In the manuals reliability coefficients are presented in terms of odd-even correlations for each grade level and form. For grades 3, 6, and 12 correlations between Forms A and B are presented. The odd-even correlations range from .90 to .97. The six alternate form coefficients range from .87 to .94. Thus, the reliability of the tests is adequate.

Evidence presented of the validity of these tests is good. The tests correlate highly with other well-known tests of intelligence. They also correlate highly with course grades and with achievement test scores.

Norms for these tests were derived from an exceptionally good experimental design. Schools and classroooms within schools were randomly selected from data obtained from the Bureau of the Census. Over 96 per cent of the classrooms selected actually provided test data. Hence, the norms can be considered representative of the well-described population sampled and are not as biased as are some other norm groups through the inclusion of only volunteering schools.

The statistical methodology employed in the standardization of these tests was excellent. The test items were carefully constructed, but represent a hodgepodge of item types and content. There are too many items asking questions about family relationships. An orphan or someone whose family had few relatives might be handicapped on these tests, whereas someone whose family devoted a great deal of time to discussing family relationships would enjoy an advantage on the Henmon-Nelson tests.

Title: Kuhlmann-Anderson Intelligence Tests
Authors: F. Kuhlmann and Rose G. Anderson
Publisher: Personnel Press, Inc.
Date of Publication: Seventh edition, 1960; sixth edition, 1952; first
                edition, 1927

The first part of this review is based primarily on the sixth-edition material. The seventh edition of the Kuhlmann-Anderson Test has comprehensive changes in booklets G and H, the booklets intended for junior and senior high school use, respectively. A paragraph at the end of the review describes these changes.

These tests were devised to measure the mental development (intelligence) of school-age children and young people. The tests are most widely used in elementary schools to test scholastic aptitude. The tests can be administered from kindergarten through the high school grades. Each of the thirty-nine tests in the Kuhlmann-Anderson scale has six to twenty-four items or trials. The thirty-nine tests are arranged generally in the order of difficulty that children have in passing half of the trials. The total scale of thirty-nine tests is arranged in nine separate booklets (test batteries), so there are overlapping segments of the total thirty-nine-test scale. Only one form of the test at each level is available.

Each of the ten pages in the test booklet is scored by counting the number of correct responses and obtaining a mental age equivalent for that number. The *median* mental age for the ten pages is then computed. This median mental age is then divided by the pupil's chronological age to obtain his intelligence quotient (IQ).

The batteries for kindergarten and first grade permit ample time for pupils to attempt every item they are capable of answering correctly. The higher level forms are speeded tests. Any of the nine batteries can be given in 45 minutes.

Odd-even reliability coefficients are reported as ranging from .88 (grade 5) to .95 (grade 9). A standard error of measurement of 5.5 IQ points was obtained in one study. The tests are sufficiently reliable for use with individuals.

Validity of the tests is demonstrated statistically through a comparison of average scores of groups of retarded, at expected grade, and accelerated pupils (average scores increase in the expected direction). There is a progressive increase in the number of pupils responding correctly to a given test through the grades. Correlations with achievement tests or school grades as evidence of concurrent or predictive validity are not given.

The earliest published norms were based on a minimum of 350 school children at each chronological age from representative Minnesota communities. Rechecks on the original norms resulted in the addition of 15,000 cases from representative Minnesota, New York, New Jersey, and Pennsylvania communities. Norms based on pupils from northern, midwestern, and eastern regions may be biased compared to norms based on a sampling of the entire United States. No evidence is available to evaluate this bias.

The new seventh-edition G and H booklets have eight tests per booklet rather than ten, and the number of items in the tests is increased.

Each booklet has four verbal tests yielding a verbal aptitude (V) score and four quantitative tests yielding a quantitative aptitude (Q) score. The V and Q scores are added to obtain a total (T) score. Grade percentile ranks are provided for the V, Q, and T scores; deviation IQ scores for three-month intervals of chronological age for the T score; and percentile rank equivalents and a classification table for the deviation IQs. Norms are provided for grades 7 to 9 on Booklet G and for grades 9 to 12 on Booklet H. The test booklets are reusable and separate IBM answer sheets may be scored either by hand or machine.

Experience and research suggest that this is an efficient and accurate test of intelligence for use in many schools.

Title: Kuhlmann-Finch Intelligence Tests
Author: F. H. Finch
Publisher: American Guidance Service, Inc.
Date of Publication: 1957

These tests were designed to measure intelligence of school children from grade 1 through high school. A battery of eight test booklets, each containing five subtests, is provided to cover the range of grades. The format of the tests is similar to that of the Kuhlmann-Anderson tests, but these tests cannot be considered a substitute for them. The tests yield intelligence quotients based on the standard deviation for the appropriate age group. Only one form is available.

Separate answer sheets can be used with Tests 4, 5, 6, the Junior High School Test, and the Senior High School Test. The subtests are scored (rights only), and the median score for the five tests is determined. This median score is used to calculate the deviation IQ.

The tests can be given in approximately 45 minutes. Each of the five subtests is separately timed.

Within age split-half reliability coefficients for ages 6 to 17 range from .86 to .92 for samples of from 110 to 250 pupils. These correlations indicate that the tests are reliable.

The only evidence for validity of these tests is the increase with age of the per cent passing the tests. Further evidence of validity is needed before the tests can be used with the confidence that they are measuring intelligence.

Norms for these tests are in terms of median mental ages (MAs) and intelligence quotients (IQs). The median MA is the chronological age corresponding to the median of the scores earned on the five subtests. The IQ is a standard or deviation score in a distribution with a mean of 100 and a standard deviation of 16. Percentile ranks corresponding to these IQs are also provided.

Title: The Ohio State University Psychological Test
Author: Herbert A. Toops
Publisher: The Ohio College Association
Date of Publication: 1919, and periodically

This test has been continually studied since 1919 with Form 26 being published in 1960. It is a verbal test of scholastic aptitude, and its 150 items have been rigorously analyzed over the years. It is one of the best scholastic aptitude tests available at the high school senior and college level. Three subtests are included: Same-Opposites, Analogies, and Reading Comprehension. Included in Forms 25 and 26 are seventy-eight items from Form 23, selected because in combination they had the highest correlation with college freshmen grades for 2,000 college freshmen. The selected seventy-eight items now comprise the Minnesota Scholastic Aptitude Test.

The Ohio State test can be used in the high school grades and in college. Forms 18 through 26 currently are available. It can be hand- or machine-scored. Scores (rights only) are obtained on all three parts and the total. The test usually is given without a time limit and most college freshmen finish in 2 hours. Separate answer sheets must be used.

The reliability of the total test is in excess of .95. The odd-even and test-retest reliability coefficients of the seventy-eight items incorporated in the Minnesota Scholastic Aptitude Test are both .93.

At Ohio State University and the University of Minnesota, the test consistently has demonstrated validity coefficients as high as .60. Validities reported at other institutions usually fall in the .45 to .55 range. This test is one of the most valid tests of its type available today.

Norms for the various forms are based on Ohio high school pupils and Ohio college freshmen. Schools using the test will want to use local norms. No attempt has been made to develop representative national norms on this test.

Title: Otis Quick-Scoring Mental Ability Tests, New Edition
Author: Arthur S. Otis
Publisher: Harcourt, Brace & World, Inc.
Date of Publication: 1954

These tests represent new editions of the Otis Quick-Scoring Mental Ability Tests. They are scholastic aptitude tests to be used in grades 1 through college. The Alpha Short Form test is for use in grades 1 to 4. The Beta test was developed from the Intermediate Examination of the much older Otis Self-Administering Tests and is suitable for use in grades 4 to 9. The Gamma test was developed from the Higher Examination of the Otis Self-Administering Tests and is for use in high school and college.

The Alpha Short Form test is available in only one form. The Beta and Gamma tests are available in two forms each, EM and FM.

Separate answer sheets are available for Beta and Gamma. These tests may be hand- or machine-scored (rights only). Alpha requires 25 minutes of working time; Beta and Gamma each 30 minutes.

Odd-even reliability coefficients for Alpha are reported as .87 and .88 in two samples. Within grade coefficients for Form EM of the Beta test range from .84 to .95. Split-half reliabilities of .92, .91, and .92 are reported for grades 10, 11, and 12, respectively, for Form EM of Gamma. A speed factor may have influenced these coefficients to an unknown degree making them overestimates.

Published evidence for the validity of these tests is meager.

The norms groups are not clearly defined in the manual. The author states that they are to be considered representative of the country as a whole. Mental age equivalents and deviation IQs are presented for Alpha and Beta. Deviation IQs are given for Gamma. Percentile rank tables are needed, but not provided.

Title: Terman-McNemar Test of Mental Ability
Authors: Lewis M. Terman and Quinn McNemar
Publisher: Harcourt, Brace & World, Inc.
Date of Publication: 1942, 1949

This test is a revision of the Terman Group Test of Mental Ability which was used for many years as a scholastic aptitude test. The present revision omits the arithmetical and numerical subtests included in the earlier test. Included are the following subtests: Information, Synonyms, Logical Selection, Classification, Analogies, Opposites, and Best Answer. Thus, this test may be considered a test of verbal ability. The test is available for use in grades 7 to 12 and with college freshmen. Two forms, C and D, are available, and the test yields a single total raw score which can be obtained by hand or machine. The test can be given in a 50-minute period, which includes 40 minutes of working time.

Split-half and interform reliability coefficients are estimated to be .96 for a single age, 14. The reliability coefficients for other age ranges were found to vary only slightly from that for age 14. The standard error of measurement is approximately 3.2 standard score points for the entire age range covered by the test.

No direct evidence of validity is presented in the manual.

Norms are based on a 10 per cent sampling of results from 148 communities in 33 states. Mental age, deviation IQ, and percentile rank tables are provided so scores may be expressed in these ways.

MULTIPLE ABILITY TESTS[1]

Title: Differential Aptitude Tests (DAT)
Authors: George K. Bennett, Harold G. Seashore, and Alexander G.
    Wesman
Publisher: The Psychological Corporation
Date of Publication: 1947; revised manual, third edition, 1959

These tests were developed to provide measures of differential ability for boys and girls in grades 8 through 12 for purposes of educational and vocational counseling. The scores provide information about abilities and aptitudes relevant to a variety of occupations and are useful for making judgments concerning pupils' probabilities of success in various training programs and jobs.

Although the tests were designed for pupils in grades 8 through 12, they also are useful with college freshmen and young adults out of school. Eight scores are derived from tests of verbal reasoning, numerical ability, abstract reasoning, space relations, mechanical reasoning, clerical speed and accuracy, spelling, and sentences. Two forms of the test are available, Form A and Form B. Separate norms are available for boys and girls, and these norms are based on 47,000 students drawn from 100 school systems throughout the country. Scoring can be done with hand stencils or with an IBM test-scoring machine. Hand scoring for a complete battery for a pupil requires approximately 10 minutes. Total testing time is 3 hours and 6 minutes; actual time for administration is slightly more than 3½ hours. The DAT tests can be ordered singly, each booklet obtainable with a separate answer sheet, or the entire battery can be ordered in combined booklets and answer sheets.

Reliability coefficients for the tests range from .85 through .93 for boys and from .71 through .92 for girls. The test with the lowest reliability for girls is the mechanical reasoning test. Correlations between scores of boys tested in grade 9 and tested later in grade 12 ranged from .59 through .87 and for girls from .58 through .82. The tests have reliabilities higher than those for most tests in differential test batteries.

The validity of the tests is based on correlations between test scores and scores on other tests of a similar nature, and a longitudinal follow-up study of students tested in grade 8 in 1948 and followed up later and a group of students tested in 1947 as juniors and seniors in high school and followed up in 1951. A mass of validity data is reported in the manual.

[1] The counselor considering the use of multiple ability tests should carefully study *The Use of Multifactor Tests in Guidance* published by the American Personnel and Guidance Association in 1958. This book was originally published as a series of articles in the *Personnel and Guidance Journal*, September, 1956, through September, 1957.

Validity coefficients tend to be statistically significant and as large as those usually found for most aptitude tests.

These tests are based on a trait theory of aptitude measurement and are designed to be of maximum assistance to the counselor rather than to depict the psychological organization of the individual within the framework of any single theory of trait organization. The traits are not designed to be "factorially pure," but their constitution does take into cognizance information derived from factor analyses of ability tests. This battery of multifactor tests has been judged by many to be the most effective one available for school use.

The manual contains a list of 105 references; most recent references are listed in *Psychological Abstracts* under "Differential Aptitude Tests."

Title: Flanagan Aptitude Classification Test (FACT)
Author: John C. Flanagan
Publisher: Science Research Associates
Date of Publication: 1953, 1957

This assembly of nineteen aptitude tests was designed to help predict success in particular tasks required in a variety of occupations. The tests have been designed for two different uses. The authors say: "(1) They can be used for vocational counseling as an aid to prediction of job success on the basis of aptitude, and as a guide for planning a suitable program of school courses. (2) They can be used for the selection and placement of employees" (Flanagan Aptitude Classification Test, Examiner Manual, 1953, p. 4).

The tests have been standardized on, and norms are available for, pupils in grades 9 through 12. The evidence for validity of the tests is based on research and follow-up studies of students tested during their senior year in a Pittsburgh, Pennsylvania high school, and the validity of the tests for students younger than this can only be inferred.

Nineteen scores are available, based on the following tests:

Inspection	Arithmetic
Mechanics	Ingenuity
Tables	Scales
Reasoning	Expression
Vocabulary	Precision
Assembly	Alertness
Judgment and Comprehension	Coordination
Components	Patterns
Planning	Coding
Memory	

Available national norms by grade are based on 11,000 students from 17 schools in 11 states. The norm group was representative of the norm group of the Iowa Tests of Educational Development. Separate norms are not provided for boys and girls, in spite of the mass of evidence that reveals sex differences in the aptitudes measured by some of these tests.

Only one form of the test is available, and information has not been reported concerning the effects of practice on these or similar tests. Consequently, no provision has been made for retesting, either to verify scores where errors of test administration are suspected or to assess growth and development in these aptitudes.

Of the nineteen tests, thirteen make use of a separate answer sheet which is machine-scored and six are answered in the test booklet and must be hand-scored.

The entire series of tests requires three half-day sessions, each requiring approximately 3½ hours. The section of the examiners manual which contains detailed instructions for test administration requires fifty pages, so much of the 14 hours of testing time is devoted to the examiners providing pupils with instructions.

The length of working time for the various tests extends from 3 minutes to 24 minutes, with two tests being untimed. The actual administration time of the various tests extends from 6 minutes to 34 minutes. Timing, although not extremely difficult, requires care and extreme accuracy.

Scoring services for the tests that are machine scorable can be ordered from the publisher. The tests where responses are entered on the test booklet can be scored directly by pupils under the supervision of the examiner. A separate booklet edition is available which provides measures of sixteen of the nineteen aptitudes in the centrally scored edition. This edition has self-scoring booklets.

The difficulty of items in some of the tests appears to be inappropriate. For example, in the National Norm Tables for the Mechanics Test, which has 30 possible points, the median scores range from 9 points for grade 9 to 11 points for grade 12, and a percentile of 99 is obtained by a raw score of 25 for the most difficult norm group (grade 12). On the Coding Test, with 120 possible points, median scores range from 105 to 114 for grades 9 to 12, and a raw score of 118 obtains the 75th percentile for grades 10 through 12. The Mechanics Test appears to have items which are too difficult, and the Coding Test items which are too easy.

Reliability coefficients of the various FACT tests vary from .52 through .86 for pupils in grade 9 and from .61 through .91 for pupils in grade 12. These reliability coefficients are considerably lower than similar coefficients reported for tests such as the Differential Aptitude Tests. When the FACT scores are combined to provide occupational scores, however, the reliability coefficients are higher, for grade 9 extending from .83 through .91, and for grade 12 from .84 through .93. Reliability coefficients for ninth-grade pupils tend to be lower than those for pupils in grade 12.

The validity of the test is based on follow-up studies of students tested in grade 12 and on correlations between FACT tests, school grades, and scores on other tests. In nine groups of occupations requiring college preparation, the correlation between indexes of progress and performance and occupational scores ranged from .04 through .65, the former correlation being obtained with clergymen, missionaries, and social workers, the latter correlation obtained with social scientists including lawyers, psychologists, political scientists, historians, and sociologists. Correlations between the criteria and occupational scores in business and clerical fields were not significant. The correlation between the expression tests and the average of all marks in English courses was .42, but the correlation between English grades and judgment and comprehension was .46, with reasoning .54, and with planning .47. The reasoning test correlated .72 with the Wechsler Adult Intelligence Scale, as did the judgment and comprehension and ingenuity tests. The evidence available suggests that the FACT test has some claim to validity, but this validity perhaps is no greater than has been found with other somewhat similar tests of earlier vintage. The battery offers most promise to counselors particularly well experienced with aptitude tests and sophisticated about occupational psychology and psychometric theory.

Title: General Aptitude Test Battery (GATB)
Author: United States Employment Service (B. J. Dvorak)
Publisher: United States Employment Service
Date of Publication: 1952

This set of tests is designed to aid in the vocational counseling of entrants into the labor market and persons considering entering occupations in which they have had no previous experience or vocational training. The test is appropriate for use with persons sixteen years of age and over who have completed at least the tenth grade. Form B-1002 consists of twelve tests which yield nine aptitude scores. The tests are Name Perception, Computation, Three-dimensional Space, Vocabulary, Tool Matching, Arithmetic Reasoning, Form Matching, Mark Making, Placing, Turning, Assembly, and Disassembly. Alternate forms of the first seven tests are available. The nine aptitude scores are labeled G—intelligence, V—verbal aptitude, N—numerical aptitude, S—spatial aptitude, P—form perception, T—clerical perception, K—motor coordination, F—finger dexterity, and M—manual dexterity. The first eight tests are paper-and-pencil tests, and the first seven are arranged in two booklets for which IBM answer sheets are provided. Test 8 is on a separate sheet and no answer sheet is required. The last four tests are performance tests. The first seven tests can be scored either by hand or with an IBM machine. Raw scores are converted to standard scores where 100 represents the average of the general working population with a standard deviation of 20. Scoring by hand requires approximately 10 minutes. The test requires approximately 2¼ hours for administration.

The tests were constructed primarily for the use of local employment offices, although arrangements have been made for the test to be used in certain schools, colleges and universities, prisons, VA hospitals, and similar nonprofit organizations. The high school counselor who wishes to help a student benefit from these test scores usually will have to refer him to a state employment office or arrange with that office to have one or more students tested locally. The counselor will find the test battery most helpful with students about to leave school to enter the labor market, although the tests have some value to aid students in planning occupational training either at the collegiate or subcollegiate level.

One study of the reliability of the battery as shown by a test-retest over a two-week interval revealed correlation coefficients varying between .81 and .93. The reliability of these tests appears to be approximately the same as those of the Differential Aptitude Tests and somewhat higher than the Flanagan Aptitude Classification Test.

Some information is available concerning the validity of these tests for predicting educational success, but it has not been widely circulated. More information is available concerning the vocational validity of this battery than is available for any other multifactor test. The United States Employment Service has made use of occupational aptitude patterns based on job analyses of occupations included in the *Dictionary of Occupational Titles,* and validity coefficients are reported for these patterns and for many families of occupations. Criteria have consisted of both measures of success subsequent to testing and indexes of status concurrent with testing. The validity information exchange section of the *Personnel Psychology Journal* from 1954 through 1960 contained numerous reports of the validity of the test. More validity information related to occupational success is available about this test battery than other aptitude tests used in counseling.

The norms for the GATB are based on a sample of 4,000 employed persons representative of the occupations held by the general working population. The population from which the norm group was obtained was restricted in age from 18 through 54 years, and from it were eliminated farmers, farm laborers, farm managers, foremen, and service workers. Separate sex and age norms are not available, but separate occupational norms for occupational scores are.

REFERENCES

Section 3 of the manual contains a list of 14 references. A description of the battery in the November, 1956, issue of the *Personnel and Guidance Journal* contains a list of 100 references, and additional references are found in *The Mental Measurements Yearbook.*

Title: Guilford-Zimmerman Aptitude Survey
Authors: J. P. Guilford and Wayne S. Zimmerman
Publisher: Sheridan Supply Company
Date of Publication: 1947

This multifactor battery of tests was designed to measure unique abilities important for success in a broad variety of jobs. The test was originally standardized using college students, and the authors have announced norms for both industrial and high school populations. The battery is designed eventually to measure twenty primary abilities. The current edition consists of seven parts providing seven scores: verbal comprehension, general reasoning, numerical operations, perceptual speed, spatial orientation, spatial visualization, and mechanical knowledge. The factors measured have been labeled verbal comprehension, general reasoning, number ability, perceptual speed, spatial relations, spatial visualization, and mechanical experience. Apparently only one form of the test is available.

The test can be scored either from responses marked on booklets or from answer sheets. IBM machine-scorable answer sheets are available for Parts 1, 2, 6, and 7. Parts 3 and 4 cannot be used with answer sheets, and the authors recommend that Part 5 be given without an answer sheet. The total time for administration and testing is approximately 3 hours.

Reliability coefficients for Parts 1 and 2, based on internal consistency estimates, were .96 and .89. Alternate forms reliability for Parts 3, 4, and 5 were .92, .92, and .88. The reliabilities appear to be at least as good as those of most multifactor tests, and somewhat better than those of others. Little evidence is available concerning the validity of these tests. The tests appear to be reasonably pure factorially and probably measure the aptitudes they purport to measure. This does not indicate, however, that the tests have predictive or practical validity in any practical situation.

Tentative norms are available only for high school eleventh-grade students and for college students.

Title: Holzinger-Crowder Unifactor Tests
Authors: Karl J. Holzinger and Norman A. Crowder
Publisher: Harcourt, Brace & World, Inc.
Date of Publication: 1955

This battery of tests was designed to measure four types of mental activity considered important in predicting academic success. From the content of the tests the primary usefulness most likely will relate directly to educational counseling and questions related to the selection of courses and curricula, although the tests promise usefulness for vocational counseling purposes also. Nine tests provide estimates of four different factors.

The titles of the tests are Word Meaning, Odd Words, Boots, Hatchets, Mixed Arithmetic, Remainders, Mixed Series, Figure Changes, and Teams. The titles of the four factors are verbal, spatial, numerical, and reasoning. Two parallel forms of the tests are available. Working time on the tests equals 40½ minutes; total time for giving the tests requires two periods each of 45 minutes. The tests can be machine- or hand-scored. All responses are recorded on answer sheets, and the test items for tests 3, 4, 5, and 6 are printed on an answer sheet.

Reliability coefficients derived from correlations between scores on paralleled forms vary from .95 to .76, and split-half reliabilities range from .88 through .96. Because of the speeded nature of these tests, this method of computing reliability is not appropriate. Reliability coefficients for these tests are slightly higher than similar coefficients for other multifactor tests.

Validity as described in the manual is based on correlations between test scores and scores on other ability and achievement tests and teachers' marks. Validity coefficients are in the expected direction and compare favorably to similar coefficients reported for other multifactor tests. This is one of the few psychological tests which in its manual discusses the effects of practice, and these effects for some of the tests are quite large.

End-of-year norms are presented in the manual for the combined sexes by grade for each grade from grade 7 through grade 12. Insufficient information is presented in the manual describing the groups upon which the norms are based.

Title: Multiple Aptitude Tests
Authors: David Segal and Evelyn Raskin
Publisher: California Test Bureau
Date of Publication: 1955

The authors describe the purpose of their test as being "To provide comprehensive differential aptitude data which can be used to help individuals understand their aptitudes and enable them to make wiser decisions in relation to the myriad of vocational, academic, and professional opportunities offered by our modern world." The general purpose of these tests is the same as that of other multifactor test batteries. The battery consists of nine tests: Word Meaning, Paragraph Meaning, Language Usage, Routine Clerical Facility, Arithmetic Reasoning, Arithmetic Computation, Applied Science and Mechanics, Spatial Relations—Two Dimensions, and Spatial Relations—Three Dimensions. The first three tests provide a factor score labeled verbal comprehension. The next two tests provide a factor score called perceptual speed. The next two tests presumably measure numerical reasoning, and the last three tests yield a factor score labeled spatial visualization. The tests are designed for use with pupils from grades 7 through 13. Only one form of the test is available, somewhat limiting its usefulness when indexes of change or development are desired or when retesting becomes necessary. The tests may be scored manually from the responses marked on the answer sheet or they may be scored with an IBM test-scoring machine. The total battery of tests requires somewhat over 3 hours, including time for administration as well as actual testing time.

Reliability coefficients are reported separately for boys and girls by grades from grade 7 through grade 13. These reliability coefficients range from .66 through .98 and in general are as high as the reliability coefficients reported for the tests included in most multifactor batteries and somewhat higher than those reported for some batteries. The reliabilities of the factor scores are reported as being considerably higher, and in general the reliability of the entire battery seems to be satisfactory for the purposes for which it was designed.

Little information is reported about the validity of the test. Correlations between the Multiple Aptitude Tests and other aptitude tests are for the most part in the expected direction and are reasonably high. Correlations between test scores and school marks are for the most part in the expected direction, many are statistically significant, but in general they are not high. Follow-up studies which provide information about the predictive value of the tests such as have been reported for other multifactor batteries are not reported in the manual of this battery and are necessary if the tests are to be useful to counselors.

Norms are based on pupils tested in sixty-four schools located throughout the country. Between 1,000 and 2,000 students were tested in each grade and the norms are based on approximately 11,000 pupils. The median intelligence quotient for pupils in the norm group is presented for each grade. Approximately 85 per cent of the pupils in the norm group were Caucasian, the remaining students belonging to minority groups such as Mexican or Negro. This type of information has not been reported for other multifactor batteries.

INTEREST AND PERSONALITY TESTS

Title: California Psychological Inventory (CPI)
Author: Harrison G. Gough
Publisher: Consulting Psychologists Press, Inc.
Date of Publication: 1956

The CPI is a personality inventory designed primarily for use with "normal" persons in high school, college, or beyond. The 480 true-false items yield eighteen scales, each of which purports to identify some aspect of the individual's social behavior. Although each scale is a meaningful entity and is included as such on the profile sheet, the scales have been grouped into four categories in order to emphasize their psychological relationship. The four categories include: (1) Poise, Ascendancy and Self-Assurance—six scales (dominance, capacity for status, sociability, social presence, self-acceptance, sense of well-being); (2) Socialization, Maturity and Responsibility—six scales (responsibility, socialization, self-control, tolerance, good impression, communality); (3) Achievement Potential and Intellectual Efficiency—three scales (achievement via conformity, achievement via independence, intellectual efficiency); and (4) Intellectual and Interest Modes—three scales (psychological-mindedness, flexibility, femininity).

Twelve of the CPI scales were empirically developed and consist of items that differentiated between criterion groups; four additional scales consist of items judged to be homogeneous and then refined by an internal-consistency analysis; and the remaining two scales consist of items forming control keys providing information about validity of responses.

The manual reports considerable scale validity data drawn from cross-validation studies, with most of the information based on comparisons of extreme groups. A reliability study of high school juniors retested a year later shows a range of coefficients for the various scales from .38 to .77, with 30 of the 36 (18 for each sex) correlations ranging from .60 to .77. The scale intercorrelation matrix for the CPI shows considerable overlapping among the scales.

The norms are based on consolidations of available samples into a single composite sample for each sex. The manual also includes mean profiles for high school and college groups, as well as statistical data on a variety of other educational, occupational, and miscellaneous samples.

The inventory can be easily administered. The questions are contained in a reusable booklet, and the answers are recorded on a separate answer sheet for which both hand- and machine-scoring forms are available. There is no time limit, but the test is usually completed within 45 to 60 minutes. Scoring and transferring the scores to the profile sheet are relatively simple clerical tasks.

Interpretation of the results of an inventory such as the CPI requires a knowledgeable and experienced user. Each individual scale meaning must be understood and the interrelationships of the scales appreciated, along with the complexities of profile interpretation, if the counselor is to derive a meaningful picture. Although the manual provides aids and suggestions, as well as sample profile interpretations which are helpful, these cannot substitute for experience and psychological sophistication.

Title: Kuder Preference Record—Vocational
Author: G. Frederic Kuder
Publisher: Science Research Associates
Date of Publication: 1934–1956

One of today's most frequently used interest tests, the Kuder Preference Record—Vocational, is extensively employed in secondary school guidance and classroom programs as a means of aiding students to begin to focus on and learn about the world of work and occupations consonant with their preferences as measured by this particular instrument.

The record consists of 168 items, each item listing three activities. The student is asked to indicate which activity in each triad he likes the most and which he likes the least.

Form C, published in 1948, provides scores in ten interest areas (outdoor, mechanics, computational, scientific, persuasive, artistic, literary, musical, social service, and clerical) plus a verification (V) score. The latter helps identify those individuals who have not followed the directions carefully or have answered carelessly, or whose results may be invalid because of a reading difficulty or because they are so atypical that the scores on the ten scales must be questioned.

The manual provides a list of occupations for each interest area and combination of two interest areas. These occupations are to be considered suggestive and not all-inclusive.

Reliabilities obtained from studies of adult and high school students range from .85 to .92.

The validity of the record is based primarily on the mean profiles of occupational groups often small in number whose representativeness of any defined population is not known. A portion of the data presented was obtained from test users, and therefore the varying conditions under which the test was given are not known. Although the manual offers some evidence to support the validity of the record, thus far the direct demonstration of validity via follow-up studies has only begun to be published.

The high school norms for Form C of the record are based on scores obtained by several thousand students (3,418 boys and 4,466 girls) enrolled in high schools located in various parts of the country. Two sets of norms for adult men have been developed. One set was based on a group of 1,000 telephone subscribers (from a stratified sample of 138 cities and towns selected from the Postal Guide and chosen from all sections of the country) who responded to the invitation to fill out the Preference Record; the other was based on the scores of 1,296 men representative of the major (75 per cent) occupations in the general population, the notable omission being the unskilled-workers group. The norms used on the adult profile sheet are those based on the telephone subscribers group. Intercorrelations of the scores of the 1,000 male adults range from —.52 to +.34. (Decimal points are omitted in the manual.) The norms for the adult women's profile sheet are norms transmuted from those for the earlier Form B by means of equations developed from a group who took both forms. Norms for the newly developed Outdoor Scale were based on a sample of 100 women.

The Kuder Preference Record can be obtained with either a self-scoring pin-punch answer pad or with separate IBM machine-scorable answer sheets.

Since the publication of the first edition of the Preference Record in 1940, studies of various facets of the validity of the instrument have appeared. Some of these investigations related preference scores to curricular choice, others to achievement or abilities, and still others to on-the-job satisfaction. While a wealth of information has been obtained, the predictive validity of the Kuder Preference Record—Vocational has not been completely explored.

There are many reasons for the extensive use of this instrument. The record is an easily administered and easily scored interest inventory, attractive in format, and relatively inexpensive. Though the reading level of the record is probably appropriate to most high school students, Kuder has found that some of the words and phrases were beyond the range of ninth graders, and these are included in a glossary of words and phrases in the test manual. A pamphlet book list of several hundred titles, fiction and nonfiction, classified by the interest measured as well as by reading-difficulty level, also adds to the attractiveness of the record.

A careful reading of the normative, reliability, and validity data for the Preference Record does not justify its use in the prediction of vocational interests. The instrument is useful, however, for initial, relatively rough screening and for early, though general, exploratory purposes.

Title: The Minnesota Counseling Inventory (MCI)
Authors: Ralph F. Berdie and Wilbur L. Layton
Publisher: The Psychological Corporation
Date of Publication: 1957

The MCI provides high school teachers and counselors with relevant information about the personality structure and dynamics and the problems of the youth with whom they work. The inventory is based on and adapted from two previously published personality inventories, the Minnesota Personality Scale and the Minnesota Multiphasic Personality Inventory. It was carefully developed for use with students in grades 9 to 13 who have at least eighth-grade reading ability.

The inventory consists of 355 statements printed in a reusable booklet with a separate sheet for marking responses, and it may be scored either by hand or by machine. The student is instructed to read each statement and decide whether it is true or false as it applies to him, marking the answer sheet accordingly. There is no time limit, but most students complete the inventory in 50 minutes. Only one form of the inventory is available, although separate norms are used for boys and girls. The profile furnished with each answer sheet incorporates the norms enabling the user to completely score an inventory and plot the resulting scores on the profile sheet in less than 5 minutes.

The nine scores are identified by the authors as being in two groups. The first group includes a "question" score and a "validity" score, both relating to test-taking attitude. The former, which is the number of omitted items, is used to determine whether or not the student has responded to enough statements to warrant the scoring of the inventory. The latter score aids in the identification of students who might be overly anxious to obtain socially favorable and acceptable results and thus represents the degree of defensiveness of the student.

The seven scales of the second group provide scores that identify several areas of adjustment, as well as give information about the *mode* of the student's adjustment. An FR (family relationships) score reflects the relations between the student and his family. The SR (social relationships) score refers to the relationships between the student and other persons. The ES (emotional stability) score reflects the emotionality of the student. The C (conformity) score is related to the student's behavior in situations requiring responsible and conforming behavior. The R (adjustment to reality) score suggests the student's manner of dealing with reality, his tendency to withdraw. The M (mood) score reflects the student's usual mood or disposition. The L (leadership) score is related to personality characteristics which are related to leadership behavior.

Two types of reliability data are reported for the seven diagnostic scales. Coefficients of correlation between scores on odd- and even-numbered items range from .56 to .95 on a sample of 800 cases (200 of each sex in grades 9 and 10, and the same number in grades 11 and 12). Test-retest coefficients of reliability were obtained for each sex from the scores of students in one twelfth-grade class who were retested after a one-month interval, and from results for a second twelfth-grade class retested after three months. These coefficients ranged from .56 to .93. In both of these reports, the lowest coefficients were found for the Conformity and Mood scales.

The reliability of the Validity scale was estimated in the test-retest studies cited above. The average reliability coefficient was .67 for boys and .64 for girls.

Data on the validity of the inventory are extensive. The validity of the test is based on comparisons between the mean scores of teacher-nominated groups, special nominated groups, contrasting groups nominated by teachers, and a sample of 200 cases selected at random from all those in two high school populations. Separate analyses were made for boys in grades 9 and 10, for boys in grades 11 and 12, and for two groups of girls in the same grade combinations.

Of the resulting 152 critical ratios presented, 119 (78 per cent) were significant at the 1 per cent level. The remainder, though not statistically significant, are all in the expected direction. Although extensive overlapping is found among groups when the distributions are compared, statistical comparisons based on mean scores indicate that the scales of the MCI have acceptable validity.

Coefficients of correlation among the seven diagnostic scales were computed for samples of each sex and for each of the two combined grade levels. The intercorrelations demonstrate the range (.04 to .79) of the relationships between various scores.

The norms consist of standard score equivalents for raw scores. As in the computation of validity and reliability coefficients, four groups were used for normative data: (1) boys in grades 9 and 10; (2) girls in grades 9 and 10; (3) boys in grades 11 and 12; (4) girls in grades 11 and 12. The 5,440 students in the norm groups were tested in twenty-five schools located in two midwestern states. The means for the norm groups were compared with those of students drawn from ten states to investigate the applicability of the norms to a wider geographic region. The means and standard deviations for the norm groups and those for the samples selected from a group more nearly representative geographically showed that the differences between the data for the norm group and the data based on a more heterogeneous geographic sample were small.

As is the case with the other personality inventories discussed, the effective use of the MCI requires a counselor sophisticated in his understanding of measurement and human behavior.

REFERENCES

Darley, J. G., & McNamara, W. J. Factor analysis in the establishment of new personality tests. *J. educ. Psychol.*, 1940, 31, 321–334.

Darley, J. G., & McNamara, W. J. *Manual of directions, Minnesota Personality Scale.* New York: Psychological Corporation, 1946.

Hathaway, S. R., & McKinley, J. C. *Manual, Minnesota Multiphasic Personality Inventory.* New York: Psychological Corporation, 1951.

Title: The Minnesota Multiphasic Personality Inventory (MMPI),
Revised Edition
Authors: Starke R. Hathaway and J. Charnley McKinley
Publisher: The Psychological Corporation
Date of Publication: 1943–1951

"The MMPI is a psychometric instrument designed to provide, in a single test, scores on all the more important phases of personality. The point of view determining the importance of a trait in this case is that of the clinical or personnel worker who wishes to assay those traits that are commonly characteristic of disabling psychological abnormality. The instrument itself comprises 550 statements covering a wide range of subject matter—from the physical condition to the moral and the social attitudes of the individual being tested." Thus do the authors describe the inventory in the introductory paragraph of the MMPI manual (p. 5).

Although the MMPI was originally developed to assist clinical psychologists and psychiatrists in their assessment and therapeutic work with patients, subsequent experience and study have clearly shown that this instrument is useful for the understanding of normal persons.

Two forms of the inventory are available: the individual (card) and the group (booklet). The individual being tested responds to each of the 550 statements (566 items in the booklet form, since for ease of machine scoring 16 statements of the original 550 are duplicated) with a "true," "false," or "cannot say" as the statement applies to him. These responses are summarized in a profile containing four validity scales and customarily ten clinical scales. The validity scales include the ? (question) score, number of items put in the "cannot say" response category; the L (lie) score, a measure of the degree to which the individual may be trying to present himself in the most socially desirable light; the F score, validity in the more general use of the term; and the K score, presumed to be a measure of test-taking attitude and used as a correction factor for several of the clinical scales.

The clinical scales originally developed and included in the profile are hypochondriasis, depression, hysteria, psychopathic personality, masculinity-femininity, paranoia, psychasthenia, schizophrenia, and hypomania. Many additional clinical and experimental scales have been developed, but only one of these has been incorporated in the format of the published profile. This latter scale, social introversion-extroversion, was derived and cross-validated by Drake (Drake, 1946; Drake & Thiede, 1948). As one can infer readily from the description of the inventory, the use of the MMPI requires a professionally trained, experienced, and sophisticated practitioner. The personality characteristics estimated by the inventory are in themselves complex; when one adds to this the dimensions of meanings of the scales, the shape, relationships, and intensity of the scales and resulting profiles, and the interpretation and use, it is clear that the user of the inventory needs to be a fully qualified person in the science of personality and human behavior.

The original normative data were derived from a sample of about 700 individuals who were visitors at the University of Minnesota Hospitals. These persons ranged in age from 16 to 55 and represented a cross-section of the Minnesota population. The authors also had data available on several other groups: precollege and college students, WPA workers, and epileptic and tuberculous patients. The scales were developed by contrasting these normal groups with some 800 clinical cases from the neuropsychiatric division of the University of Minnesota Hospitals.

Reliability and validity of a personality inventory are difficult to assess. On the one hand, unless a test has a demonstrable statistical reliability and validity, we do not consider the test a "good" instrument; but on the other hand, when these tests measure personality characteristics which are unstable or modifiable and we wish to make estimates of these characteristics, then we must sacrifice the customary demonstrable statistical significance.

The MMPI manual reports the results of several test-retest studies: two based on samples of unselected normals and one based on a sample of unselected psychiatric patients. Although the form and time intervals between test and retest varied, the reported results of the reliability coefficients provide an estimate of the reliability of the inventory. As one would expect, the reliability coefficients vary by scale and by the constituency of the sample population. The reported test-retest reliability coefficients range from .46 to .93 with the majority lying between .70 and .90.

The validity of the inventory was observed by determining the effectiveness with which a high score on a scale predicted the clinical diagnosis of newly admitted psychiatric patients. In other words, the authors addressed themselves to the question, "Can the obtained high-scale score successfully differentiate among various kinds of clinical patients?" It was found that in more than 60 per cent of the cases a high score on a scale positively predicted a corresponding clinical diagnosis.

Since its publication in 1943, the MMPI has been used and studied in business and industrial personnel settings, educational counseling agencies, and hospital and clinical practice. As Albert Ellis writes in his review of the MMPI in *The Fifth Mental Measurements Yearbook* (p. 166), "it can confidently be stated that in the whole history of modern psychology there has been no other personality inventory on which so much theoretical and practical work has been done."

The group form of the inventory is used with separate answer sheets which can be either machine- or hand-scored. There is no time limit, but most students complete the inventory in 45 to 90 minutes.

REFERENCES

Dahlstrom, W. G., & Welsh, G. S. *An MMPI handbook*. Minneapolis: University of Minesota Press, 1960.

Drake, L. E. A Social I.E. scale for the MMPI. *J. appl. Psychol.*, 1946, **30**, 51–54.

Drake, L. E., & Oetting, E. R. *An MMPI cookbook for counselors*. Minneapolis: University of Minnesota Press, 1959.

Drake, L. E., & Thiede, W. B. Further validation of the Social I.E. scale for the MMPI. *J. educ. Res.*, 1948, **41**, 551–556.

Hathaway, S. R., & Meehl, P. E. *An atlas for the clinical use of the MMPI*. Minneapolis: University of Minnesota Press, 1951.

Hathaway, S. R., & Monachesi, E. D. *Analyzing and predicting juvenile delinquency with the MMPI*. Minneapolis: University of Minnesota Press, 1953.

Welsh, G. S., & Dahlstrom, W. G. *Basic readings on the MMPI in psychology and medicine*. Minneapolis: University of Minnesota Press, 1956.

Title: Mooney Problem Check List (PCL)
Authors: Ross L. Mooney and Leonard V. Gordon
Publisher: The Psychological Corporation
Date of Publication: Junior High School Form, 1942–1950
                     High School Form, 1941–1950
                     College Form, 1941–1950

The Mooney Problem Check List is a self-administering, untimed inventory comprised of lists of problems. The pupil is asked to read and mark each problem which is troubling him. Each form is printed on a six-page folder, three pages of which list the problems with the directions clearly given on the first page, with the remaining pages presenting questions or summary statements that the respondent is asked to answer. For most purposes the consumable edition of the check list will be used.

The manual states: "Experience indicates that about two-thirds of a group will finish checking in 35 minutes and practically all of the group in 50 minutes." The Junior High School Form contains 210 items, 30 in each of the following areas: (1) health and physical development; (2) school; (3) home and family; (4) money, work, the future; (5) boy and girl relations; (6) relations to people in general; and (7) self-centered concerns. Included also are three open-ended questions which ask the pupil to comment on his problem(s), to indicate his need to resolve his problem(s), and to indicate his willingness to discuss his problem(s) with someone else.

The High School and College Forms contain 330 items, 30 each in 11 categories which are similar to the Junior High School Form categories. The open-ended questions with which these problem check lists conclude are similar to those of the Junior High School Form, but are stated more extensively and require more sophistication to complete.

The PCL is a form of self-report or tabulation of self-description and is easily counted and summarized. The results can provide the counselor or school administrator data which can be utilized in counseling, in group-guidance programs, and for survey and research purposes. The items included in the check list were obtained by the authors' analysis of material provided by students about their personal problems and needs from case records, counseling interviews, check-list responses, and several other sources.

Even though the Problem Check List is not a test, but "rather . . . a form of simple communication between the counselee and counselor designed to accelerate the process of understanding the student and his real problems" (manual, p. 5), validity and reliability are nevertheless relevant. The manual in discussing the validity of the PCL reports the results of some studies concerning several assumptions felt by the authors to be meaningful and appropriate in the evaluation of this instrument. Thus, for example, the authors assumed that "responsiveness" was a necessary component of the value of their check list, and data are reported evaluating this aspect of the PCL. Similarly, the authors discuss the other "validity" assumptions which they held. The reliability of the instrument is likewise difficult to ascertain, for if the check list is an indication of the student's perception of himself and his problems at the time he completes the list, then it follows that repeated administration should reflect changes in the items checked.

The authors report group-measure data of two varieties. First, the rank order correlation coefficients of the mean number of problems marked in the eleven problem areas drawn from repeated administrations one to ten weeks after the initial administration range from .90 to .98. Second, when the frequency with which each item was marked on the first administration to 116 college students was correlated with the frequency with which each of the same items was checked on a second administration, the resulting correlation coefficient was .93.

Norms are not reported, for the authors consider that such information would be neither helpful nor useful. The development of local norms and problem surveys are encouraged.

The booklets are obtainable in either the reusable edition with a separate answer sheet or in the nonreusable edition.

Title: Strong Vocational Interest Blank for Men, Revised
Author: Edward K. Strong, Jr.
Publisher: Consulting Psychologists Press
Date of Publication: Original 1927, revised 1938

Probably the most widely used and extensively studied of the interest inventories, the Strong Vocational Interest Blank provides a measure of the similarity of the interests of an individual to the interests of individuals successfully engaged in a given occupation. The basic assumption underlying Strong's development of this blank was that the interests of men in an occupation could be distinguished from those of men in general. Not only has this assumption been validated, but more recent data have borne out the occupational predictive ability of the scores obtained by individuals who had previously completed the inventory.

Four hundred items comprise the Strong Vocational Interest Blank. These include occupations, school subjects, recreational activities and hobbies, kinds of people, and personal abilities and characteristics. The respondent indicates his reaction to each item by an expression of liking, disliking, or indifference, with the exception of the items in the latter two categories above in which he is asked to rate himself. The blank is largely self-administering and untimed, requiring 30 to 50 minutes to complete. Although hand scoring is possible, the task is so time consuming that most users of the blank rely on machine scoring and avail themselves of the existing professional scoring services.

Currently scores are available on forty-eight occupations, six groups of occupations, and four special scales. The occupational scales have been grouped on the basis of scale intercorrelations into eleven groups of occupations. These groups have been labeled by Darley as follows:

I Biological Sciences
II Enginering and Physical Sciences
III Production Manager
IV Technical-Mechanical
V Social Service
VI Musician
VII Certified Public Accountant
VIII Business Detail
IX Business Contact
X Verbal-Linguistic
XI President of Manufacturing Concern

The four special scales include Interest Maturity, Occupational Level, Masculinity-Femininity, and Specialization Level. Scores on all scales are reported on a profile which by its format indicates the significance of the score. That is, the profile shows the point where a particular score falls on the continuum of similarity to the interests of men successful in that occupation. The profile also includes a gray or shaded area for each scale. Scores which fall within this area may be interpreted as chance scores and therefore indeterminate in meaning.

The manual contains an excellent section on the interpretation of the blank, providing not only data and suggestions as to the meaning of various scores, but also some typical case studies.

Hundreds of studies dealing with the reliability and the validity of the Strong Vocational Interest Blank have been reported; and although there are variations or differences among the research findings, the evidence supports the blank as a reliable and valid instrument. The odd-even technique applied to the records of 285 Stanford seniors resulted in an average coefficient of reliability of .877 for the thirty-six revised scales. Test-retest correlations on seventeen scales over an eighteen-year period have a median of .69. The median test-retest correlation of scores reported in the manual for eleventh-grade boys tested twice over two and three years is .81. The study of the validity of the blank has been approached in several ways: percentage of overlapping, intercorrelations between the scores of occupations, and the relationship between interest scores of college and high school students and the occupations engaged in years later. The findings show that the interest scales successfully differentiate members of an occupation from men in general and the occupations from each other. Further, Strong has been able to demonstrate that interest scores obtained by students in college predicted occupations in which they were engaged eighteen years later.

This blank differs, then, from many other interest inventories or tests, for it has demonstrated reliability and validity, including predictive validity. This blank has much to recommend it, and the counselor would do well to become thoroughly familiar with its literature and use.

REFERENCES

Darley, J. G. *Clinical aspects and interpretation of the SVIB*. New York: Psychological Corporation, 1941.

Darley, J. G., & Hagenah, Theda. *Vocational interest measurement: theory and practice*. Minneapolis: University of Minnesota Press, 1955.

Layton, W. L. Counseling use of the SVIB. In E. G. Williamson (Ed.), *Minnesota Studies in Student Personnel Work*. Minneapolis: University of Minnesota Press, 1960. No. 10.

Strong, E. K., Jr. *Vocational interests of men and women*. Stanford, Calif.: Stanford, 1943.

Strong, E. K., Jr. *Vocational interests eighteen years after college*. Minneapolis: University of Minnesota Press, 1955.

Title: Strong Vocational Interest Blank for Women, Revised
Author: Edward K. Strong, Jr.
Publisher: Consulting Psychologists Press
Date of Publication: Original 1935, revised 1947

The Strong Vocational Interest Blank for Women, like the Blank for Men, contains 400 items (of which 263 appear in both forms) covering a variety of activities and subjects to which the person for the most part responds by an expression of like, dislike, or indifference. The blank is easy to administer and can be completed within the time limits of the usual class period. Machine scoring is preferred to the more tedious hand-scoring process.

Scores are now available for twenty-nine occupations and one non-occupational scale. Although the Strong Vocational Interest Blank for Women is a counterpart of the Blank for Men in its development, some differences between the two forms are apparent. The occupational scales for the women, rather than being grouped as they are on the men's blank, are listed on the profile on the basis of their closeness of relationship. Consequently, there is no identification or labeling of groups. The interpretation of women's scores, therefore, is somewhat more focused on individual scales than is the case with the identifiable group and individual scale format of the men's profile. The only nonoccupational scale available for the women's blank is the Femininity-Masculinity Scale.

Odd-even reliability coefficients on nineteen of the original scales, considered comparable to the revised scales now used, ranged from .74 to .94 with a median of .86. A study of the percentage overlap of the members of each occupation and women in general shows that the percentage approximates a biserial r of .85. A further investigation of the validity of the blank reveals that "the average overlapping between each occupation and the occupations scoring least like it is 12%" (manual, p. 21). These data suggest the tenability of inference that the reliability and validity are acceptable.

The unsophisticated user of the Strong Vocational Interest Blank for Women may find the scores disappointing. Many women do not have well-developed or strong occupational or career interests. Thus, it should not be surprising that many women score a high similarity of interests only in the "premarital" or "women's role" occupations: elementary school teacher, office worker, stenographer-secretary, and housewife. Such a finding is as significant to the counselee as is any other pattern. Indeed, this same frequency of similarity of interests to those in the premarital occupations should heighten the significance of those high scores found on the nonpremarital occupational scales.

The Strong Vocational Interest Blank for Women, like its counterpart, the Strong Vocational Interest Blank for Men, is an invaluable aid in counseling high school students.

EDUCATIONAL ACHIEVEMENT TESTS

Title: The Iowa Tests of Educational Development (ITED)
Authors: E. F. Lindquist, Miriam M. Bryan, Julia J. Peterson
Publisher: Science Research Associates
Date of Publication: 1952

The Iowa Tests of Educational Development is a battery of nine tests intended for administration in an annual testing program to all pupils in grades 9 through 12. The purposes of the battery are to enable teachers and counselors to keep themselves better acquainted with the educational development of each pupil and to provide the school administrator with a dependable and objective basis for evaluating the total educational offering of the school.

The nine tests of the ITED are:

1. Understanding of Basic Social Concepts
2. Background in the Natural Sciences
3. Correctness and Appropriateness of Expression
4. Quantitative Thinking
5. Interpretation of Reading Materials in the Social Studies
6. Interpretation of Reading Materials in the Natural Sciences
7. Interpretation–Literature
8. General Vocabulary
9. Use of Sources of Information

The full length battery requires 7 hours and 40 minutes of working time. The shortest test, General Vocabulary, requires 22 minutes, and the longest, Quantitative Thinking, 65 minutes. A shortened version of the regular battery, discussed more fully later, requires 6½ hours. In the short version, tests 1 to 7 all have 40-minute time limits, and tests 8 and 9 have the same time limits as in the full-length battery, 22 and 27 minutes respectively.

In addition to the scores for each of the nine tests, a composite score is based on tests 1 to 8. Test 9 is not included in the composite score, since it differs from the other eight tests. Iowa test results are reported as standard scores in a system in which the approximate mean is a standard score of 15 and the approximate standard deviation is 4 standard score points. The range (difference between the highest and lowest standard scores) is approximately 30. The use of the standard score scale permits comparability of performance from test to test for a given student and for a given test among several students.

The Iowa test battery has already been discussed in Chapter 7 on National Testing Programs. It may be obtained as part of a national program in which all materials, scoring services and reports are provided by the central agency.

Currently the Iowa tests are available in Forms X-3, Y-3, X-3$_S$, Y-3$_S$, X-4, and Y-4. The "S" subscript refers to a shortened version of the regular Forms X-3 and Y-3 in which each test requires 45 minutes or less, and each can be given in a regular class period. The short or class-period version is designed as an administrative convenience. Whether the regular form or short form should be chosen should be decided in terms of the reliability and the validity of the respective forms, not on administrative convenience. Presumably, if the short-version tests provide nearly equal statistical reliabilities and validities as do the tests of the longer version, the longer version could be dispensed with on this basis. However, the validity of the actual content of an achievement test is one of its prime requisites. In terms of the objectives which the Iowa test authors set out to measure, they have achieved an excellent instrument. The counselor or administrator, in trying to choose between the regular and the short version, is advised to consult with his teachers and carefully evaluate the two forms item by item. Do the items eliminated in developing the short form seriously curtail the measurement of certain content and thus not test some of the outcomes which they consider important to be tested?

The several forms of the Iowa tests are equated through the standard score scale. This means that an Iowa test standard score, whether obtained from Form X-3, Y-3, X-3$_S$, Y-3$_S$, X-4, or Y-4 can be interpreted in the same way by entering the appropriate norms tables. Two sets each of national norms and norms for the state of Iowa are available for the Iowa tests, one set for schools testing in the beginning of the year and one set for schools testing at the end of the year.

The content validity of the Iowa tests is of major importance. The tests' authors and publishers are explicit in the statements of their objectives, that they are trying to measure the complex generalized outcomes of the educational process, obtained not just from the classroom but from informal contacts, out-of-school experiences, and self-education. The prospective user must decide whether this content coincides with the objectives of education which he considers important. A considerable number of studies show that the ITED have a significant relation to college grades. The ITED administered to ninth-grade students shows correlation coefficients ranging from .50 to .60 between the composite score and first-year college grade averages. For results obtained on twelth-grade students, similar correlation coefficients range from .45 to .70.

The reliabilities of the individual Iowa tests in the long version are adequate for individual counseling, most of them being .90 or higher. Test 4, Ability to Do Quantitative Thinking, and Test 9, Use of Sources of Information, are exceptions showing reliability coefficients of about .85 and .81 respectively. The composite score has reliability of about .95. This is obtained by estimating its reliability through the individual test reliabilities and the correlations from the intercorrelation matrix.

In addition to these reliabilities the manual presents reliabilities of score differences. The average reliability of all possible score differences is .71. However, the intercorrelation coefficients are quite high, most of them falling in the .50 to .75 range. Correlations of individual test scores with the composite score range from .75 to .88. Such high intercorrelations mean that quite sizable differences must obtain between ITED scores for a given individual before these differences can be considered significant. The above discussion of reliabilities refers only to the long forms of the tests. No reliabilities are presented for Forms X-3$_8$ and Y-3$_8$ in the current manuals.

Title: California Achievement Tests
Authors: Ernest W. Tiegs and Willis W. Clark
Publisher: California Test Bureau
Date of Publication: 1950, 1957

The purpose of the California Achievement Tests is to provide accurate and objectively measured student achievement in the fundamental skills of arithmetic, language, and reading. In addition, the tests are designed to provide bases for planning remedial instruction in the areas where individual students appear to be deficient.

Published in 1950 and revised in 1957, this test battery replaces the former Progressive Achievement Tests in Reading, Arithmetic, and Language. The 1950 edition is still available. The new edition continues to provide measures of the basic skills in the areas of reading, arithmetic, and language from grades 1 through 14. Five test batteries or levels are available: Lower Primary (grades 1 to 2), Upper Primary (grades 3 to 5), Elementary (grades 4 to 6), Junior High (grades 7 to 9), and Advanced (grades 9 to 14). Two forms, W and X, are available for each of the primary batteries, and four forms, W, X, Y, and Z, for each of the other three batteries. The tests can be ordered as a complete battery, or the Reading, Arithmetic, and Language Tests can be ordered separately or in combination with each other.

The California Achievement battery provides eleven scores: reading vocabulary, reading comprehension, reading total, arithmetic reasoning, arithmetic fundamentals, arithmetic total, total (entire battery), and handwriting. Scores are furnished in terms of grade placement norms, age norms, and percentiles. In addition to the eleven scores listed above, each of the skills scores can be broken down into subscores for the essential functional elements being measured by a few items. The California tests also provide an anticipated achievement grade placement, the test performance which a student should obtain. Anticipated achievement is based on the norm performance of a nationwide sample of students in the same school grade having comparable chronological age and mental ability characteristics.

Administration time (actual working time plus distribution, direction, and collection time) is approximately 110 minutes for the Lower Primary, 145 minutes for the Upper Primary, 165 minutes for the Elementary, and 180 minutes for both the Junior High and Advanced batteries. There are many subdivisions of the tests that require separate timing.

The authors of the California Achievement Tests claim content validity in that the tests measure many of the universal subject-matter objectives of the curriculum. Though curricula in science and social studies may vary considerably in different school systems, basic skills or tasks of learning are much the same from school to school, and it is these basic skills the tests purport to measure. The authors also show correlation coefficients of the California tests with corresponding tests of other achievement batteries at corresponding grades. Typically these are .60 or higher. Correlation coefficients are also shown for scores on the California Achievement Tests versus the appropriate level language and nonlanguage test scores of the California Test of Mental Maturity (CMM). For the junior high level tests, correlation coefficients for the Reading Test scores versus the CMM language and nonlanguage scores range from .70 to .86; for Language Test scores versus the CMM scores, the coefficients range from .49 to .68; and for the Arithmetic Test scores and the CMM scores, they range from .62 to .73.

Most of the reliability coefficients of the skill scores and total scores are .90 or higher and are satisfactory for individual guidance and counseling, but a few, especially for the lower-level tests, fall below .80. However, throughout the manuals of the California Achievement Tests, the use of the test results for diagnostic purposes is stressed. The diagnostic profile permits plotting of grade-placement scales against the number of items correct for subtests, for which the total possible score in many instances is only 10. The test user must not fall into the error of assuming reliability of these subtest scores based on so few items. The test authors also caution about the use of these subtest scores, suggesting that low subtest scores may merely help to indicate areas of possible weakness for further exploration.

The California tests were standardized on a stratified sample of pupils from 341 school systems in 48 states. The stratification variables were geographical location, size of community, grade assignment, chronological age, and mental age. The latter was obtained by administering the California Test of Mental Maturity to all pupils in the standardization groups. Pupils in accelerated and retarded classes were not used, nor were pupils from adjacent grades in the same school system. The careful norming procedures followed would appear to provide a nationwide sample group of very stable characteristics.

The California Achievement Tests, either as a battery, or used as individual tests, are well worth considering for inclusion in a school's testing program. The would-be user must carefully review their content to see if the objectives measured are the ones he considers important. With the appropriate cautions cited about the subtest scores, the tests can provide useful diagnostic information. The concept of anticipated achievement provided by these tests is a useful one and merits careful study by the user.

Title: Cooperative Achievement Tests

The Cooperative Achievement Tests afford such a wide array of both general and specific subject-matter achievement tests that it is beyond the scope of this text to describe all of them in the detail given to other tests and test batteries in this chapter. The Sequential Tests of Educational Progress (STEP) have been partially described in Chapter 8 as part of the National Guidance Testing Program as well as in this chapter. The other cooperative tests will be described as a group, and the reader will need to make use of the references given to evaluate individual tests.

Author

The cooperative tests were originally so named because they represented the cooperative efforts of teachers, other subject-matter experts, and technical test specialists. Each test carries the name or names of one or several individuals as author(s) or may simply be credited to a committee, institution, or publisher.

Publisher: The Educational Testing Service

The cooperative tests are aimed at measuring the achievements, skills, and outcomes in a variety of subject matters primarily in grades 7 to 14. However, with the advent of STEP, cooperative tests are now available in elementary grades 4 to 6. What the tests measure may range from broad educational outcomes and general achievement to specific and factual subject-matter knowledge. The several tests available in each field offer considerable latitude in choice of a specific instrument. As with any test to be considered for a school program or an experimental project, the cooperative tests must be carefully evaluated in terms of the objectives the test user himself most desires to measure. The working time, costs, scoring format, forms of the test, reliabilities, validities, and norms available for any cooperative test can be determined by obtaining specimen kits and reading reviews of the tests in the standard test references.

Many of the cooperative tests have been in use for some time and reflect time-tested values of traditional education. However, cooperative tests reflecting recent emphases and new educational developments constantly are becoming available. Schools teaching the physics curriculum sponsored by the Physical Science Study Committee (PSSC) should be aware that cooperative tests are available covering the various topics of the PSSC course. Also mathematics tests covering the new School Mathematics Study Group (SMSG) approach are available.

REFERENCES

The would-be user is advised to consult the latest Educational Testing Service catalog, to obtain specimen sets of those tests in which he is interested, and to refer to Buros's *Mental Measurements Yearbooks* for reviews by test experts.

Title: The Sequential Tests of Educational Progress (STEP)
Author:[2]
Publisher: Educational Testing Service
Date of Publication: 1957

The Sequential Tests of Educational Progress were developed to provide tests long enough and broad enough for individual interpretation, to afford continuity of measurement over nearly all the years of general education, to focus on the outcomes of instruction rather than content, and to test the ability to apply learning, not simply recall it.

With these purposes in mind a battery of seven separate tests was developed to cover grades 4 through 14. The seven tests are Essay Writing, Listening Comprehension, Reading Comprehension, Writing, Science, Mathematics, and Social Studies. Two forms are available for each of the seven tests at each of four different levels. These are:

STEP 4A, 4B—For grades 4 to 6
STEP 3A, 3B—For grades 7 to 9
STEP 2A, 2B—For grades 10 to 12
STEP 1A, 1B—For grades 13 and 14

Each test is a work-limit measure allowing 70 minutes in two individually timed sections of 35 minutes each which may be administered separately. The one exception is the Essay Writing Test which has only one 35-minute section. The same answer sheet can be used for any STEP test at any level, a unique feature making for ease of ordering supplies

[2] No single author or even three or four authors can be ascribed to STEP. The tests are a cooperative effort of the Educational Testing Service and many individuals. The prospectus says: "To discover what educators regard as important in the measurement of student achievement, the Educational Testing Service consulted literally hundreds of teachers and researchers at all levels of the educational ladder. Out of this inquiry grew a pattern of commonly-held assumptions about both teaching and testing."

and administration. These answer sheets can be scored either by hand or IBM machine. Combinations of STEP tests with each other and with the SCAT test described on pages 237–238 can be ordered as part of the National Guidance Testing Program as described in Chapter 8. A single answer sheet containing space for all the answers for the STEP and SCAT tests, and scorable on high-speed electronic equipment, is provided in the NGTP. This answer sheet is not suitable for hand scoring or the usual IBM machine scoring.

STEP scores are reported in terms of converted scores. Converted scores range from about 230 to about 330. For NGTP users the reports come with converted scores. For schools using STEP apart from NGTP, raw-score to converted-score scales are provided on the scoring stencils. The converted-score scale is test defined, not normative, and can only be interpreted by reference to appropriate norms.

National norms for fall testing are available for each grade from 4 through 14. The converted scores permit use of the norms with results from any form of STEP. A unique feature of the STEP norm tables is a percentile-rank band rather than a single percentile rank. The intent of the STEP publishers in using the "band" concept is to focus the test user's attention on the inexactness of a test score and to avoid interpretations of scores as single fixed points. The percentile-rank bands representing each converted score correspond to the percentile ranks for converted scores approximately ± 1 SE Measurement above and below the midpoint of the converted-score interval. Consistent with both statistical theory and empirical findings, the band is larger for scores in midrange and smaller for scores at extremes of the range. The band interpretation provides some aid in comparing two or more STEP scores for the same individual. When the percentile-rank bands overlap, it is impossible to say with assurance that a student's standing on one STEP test is higher or lower than on another STEP test. When the bands do not overlap, one can with considerable assurance consider the results significantly different. The interpretative materials for STEP focus considerable attention on the importance of local norms and how to develop them, since the publishers feel the use of both local and national norms will considerably increase the usefulness of the test results.

As with other achievement tests and test batteries, the content validity of the test is of primary importance. The publishers feel that reliance on well-qualified persons in constructing the tests ensures valid content. The would-be user of the STEP tests must carefully review the test or tests he wishes to use to see if enough of the objectives measured by STEP coincide with the objectives he is interested in measuring. The separate manuals for each STEP test facilitate this review by clearly describing what objectives the test writers felt were important to measure. The

Technical Manual provides correlations of all of the STEP tests for each grade and each form with the verbal, quantitative, and total score of the School and College Aptitude Test (SCAT).

Relationship of STEP scores with school grades and results from studies predicting school grades with STEP scores are not included in the STEP manuals. STEP users are urged to be alert for reports of such studies in educational and psychological journals.

All of the STEP tests are power tests and scores are little affected by speed. Reliabilities were obtained for Form A of the STEP tests for grades 5, 8, 11, and 13 using the Kuder-Richardson Formula 20. For the six STEP tests (Essay Writing not included), nine of the coefficients are above .90, eight between .85 and .89, six between .80 and .84, and one is .74. Though only Form A results were analyzed, the publishers state that the reliabilities should characterize Form B results as well, since the item content for each test at the same level is very similar. These reliabilities are satisfactory for group measurement, but those tests for which reliabilities are below .85 need to be used with caution for individual measurement.

Title: The Essential High School Content Battery
Authors: David P. Harry and Walter N. Durost
Publisher: Harcourt, Brace & World, Inc.
Date of Publication: 1951

The Essential High School Content Battery is a comprehensive battery of achievement tests covering, in a single test booklet, the four basic areas: mathematics, science, social studies, and English. It is intended as a survey type of instrument from the end of grade 9 through the end of grade 12. The basic premise of the battery is that there is a common body of knowledges and skills which it is reasonable to expect a high school graduate to possess, and it is the purpose of the test to measure the growth and development of these knowledges and skills.

Two forms of the test are available: AM and BM. Scores are the number of correct answers. The tests can be either hand- or machine-scored, the same scoring stencils being used for either method. Standard scores are used in interpreting the tests and are obtained by circling the appropriate scores on a raw to standard-score scale provided on each answer sheet. Though four areas are tested, five separate testing sessions are required, one of 45 minutes for the Mathematics and one of 40 minutes each for the Science, Social Studies, and two parts of the English Test. The time requirements will permit administration of one section in the usual 50- to 60-minute class period. Though the authors provide a topical breakdown of the items in each test, the use of any part scores is inadvisable, with the possible exception of the English Test. Even here, because of low reliabilities, the part scores should not be used for individual diagnosis.

The validity provided for the test is primarily content validity or curricular validity. Detailed descriptions are given of the topics the items measure, the reasons for measuring such topics, and the sources to which most weight was given when the topics and items were determined. The authors appropriately stress that the test user must evaluate the objectives of this test battery in terms of the objectives which he wishes to measure. They discuss frankly what the test does and does not measure and provide useful suggestions as to how information from these tests may help the school.

The test was standardized on 46,000 students in 288 high schools in 38 states. The number is adequate for stable norms, but does not guarantee representativeness of the grades for which the tests are intended. Median Terman-McNemar IQs ranging from 100.6 for grade 9 to 105.8 for grade 12 make the assumption reasonable that the standardizing populations are typical of the grades they represent. In addition the normative data were weighted, so that the final norms are based on a group whose geographical distribution corresponds closely to that of the national high school population. The publishers will furnish upon request detailed information on the standardizing group and the standardizing procedure.

Norms are provided for each grade from 9 to 12 in terms of the standard score. One norms table is provided for the total school population, one for students taking academic and scientific courses, and another for students taking commercial and general courses. For the mathematics and science test, mean scores are provided by grade according to the number of semesters instruction in these courses. In addition, tables of the distributions of the average standard scores for schools are provided for each test.

Two reliability coefficients are reported for each test for each of grades 10 through 12. One is a split-half reliability corrected by the Spearman-Brown formula, and two are alternate form reliabilities. The odd-even split-half reliabilities are all above .87, with the exception of a .76 for the tenth-grade science test. The alternate form reliabilities range from .78 to .92, again with the exception of the tenth-grade science test which shows .67. These reliabilities are satisfactory for group analyses, but some are low enough to require much caution in using the results for individual guidance. Reliability coefficients also are given for part scores of the English Test. These range from .36 to .78, and most of them are so low that the test results should not be used for individual diagnosis. A high school well may find this a satisfactory battery to use in its testing program when it wishes tests of specific subject-matter knowledge and skills.

Title: The Iowa Tests of Basic Skills (ITBS)
Authors: E. F. Lindquist and A. N. Hieronymous
Publishers: Houghton Mifflin Company
Date of Publication: 1955

The Iowa Tests of Basic Skills attempt to provide measurements of the crucial skills involved in reading, work-study, language, and arithmetic. Through the objective and dependable results, teachers and school officials are able to become more quickly acquainted with the educational accomplishments of each of their pupils. The test results also supply the teacher, counselor, parent, and pupil with important information for educational guidance. The intent of the ITBS authors is to measure generalized intellectual skills and abilities, not to provide separate measures of achievement in content subjects such as literature, social studies, or general science.

The skills measured by the ITBS are classified into five major areas. Under these five areas, eleven subtest scores are available: vocabulary skills (one score), reading skills (one score), language skills (four scores for spelling, capitalization, punctuation, and usage), work-study skills (three scores for map reading, reading tables and graphs, and knowledge and use of references), and arithmetic skills (two scores for concepts and problem solving). In addition to grade-equivalent norms for individual students, grade-percentile scores are available for individual students, and grade-percentile norms for school averages. These norms are provided for the beginning, middle, and end of the school year administration.

The ITBS has two forms available and each form provides a separate battery of tests for each grade from 3 through 9. When the tests are used every year, no two successive school grades take exactly the same test. The pupils in each grade take only items which are appropriate in difficulty and content for their particular grade level. A unique feature of the ITBS booklet is that it contains the tests for all skills for all grades in one booklet, 1,232 items in all. This means that there is one continuous test for all grades and that pupils in different grades begin and stop at different items on a continuous test. The overlap of items from one grade to the next for a given test is intended to provide a measure of the actual overlap of objectives and content of instruction and yet permit introduction of advanced objectives at higher levels.

To judge the validity of the individual ITBS tests, the user must carefully scrutinize the actual concepts measured by the items in each test. Do the objectives measured by the various tests of this battery correspond with the objectives which the user considers important? The authors of ITBS have considerably lessened the task of examining the test content by providing an unusually complete description of the tests' development, showing item difficulty indexes by grade level, and carefully describing the concepts that the test items measure. They strongly urge, as do the authors of this text, that each potential user examine this data to assure himself that this test battery measures the things he considers important.

Studies of the validity of the ITBS as predictors of future school success have not yet been made. Validity coefficients can be inferred from the eighth-grade Iowa Every-Pupil Tests of Basic Skills, a predecessor of the ITBS. These tests were studied in forty-nine Iowa school systems. Correlation coefficients were .80 for predicting the grade 12 composite score of the Iowa Tests of Educational Development; .59 for predicting four-year high school grade averages; .54 for predicting first-year grade-point averages in three state-supported institutions of higher education in Iowa; and .47 for predicting first-year grade-point averages in all junior colleges, colleges, and universities attended. This lends indirect evidence to the validity of the ITBS battery as a predictor of subsequent school grades, but the user should be alert for new evidence on the tests themselves.

The ITBS authors provide reliability data for the tests and subtests in terms of reliability coefficients and standard errors of measurement. The scores for the five major skills areas and the composite score show reliability coefficients usually of .90 or better. The verbal score for the third and fourth grades are exceptions, having reliability coefficients of about .85. The skill scores possess adequate reliability for individual usage. The subtest scores have coefficients ranging from .70 to above .90. Most often the subtest coefficients appear adequate for individual use of the test results, but the test user should examine the reliability data to see which subtests at which grade level have reliability coefficients in the low .70s. The standard error of measurement is shown in both raw-score and grade-equivalent units. The ITBS user should familiarize himself with these standard errors. They spell out specifically what the reliabilities mean in terms of the scores themselves. They also help the user to focus on the test score, not as a single fixed point, but as a measure which falls within a range of score units.

To help the user make differential use of the various ITBS test and subtest scores, intercorrelations are shown for grade 4 and grade 7. The coefficients are generally high; for the skill scores nearly all coefficients are above .70. Most of the intercorrelations for the subtest scores are in the .40 to .70 range.

The norms for the ITBS appear to have been well developed and are based on adequate numbers. The population which the norms represent is based on all the children in regular attendance in each grade from grade 3 through 8 in public elementary schools throughout the United States. It does *not* include pupils attending denominational schools, private schools, or schools associated with teacher-training institutions. The norms sample was controlled on the factors of community size and geographical region. Within the strata of geographical region-community size, schools were drawn strictly at random until enough students were provided to furnish a number proportional to the population of each strata in the United States population. A total in excess of 74,000 students were used, from 11,000 to 13,000 in each grade from the third through the eighth.

Title: Metropolitan Achievement Tests (MAT)
Authors: Harold H. Bixler, Walter N. Durost, Gertrude H. Hildreth, Kenneth Lund, and J. Wayne Wrightstone
Publishers: Harcourt, Brace & World, Inc.
Date of Publication: 1959

The Metropolitan Achievement Tests are a general achievement series purporting to measure the important general outcomes of elementary education: the essential skills of reading, arithmetic, and language, as well as study skills. At the appropriate grade level, MAT also measures the mastery of science and social studies content. MAT consists of five test batteries in a series providing measurement for grades 1 through 9. The five batteries are Primary I, for last of first and beginning of second grade; Primary II, for last of second and beginning of third grade; Elementary, for grades 3 and 4; Intermediate, for grades 5 and 6; and Advanced, for grades 7, 8, and beginning of 9. Five forms, A, B, C, D, and E, are available for each series.

Several scores are available from MAT. Primary I and Primary II are similar, providing four scores in common: word knowledge, word discrimination; reading—sentences; reading—stories; and arithmetic concepts and skills. Primary II provides three additional scores: arithmetic —computation, arithmetic—total, and spelling. The Elementary battery provides nine scores: word knowledge, word discrimination, reading, arithmetic—computation, arithmetic—problem solving and concepts, spelling, language—usage, language—punctuation and capitalization, and language—total. The Intermediate and Advanced batteries are quite similar, the Intermediate battery providing thirteen, and the Advanced battery fourteen scores. Common to both batteries are scores on word knowledge, reading, spelling, language—usage, language—parts of speech, language—punctuation and capitalization, language—total, language study skills, arithmetic computations, arithmetic problem solving and concepts, social studies information, social studies skills, and science. In addition to these, the Advanced battery provides a language score on kinds of sentences.

Working time for Primary I is 1 hour and 45 minutes, for Primary II slightly less than 2 hours, for Elementary 2 hours and 45 minutes, for Intermediate 4 hours, and for Advanced 4 hours and 15 minutes. Intermediate and Advanced partial batteries are also available using only tests on the tool subjects: Reading, Language, Spelling, Arithmetic, and Study Skills. The tests of the partial batteries are identical to the corresponding tests of the complete battery. Administration time for the Intermediate partial battery is 3 hours and 30 minutes, and for the Advanced partial battery 3 hours and 45 minutes. In addition, separate subjects tests are available. Since the times quoted are actual working times, 10 to 20 per cent more time will need to be allowed for distribution and collection of material and for reading directions. The tests can be given singly or grouped in four or five sittings. The manual for each battery gives recommended groupings for administration. The administrator is advised not to give a complete battery in a single day, and though he can use his own groupings, he must adhere to the detailed directions for opening and closing a given sitting and for administering the individual tests.

Norms for MAT purport to describe the achievement of pupils "representative" of the nation's public school population. Characteristics of the national public school population for which an attempt was made to obtain representativeness in the norm sample were size of school system, geographical location, type of community (rural or urban), intelligence level of pupils, and type of system (segregated or nonsegregated). Every pupil tested in the experimental program also took the appropriate Pintner General Ability Tests so that the mental ability level of the normative group could be specified. Over 500,000 pupils from 225 school systems in 49 states were tested in the standardization program. A 25 per cent random sample was selected from each class tested, and students in each grade who were markedly over- or underage for their grade were eliminated. The modal-age group for each grade was defined as the 18-month age range in which the greatest percentage of pupils would be included. The age-controlled grade sample included from 81 per cent of the pupils in grade 9, to 91 per cent of the pupils in grade 2. The N of the norm-group ranges from 2,800 in grade 9 to 14,600 in grade 4.

The validity of the MAT tests is primarily a content validity. The tests measure those outcomes of instruction which, according to authoritative judgment and concensus of current practice, are the important goals of elementary instruction. In the tryout of the experimental forms of the tests, teachers were asked to criticize the appropriateness of the content for the grade to which the tests were administered.

Reliability coefficients were computed separately for pupils in each of several school systems, and standard errors of measurement were calculated in raw-score terms. Ranges and medians for the tests and the subtests of each battery are shown for both the reliability coefficients and the standard errors of measurement. Most of the median reliability coefficients are .85 or better, many above .90, and one can use the test results satisfactorily for individual guidance. However, some of the subtest scores have median reliability coefficients well below .80, and the MAT user needs to exercise caution when using these subtest scores for individual guidance. Inclusion of the standard errors of measurement is commendable, but it would be more helpful if the standard errors had been computed in the same score units as are reported to the user.

The MAT battery represents a careful job of test development and good standardization. As with all other tests, the would-be user needs to carefully review the tests and the items themselves to determine if this battery measures the objectives he considers important in his school system.

Title: Stanford Achievement Test (SAT)
Authors: Truman L. Kelley, Richard Madden, Eric F. Gardner, Lewis M. Terman, Giles M. Ruch
Publisher: Harcourt, Brace & World, Inc.
Date of Publication: 1953

The Stanford Achievement Test is designed for the measurement of growth and for the analysis of broad areas of strength or weaknesses of individual pupils. Five forms of the test (J, K, L, M, and N) are available in four batteries or levels; the Primary Battery is intended for the last half of grade 1, grade 2, and the first half of grade 3. It consists of five tests in a single eight-page booklet and requires 80 minutes of working time. Its tests are Paragraph Meaning, Word Meaning, Spelling, Arithmetic Reasoning, and Arithmetic Computation. The Elementary Battery is for grades 3 and 4, consists of six tests in a single booklet of twelve pages and requires about 2 hours and 15 minutes of working time. Five of its six tests measure the same areas as the tests of the Primary Battery, and in addition it includes a language test. The Intermediate Battery is for grades 5 and 6, consists of nine tests in a single twenty-four-page booklet, and requires about 3 hours and 35 minutes of working time. It measures the same six areas as the Elementary Battery, but adds three tests for social studies, science, and study skills. The Advanced Battery is for grades 7, 8, and 9 and has the same format, kinds of tests, and time requirements as the Intermediate Battery. A battery for high school pupils is in preparation.

Subject tests in arithmetic and reading are also available for the three upper levels in hand-scorable editions. A table of corrected split-half (odd-even) reliability coefficients shows median reliabilities for single grades. For the Primary Battery the coefficients range from .83 to .94, with the exception of the Arithmetic Reasoning Test which has a reliability of .73. For the Elementary Battery they range from .87 to .95, for the Intermediate Battery from .81 to .93, and for the Advanced Battery from .84 to .94. Of the 29 reliability coefficients reported, 14 are .90 or higher, and 9 are between .85 and .90. Thus, most of the tests have satisfactory reliability for individual counseling. Although all tests are time-limit tests, the authors think the time limits are generous enough to avoid spurious split-half reliabilities due to speededness.

Validity content again must be judged by the would-be user in terms of the objectives he wishes to measure. The authors state with admirable restraint that the tests do not measure all of the desirable aspects of pupil growth, but that the tests reliably measure generally accepted objectives of education. Correlation coefficients with course grades or information about the ability of scores to predict subsequent school success are not presented in the manual. Intercorrelations of the tests for the same grade are not provided, and thus we cannot tell how much the different achievements overlap with each other. It is difficult to deduce relationships among achievements in various curricula which might help to chart progress from grade to grade nor can inferences be made about the ways in which the tests would operate if used together for predictive purposes in multiple-regression equations.

A raw score is first obtained for the test, and this is converted into a grade score used in all subsequent interpretations of the test result. The grade score can in turn be converted to a modal-age grade equivalent, a total-group grade equivalent, an age equivalent, or a percentile. In addition, for research purposes a K-score table provides measures which are approximately equal throughout the entire range of abilities being measured. The K scale permits a more accurate measurement of growth.

To obtain norms and derive the various converted scores, Form J of the SAT test was administered to over 460,000 pupils in 363 school systems in 38 states. The eventual norm group consisted of an approximate 25 per cent random sample of all the students tested in 340 of the 363 school systems. The school systems were determined by reference to geographic distributions, types of school systems, numbers of pupils desired per grade, and the extent of participation within cooperating systems. Pupils in segregated Negro school systems were not used. In participating schools, every pupil in at least three consecutive grades was included in the standardization program. This precluded selection within systems. The norms samples have N's ranging from 3,300 at the ninth grade to 16,200 at the fourth grade, and modal-age groups have N's ranging from 2,100 at the ninth grade to 11,100 at the fourth grade. The N's are large enough to give stable norms and appear representative of a national population of public and private school pupils, not including pupils from segregated Negro schools.

REFERENCES

Buros, O. K. (Ed.) *The nineteen thirty-eight mental measurements yearbook.* New Brunswick, N.J.: Rutgers, 1938.

Buros, O. K. (Ed.) *The nineteen forty mental measurements yearbook.* Highland Park, N.J.: Gryphon Press, 1941.

Buros, O. K. (Ed.) *The third mental measurements yearbook.* New Brunswick, N.J.: Rutgers, 1949.

Buros, O. K. (Ed.) *The fourth mental measurements yearbook.* Highland Park, N.J.: Gryphon Press, 1953.

Buros, O. K. (Ed.) *The fifth mental measurements yearbook.* Highland Park, N.J.: Gryphon Press, 1959.

Super, D. E., and Crites, J. O. *Appraising vocational fitness.* New York: Harper & Row, 1962.

INDEX

281